Schumpeter's Price Theory

Joseph Alois Schumpeter has long been recognised as one of the great economists of the twentieth century, and his truly revolutionary approach to economic development continues to gain appreciation. This is particularly due to the emphasis he places on innovation and creative destruction as drivers of economic development. Yet, aspects of his theory remain neglected and poorly understood, especially his treatment of prices and price dynamics.

This book provides a comprehensive and critical examination of Schumpeter's price theory as well as providing suggestions for the further development of the theory. While Schumpeter's theories of economic development, entrepreneurship and the business cycle have received substantial attention in the literature, his price theory has been neglected. Yet, he proposes a price theory that is as radical as his treatment of other topics. The holistic nature of his theory also naturally means that a better understanding of his price theory will provide extra insight into other aspects of his theoretical framework.

This volume is of great interest to those who study Schumpeter's work, as well as those who have an interest in history of economic thought, economic theory and philosophy and political economy.

Harry Bloch is currently John Curtin Distinguished Emeritus Professor at Curtin University, Australia, having previously been Professor of Economics (1997 to 2012) and Dean for Research and Development (2012) in the Curtin Business School as well as founding director of the Centre for Research in Applied Economics (2006 to 2009). He is a Fellow of the Academy of the Social Sciences in Australia and an Honorary Fellow of the Economic Society of Australia.

Routledge Studies in the History of Economics

For a full list of titles in this series, please visit www.routledge.com/series/SE0341

Schumpeter's Price Theory

Harry Bloch

Routledge
Taylor & Francis Group

LONDON AND NEW YORK

First published 2018 by Routledge

2 Park Square, Milton Park, Abingdon, Oxfordshire OX14 4RN
52 Vanderbilt Avenue, New York, NY 10017

Routledge is an imprint of the Taylor & Francis Group, an informa business

First issued in paperback 2019

Copyright © 2018 Harry Bloch

The right of Harry Bloch to be identified as author of this work has been
asserted by him in accordance with sections 77 and 78 of the Copyright,
Designs and Patents Act 1988.

All rights reserved. No part of this book may be reprinted or reproduced or
utilised in any form or by any electronic, mechanical, or other means, now
known or hereafter invented, including photocopying and recording, or in
any information storage or retrieval system, without permission in writing
from the publishers.

Notice:
Product or corporate names may be trademarks or registered trademarks,
and are used only for identification and explanation without intent to
infringe.

British Library Cataloguing-in-Publication Data
A catalogue record for this book is available from the British Library

Library of Congress Cataloging-in-Publication Data
A catalog record for this book has been requested

ISBN: 978-1-138-85037-8 (hbk)
ISBN: 978-0-367-87212-0 (pbk)

Typeset in Times New Roman
by Apex CoVantage, LLC

To Mary and Margaret

Contents

Abbreviations

BC   *Business Cycles* (Schumpeter, 1939)
CSD *Capitalism, Socialism and Democracy* (Schumpeter, 1976 [1942])
HEA *History of Economic Analysis* (Schumpeter, 1954)
TED *Theory of Economic Development* (Schumpeter, 1961 [1934])
TM   *Treatise on Money* (Schumpeter, 2014)

Preface

This book represents the culmination of a long journey of discovery or, perhaps more appropriately, rediscovery. I was first introduced to Schumpeter's work as an undergraduate at the University of Michigan, mostly in terms of the "Schumpeterian hypothesis" relating market concentration to research and development activity. *Capitalism, Socialism and Democracy* appeared on the reading list and creative destruction was certainly mentioned at some point. However, Schumpeter's ideas were cast in the dominant static structure-conduct performance (SCP) approach to competition.

Matters were little different during my postgraduate studies at the University of Chicago. Even though one might expect a natural affinity to Schumpeter's emphasis on dynamic competition, there was more interest in static models of perfect competition and monopoly. My PhD thesis, *Advertising, Competition and Market Performance*, was rooted in a static model of competition, even though in retrospect the subject could have been better dealt with using Schumpeter's dynamic approach. I now see that the empirical content, a case study of consolidation in the US brewing industry and a regression analysis of the relationship between advertising and profitability, would not have turned out much different if built on Schumpeterian foundations. The same can be said for much of the empirical research on pricing and market structure I published in the 1970s and 1980s.

When I began lecturing on industrial organisation, I still very much concentrated on static models of competition in the SCP mode. Gradually I became interested in post-Keynesian models that linked pricing to the investment strategies and growth plans of firms. However, it was not until the work of Josef Steindl was brought to my attention by colleagues, particularly David Levine, Pam Wolfe and Marcellus Andrews, at the University of Denver in the early 1980s that I started to seriously focus on the dynamics of competition and this brought my attention back to Schumpeter. Here, I greatly benefitted from the work of Dick Nelson and Syd Winter that culminated in their seminal contribution to evolutionary economics, *An Evolutionary Theory of Economic Change* (Nelson and Winter, 1982). Also useful was time spent during a sabbatical at Warwick University in 1983, where I had long conversations with Keith Cowling regarding Steindl's work and its impact on subsequent research, including *Monopoly Capital* by Paul Baran and Paul Sweezy (Baran and Sweezy, 1966) and Keith's own *Monopoly Capitalism* (Cowling, 1982).

My move to Australia in 1985 diverted my attention to issues important to the Australian economy, particularly the pricing of manufactured products in a protected domestic market and also factors affecting prices of primary commodities in world markets. However, research on these "applied" topics and also on topics in industrial economics conducted by PhD students I supervised at the University of Tasmania and Curtin University increasingly pointed to weaknesses in the conventional structure-conduct-performance model of industrial economics. Four anomalies in particular stood out: high variance in productivity across firms within the same manufacturing industry, high variance in rates of productivity growth across manufacturing industries, stability over time in the price-cost margin in manufacturing industries, and large swings over periods of several decades in the price of primary commodities relative to the average price of manufactured goods.

In the search for a framework in which to explain these anomalies, I resumed my research on Schumpeter and Steindl. In this pursuit I was particularly assisted by two collaborations, first with John Finch, who brought to my attention developments in the literature on managerial capabilities building on the work of Edith Penrose, and then with Stan Metcalfe, who filled in many gaps in my knowledge of modern evolutionary economics, especially the use of replicator dynamics to analyse the co-evolution of market structure and prices. Encouraging results for the empirical potential of the Schumpeterian framework have come from application in collaboration with Dave Sapsford to analysing trends and cycles in time-series data on the terms of trade for primary products (see Bloch and Sapsford, 2011, 2013).

Among the many individuals who have provided helpful comments on various papers and presentations that contain elements incorporated into this book are Siobhan Austen, Michael Brooks, Ben Callegari, Uwe Canter, Jerry Courvisanos, Kurt Dopfer, Mardi Dungey, John Foster, David Haas, Joseph Halevi, Geoff Harcourt, Neil Hart, Therese Jefferson, John King, Karen Knight, Peter Kreisler, Heinz Kurz, David Levine, Michael McLure, Brendan Markey-Towler, Bob Marks, Stan Metcalfe, Greg Moore, Phil O'Hara, Michael Olive, John Phillimore, Dave Sapsford, Michael Schneider, Hugh Sibly and Ulrich Witt. Also important have been comments from anonymous reviewers of Bloch (2016a), Bloch (2016b) and Bloch and Metcalfe (2017), which deal with aspects of the material in this book. I also benefitted from the contributions by participants in the discussion of my presentations at the History of Economic Thought Society of Australia conferences in 2009 and 2013, the Society of Heterodox Economists conferences in 2010 and 2015 and the International Schumpeter Society Conference in 2014 and 2016, as well as at seminars at the University of Birmingham, the University of California at Berkley, Curtin University, Federation University (Australia), the University of Manchester, Monash University, the University of Tasmania and Victoria University (Australia).

Funding from an Australian Research Council Discovery Grant over the period 2006 through 2009 supported my early research on Schumpeter's price theory as part of a larger project on the dynamics of industry development. I have also benefitted enormously from being able to have collaborators spend substantial amounts of time at Curtin under the Curtin Business School's generous visiting fellowship scheme and from being supported for visits abroad through Curtin University's outside studies programme.

Maria Mangano provided able assistance in researching literature on Schumpeter during the early stages of preparing papers that have led to this volume. Margaret Bloch has proofread the manuscript and provided wise counsel and support throughout the preparation of the book as she has for all my projects over many years.

At Routledge, I am particularly indebted to Emily Kindleysides. I doubt this volume would have eventuated without her suggestion to convert a conference paper into a book and then her persistence in urging me to submit a concrete proposal. Laura Johnson ably handled the details of organising the production process.

This book could well have been written, although not by me, in my student days of the 1960s or even a decade or two earlier. Had this been the case, it might have appeared as a contribution to the frontiers of economic theory. Now, it is appearing in a series on the history of economic thought. Yet, I am firmly of the view that its relevance to the further development of economic theory is just as alive now as it would have been then. Economic theory has become much more sophisticated and refined, but with rare exceptions it has yet to seriously tackle the issues that arise in economies undergoing development through the evolutionary process of the introduction, diffusion and absorption of innovations.

Schumpeter fully realised that economics is a social science and built this insight into the foundations of his price theory through the creative influence of the behaviour of entrepreneurs, the institutional arrangements for financing innovations and the disruptive impact of the diffusion of innovations. I hope this volume will contribute to the increased awareness of the power of Schumpeter's vision and encourage further efforts to employ his theory and methods in developing economics as a social science.

1 Introduction

Schumpeter's distinctive approach to price theory

What is Schumpeter's price theory and why does it matter? These are the questions that I attempt to answer, at least in part, in the pages that follow.

In spite of Schumpeter's fame, which continues to grow, his price theory remains in the shadows. His concept of creative destruction is well known and its implications in terms of downward pressure on prices of established products widely acknowledged. Also, well known is his proposition that credit is the fundamental source of finance for innovation, which he relies on in associating bursts of innovation with generally rising prices. Yet, the connection of these downward and upward influences on prices with the more general theoretical relation between innovation and the movement of prices has been largely ignored.

Price theory is at the core of classical, neoclassical, Marxian and post-Keynesian analyses of the economy. The same is true of Schumpeter's analysis as laid out in *The Theory of Economic Development* (*TED*) (Schumpeter, 1961 [1934]) and in *Business Cycles* (*BC*) (Schumpeter, 1939). Indeed, in Schumpeter's analysis, prices have a pattern of movement over time that is relatively well defined compared to other economic magnitudes, which make them particularly symptomatic of the course of economic development. My objective in this volume is to treat Schumpeter's theory of prices in a manner corresponding to the treatment given to price theory in other approaches to economic theorising, thereby providing a basis for comparing the strengths and weaknesses of each approach.

Just as with other approaches to economic theorising, Schumpeter's price theory is part of an interdependent analysis of consumption, production and distribution that determines prices, quantities and the distribution of income. A key distinction is that in Schumpeter's analysis the interdependencies are driven by the process of economic evolution rather than by the structure of production and demand as in the case of classical and neoclassical theory or by institutions and market power as in the case of Marxian and post-Keynesian theory. Schumpeter's theory is one of prices in motion without fixed destinations as compared to the tendency towards equilibrium or convergence to the naturally or institutionally determined levels of other approaches.

Schumpeter was a visionary. This is most obvious in his prediction in *Capitalism, Socialism and Democracy* (*CSD*) (Schumpeter, 1976 [1950]) that capitalism would eventually decline due to its own successes and be replaced by socialism. More generally, a visionary approach pervades his analysis of the capitalist process. He sees the past and future as part of the ongoing evolution of the social, political and economic structures in which we live. He thus follows a tradition, which can be traced back through Veblen, Marshall, Marx and Smith, of economists who understand economic development as involving broader changes in society than just the equilibrating of supply and demand or accumulation in the stock of physical, human or technological capital.

In dealing with the economy, Schumpeter identifies innovation as the major driver of development. Included in the array of innovations are new techniques of production, new products, new markets, new sources of supply of inputs to production and new forms for the organisation of production and distribution. Importantly, these innovations are viewed as endogenous to the capitalist process rather than being external influences. However, there are no simple cause and effect relationships leading to the innovations. Rather, innovations are the highly uncertain outcomes of complex processes operating in historical time. Innovation is an emergent property of the capitalist system.

The emphasis that Schumpeter places on the importance of innovation in explaining growth and structural change in modern economies is now widely shared both inside and outside the economics discipline. However, his analysis of the mechanism that drives economic development has never been widely embraced by mainstream economists. This is most clearly illustrated in the mixed reception, and subsequent relative neglect, afforded to the most advanced and detailed explanation of his theory in *BC*, with its two volumes and more than one thousand pages of theoretical, historical and statistical analysis. It is in *BC* that Schumpeter provides his most detailed exposition of his price theory.

There are two aspects of Schumpeter's analysis that have proven particularly unpalatable to mainstream economists. First, resource or technological constraints become ephemeral when innovation is directed towards their obliteration. Externally determined limits provide closure in economic models of decision-making based on constrained optimisation, allowing the determination of equilibrium solutions. Without constraints, there is no obvious alternative source of closure to these models. This does not worry Schumpeter, as he views the economy as an open system with emergent properties that only become concrete in a historical context, hence, his emphasis on historical material in *BC*.

Shifting focus from equilibrium properties of a model of market coordination to understanding economic development as a historical process reflects Schumpeter's view of the nature of the "economic problem".[1] Instead of taking the task of theory to be characterising the stability and efficiency properties of a fully coordinated market system with well-defined resources, preferences and technology, Schumpeter returns to the broader classical concern with the causes of the wealth of nations. Here, Schumpeter is in no doubt that innovation acts as the primary cause, so his theory is directed at understanding the process that generates innovations and then at analysing the implications of the diffusion of innovations throughout the economy.

The second, and perhaps more, unpalatable aspect of Schumpeter's analysis from a mainstream perspective is his emphasis on the distinction between adaptive and creative responses (Schumpeter, 1947). In mainstream analysis, individual behaviour is universally rational. Adaptive or rational response is choosing the best among all possible actions based on evaluating consequences of each action, with probabilities attached to alternative outcomes from the action. In all cases, there is a direct link to observations about phenomena including, in the case of rational expectations, an exact link to phenomena yet to be observed. The decision maker observes then acts rationally (adaptively) based on observations.

Creative responses lead to different actions than do adaptive responses and so are presumably outside the scope of "rational" action from the perspective of mainstream theory. Terms that are foreign to the mainstream modelling process, such as conjecture, uncertainty, instinct and imagination, have been applied in discussions of innovative behaviour. For Schumpeter, the activity associated with creative responses is primarily discussed in the context of his agent of change, the entrepreneur, who is added to capitalist, manager, worker and landowner as categories of roles undertaken by individuals in capitalist production. Individuals can perform a single role or multiple roles, with the role of the entrepreneur being that of undertaking innovations.

Innovation as an entrepreneurial activity is viewed by Schumpeter as a creative response to challenges from the economy. An adaptive response, say an increase in a farmer's planting of corn in response to a rise in price, occurs in the context of the usual constraints of economic analysis, including given technology. A creative response involves an entrepreneur innovating to alter the constraints, for example introducing a new production method, such as hydroponic cultivation or the genetic engineering of new varieties.

Not all technological breakthroughs become product or process innovations. Action is required to bring new ideas to the market. This process involves a particular sort of behaviour that extends beyond the optimal calculation based on observed conditions as applied in mainstream economics. Not surprisingly the few mainstream economists who have tried, have struggled to incorporate entrepreneurs into their analysis. Also, the action of entrepreneurs requires financing, which in Schumpeter's theory introduces a non-neutral role for credit and money creation into the process of economic evolution.

Resistance to Schumpeter's reformulation of the "economic problem" and the absence of a role for his entrepreneur within the standard theory of rational action have led to his theoretical analysis never being fully integrated into mainstream theory. This is particularly true of his analysis of prices. In Schumpeter's price theory, innovation leads not only to structural changes in relative prices but to distinctive movements in the price level in his theory of the business cycle.

Mainstream theory recognises that product innovation may lead to a price above cost as the innovator has a monopoly in the new product. Likewise, an innovator in process technology can receive a rent to their specialised knowledge that allows production at a cost below that of their competitors. There is an acknowledgment that the profit or rent might be temporary, but no inevitability of such outcome and no specifics about the dynamics of dissipation. The reviews of *BC* suggest hostility to the notion that innovation could result in cycles in the price level or any other business cycle phenomena.

A synopsis of Schumpeter's price theory

Schumpeter's most explicit statement of his price theory is found in *BC*. Here, Schumpeter treats the price level and the price system as each having characteristic features. Analysis of the price level is carried out in terms of macroeconomic magnitudes, where movement in the price level is related to cyclical variation in the creation of credit to finance investments in innovations that impact on demand for productive inputs and, later, on the supply of products. In contrast, the analysis of the price system is in terms of the microeconomics of the demand and supply for individual products or for groups of related products.

Schumpeter argues that the price level has a clear cyclical and secular pattern.

> Price level should rise in prosperity – under the pressure of credit creation, which, under the conditions embodied in the pure model, would not be compensated either by an increase in output or by any fall in "velocity" – and fall in the downgrade – under the pressure of autodeflation and of increase in output – *more than it had risen in the preceding prosperity.*
>
> (Schumpeter, 1939, p. 462, quotation marks and italics in original)

Here, the cyclical nature of price level movement is tied to economic evolution driven by the effects of investments in innovation as well as to the associated pattern of credit creation and withdrawal (autodeflation). The secular downward trend of the price level reflects the effects of expanding output from entrepreneurs combined with the temporary nature of the addition to credit.

With regard to the price system, Schumpeter recognises a more complex pattern than for the price level. This is associated with the unevenness of development across commodities. In particular, patterns of movement in price and associated quantities are classed into those commodities directly affected by innovation, the innovating commodities, and those that are induced by innovation. The latter patterns of movement are reactions to the economy-wide changes that result from the disruption caused by the innovation. Whatever regularity exists is with those price-quantity variations that flow from economy-wide changes, but even here Schumpeter cautions that every industry has its own peculiar structure that influences the way in which it reacts to common influences (op. cit., pp. 520–28).

Much discussion of business cycles or long waves in economic activity focuses on movements in quantities, especially at the aggregate level, such as industrial production, employment or aggregate investment. Schumpeter is notable for giving at least equal attention to prices. This reflects not only the interdependence between prices and quantities that features in most approaches to price theory, but a special role that Schumpeter identifies for price movements in connection with the ebb and flow of innovations financed by credit.

Schumpeter views Walrasian general equilibrium or Marshallian long-time equilibrium as appropriate for determining the prices for the circular flow of the stationary state. However, once a cluster of innovations disrupts the stationary state, a different type of theory is required to determine prices for an economy undergoing development from within through a process of uneven growth and structural change. Schumpeter's price theory is thus a theory for an economy in motion rather than in equilibrium.

Nonetheless, the motion in Schumpeter's theory is motion from and towards normality. Entrepreneurs cannot reliably calculate the profit that would be reaped from their innovation when the price system is disrupted, nor can they convince their bankers to finance the innovations under these conditions. Instead, prices need to approach those that Schumpeter associates with the "theoretical norm" for the economy. Thus, achieving a situation in which the economy is near its "theoretical norm" is viewed by Schumpeter as a precondition for a spurt of entrepreneurial activity.

A contradiction occurs because a spurt in entrepreneurial activity disturbs normality and moves prices away from those associated with the "theoretical norm", so prices no longer provide a reliable basis for calculating future costs and revenues. This feedback process between normality and entrepreneurial activity lies very much at the heart of Schumpeter's analysis of the business cycle.

> Just as the struggle towards a new equilibrium position, which will embody the innovations and give expression to their effects upon the old firms, is the real meaning of depression as we know it from experience, so it might likewise be shown that this struggle must actually lead to a close approach to an equilibrium position: on the one hand, the driving impulse of the process of depression cannot theoretically stop until it has done its work, has really brought about the equilibrium position; on the other hand, no new disturbance in the form of a new boom can arise out of the period of depression until then.
>
> (Schumpeter, 1961 [1934], p. 243)

Schumpeter argues the "theoretical norm" approached at the end of depression is Walrasian equilibrium, which has prices covering costs and remaining stable. However, he notes that, 'the position reached never completely corresponds to the theoretical picture of a system without development, in which there would no longer be income in the form of interest' (op. cit., p. 244). Thus, there are allusions to "natural", or cost-based prices from classical economics as well as to general equilibrium or long-time prices from neoclassical economics, but no firm commitment to either.

In the context of economic evolution, Schumpeter's suggestion that normality is associated with prices approximately equal to costs raises at least two difficult questions about costs: which costs and whose costs. Which costs has both an output dimension and a time horizon dimension. If innovation disrupts competitive equilibrium, marginal and average costs can be expected to differ at most output levels. Further, innovation alters costs over time at any level of output, which means historical cost, current best-practice cost and expected future cost generally differ. This helps to explain Schumpeter's insistence that a slowdown in innovations is a requirement for the economy to approach its "theoretical norm".

Without innovation it becomes at least logically possible to have both an approach to long-run competitive equilibrium with marginal cost equaling average cost and the convergence across the time horizons of historical, best-practice and expected costs.

Whose cost determines price is problematic because with innovation, firms have heterogeneous costs, even when they are producing similar products. If market arbitrage limits opportunities for variation in prices across firms, whose costs among the firms determines the "theoretical norm" for price? By emphasising the role of creative destruction in eliminating unfit firms, Schumpeter suggests the answer is that the cost basis for the "theoretical norm" for price can only be determined when cost heterogeneity has been radically reduced.

After critically reviewing Schumpeter's price theory, I argue that there is a need for further theoretical advancement. Schumpeter assumes the theoretical norms for a developing (or evolving) economy do not differ fundamentally from those of the Walrasian equilibrium of the stationary economy. Obstacles to both the elimination of profit and the convergence of costs imply that perfectly competitive Walrasian equilibrium is not the proper norm for determining of prices when innovative activity is at its ebb at the beginning and end of the long business cycle, much less at other times. There is a need to extend Schumpeter's price theory to provide more guidance on the determinants of prices over all phases of the business cycle. In the penultimate chapter of this book I provide some suggestions on how this might be achieved through adaptation of elements of the post-Keynesian theory of administered prices and the Sraffian theory of prices of production.

Schumpeterian themes in mainstream analysis

Several Schumpeterian themes have become fashionable in mainstream economics. In particular, endogenous growth, technological change and dynamic competition have received substantial attention from mainstream economists over recent decades. However, there are sharp differences in assumptions between mainstream theorising on these topics and Schumpeter's theory that covers the same ground, which creates potential confusion regarding the theoretical basis for Schumpeter's treatment of economic development, innovation and creative destruction.

Schumpeter's qualitative distinction separating economic development from other economic phenomena has never been accepted by mainstream economists. To them economic theory is universal. It applies at all times, to all countries and to all economic problems. Schumpeterian themes only enter into discussion when they are situated within traditional theory, which generally involves subtle, or not so subtle, changes in meaning.

Anne Mayhew (1980) provides a nice example of how mainstream economics has misused Schumpeterian themes in her critical review of the "Schumpeterian thesis", which is interpreted as implying that large firms are more innovative than small firms. Mayhew notes Schumpeter never said anything like this and it is, at best, a misunderstanding of Schumpeter's views on the causality between innovation and firm size. At worst, it is a deliberate misrepresentation to protect mainstream views on the application of static analysis to antitrust policy, which rely on the absence of a positive linear empirical relationship between firm size and innovative activity at a point in time.

A key feature of Schumpeter's theory is that development is endogenous. He states, 'By "development," therefore, we shall understand only such changes in economic life as are not forced upon it from without but arise by its own initiative, from within' (Schumpeter, 1961 [1934], p. 63). The mainstream theory of endogenous growth captures this insight, but insists on individual agents making optimising decisions. A difficulty arises in that equilibrium for individual producers requires decreasing returns to scale, at least under the usually assumed perfectly competitive market conditions. However, for growth to continue indefinitely, there needs to be increasing returns to scale at the country or world level. One solution has been to assume (without historical evidence) the inability of firms to appropriate positive externalities in the production of knowledge, which are in turn, strong enough to offset decreasing returns for the individual producer.

More generally, in the mainstream analysis of technological change, the outcome of research and development expenditure is not known in advance, but the individual firm nonetheless optimises the amount of its expenditure. To allow for an optimum solution, a probability distribution of outcomes is assumed, often imposing rational expectations in the sense that the true probability distribution is correctly predicted by the decision maker. Even though the decision-making is rational, the resulting total spending may still be too little for an optimum to arise. However, as noted above, mainstream theory treats this outcome as due to positive externalities in the production of knowledge and the problems firms have in appropriating all benefits, rather than admitting the impossibility of optimal decision-making regarding technological change.[2]

Particularly notable (but rare) examples of mainstream attempts to model Schumpeterian competition are those of William Baumol (2002) and Philippe Aghion and Peter Howitt (1992, 1998, Chapter 2). Baumol emphasises the pressure on firms in hi-tech oligopolies to engage in research and development to beat their rivals to the next big thing, while Aghion and Howitt model the impact of new innovations in capital goods on the obsolescence of existing capital goods. Both approaches pick up on hints from Schumpeter in *CSD* regarding the nature of competition among large-scale enterprises in the modern era. However, both blunt Schumpeter's clear distinction between invention and innovation from *TED* and *BC* by having firms investing in invention to maximise their long-term prospects rather than profiting from their creative ability to imagine and implement inventions that need not be their own.

The mainstream reinterpretations of Schumpeter's ideas are often ingenious and sometimes suggest hypotheses that can be empirically tested, occasionally with supportive findings. However, all of these analyses assume that optimisation can be applied to the analysis of economic development as it is applied to any other economic decision problem, only the characterisation of the benefits and costs are altered in terms of risk (a probability distribution of outcomes as compared to a deterministic outcome) or the extent to which the benefits or costs go to the decision maker (the appropriation issue). Schumpeter clearly and emphatically denies that application of what he terms "static" theory is valid when there is discontinuous change,

> But "static" analysis is not only unable to predict the consequences of discontinuous changes in the traditional way of doing things; it can neither explain the consequences of such productive revolutions nor the phenomena that accompany them. It can only investigate the new equilibrium position after the changes have occurred. It is just this occurrence of the "revolutionary" change that is our problem, the problem of economic development in a very narrow and formal sense. The reason why we so state the problem and turn aside from traditional theory lies not so much in the fact that economic changes, especially, if not solely, in the capitalist epoch, have actually occurred thus and not by continuous adaptation, but more in their fruitfulness.
>
> (Schumpeter, 1961 [1934], pp. 62–63, quotation marks in original)

The assumptions behind general equilibrium theory in economics are widely recognised as unrealistic, but accepted by the mainstream as abstract devices for capturing essential aspects of behaviour and outcomes. Schumpeter makes the point that these assumptions and the resulting theory are not fruitful in dealing with discontinuous change and, therefore, the theory must be abandoned in favour of an alternative. Stan Metcalfe (2014, p. 16) puts the futility of the mainstream approach in the following prosaic terms, 'the economist's fabled stationary state is a fiction that far from being an analytical masterstroke serves only to disguise the fundamentals of capitalism as a system that develops from within.'

Whether one agrees with Schumpeter that economic development is a qualitatively different phenomenon from equilibrium or the adjustment to equilibrium, it is clear his insights into the process of economic development are not the product of traditional theorising. Entrepreneurship, innovation and creative destruction as they appear in Schumpeter's theory are outcomes based on a different set of assumptions than those that lie behind the theory of general economic equilibrium.

Richard Nelson (2012) blames Schumpeter, at least in part, for the mainstream's failure to fully embrace his approach, particularly his approach to price theory.

> Put baldly, the supposition Schumpeter seemed to be leaving with the readers of his TED that his theory of innovation driven development, and the price theory of the economic classics and the rising neoclassical economics, could fit together nicely, with the latter providing a theory of the determinants of prices and the allocation of resources at any time, and the former the dynamics of change, just does not work. If economic development is as Schumpeter characterized it and is going on all the time, then there is something basically wrong with a theory of the determinants of prices and the allocation of resources that assumes equilibrium. Schumpeter's characterization of the

dynamics of change calls for a different kind of price theory. And Schumpeter did not provide one.

(p. 905)

Flaws in Schumpeter's theory can also be used to explain the limited development of price theory among evolutionary economists. As Nelson (2013, p. 17) comments elsewhere in reference to the work of evolutionary economists, 'we have done little work directly on the subjects treated in conventional price theory, that is on how markets determine the configuration of prices and quantities produced and sold that one observes at any point in time.' There is very limited attention paid to price theory in the large and rapidly growing Schumpeterian or neo-Schumpeterian literature on the causes and impacts of technological change or on the management of such change within firms and by governments.

The scope and plan of the book

Nelson's criticism of Schumpeter's treatment of price theory cited above neatly identifies the scope of the issues addressed in this book. Schumpeter's price theory is flawed, particularly in regard to his attempt to treat the theory of Walrasian equilibrium as compatible with his own theorising regarding price movements generated by the process of economic development. However, there are clearly elements in Schumpeter's analysis of prices that do not depend on the linkage to equilibrium theorising and that point to a theory of price that is compatible with, indeed necessary for, analysing the process of economic development. My objective is to identify these non-equilibrium elements through the critical examination of Schumpeter's work on the theory of economic development, business cycles and money. I then suggest how Schumpeter's price theory might be reconstructed in a form distinct from equilibrium theory and suitable for use in analysing developing economies.

Before laying out the plan for the various chapters that follow, it is worth pointing to topics that do not receive much coverage in what follows. Among topics central to the burgeoning Schumpeterian or neo-Schumpeterian literature, I give scant attention to the topics of research management and policy. Partly this reflects the neglect of price theory in the literature on these topics and partly the need to keep my project manageable in scope. Topics related to the introduction and diffusion of technology, such as national innovation systems, are also largely ignored except as they concern the relationship between pricing and the relative growth of innovative and established firms.

Among topics central to mainstream price theory but neglected here, first and foremost is the theory of consumer demand. While mainstream economics puts much emphasis on consumer preferences and choice, the entrepreneur and innovations on the supply side of the market hold centre stage in Schumpeter's theory of economic development. Consumer income or purchasing power and expenditure get attention in the theoretical, statistical and historical discussion of *BC*, but consumer preferences are ignored. I follow Schumpeter's lead in not explicitly considering the consumer or her preferences, even though some Schumpeterians argue that consumer demand requires more attention than Schumpeter provides (see for example Nelson and Consoli, 2010).

I also follow Schumpeter in giving scant attention to the theory of exchange and its implications for economic efficiency. As noted in the introduction to this chapter, Schumpeter's focus is on the classical economic problem, analysing the causes of the wealth of nations, rather than the neoclassical alternative of analysing the efficiency of the allocation of scarce resources among competing ends. As Schumpeter notes in dismissing concerns about the impact of oligopolies on efficiency in *CSD*, 'the problem that is usually being visualized is how capitalism administers existing structures, whereas the relevant problem is how it creates and destroys them' (Schumpeter, 1976 [1950], p. 84).

Another point worth bringing to the reader's attention early on is that Schumpeter's analysis of movements in the price level is only loosely connected to contemporaneous movements in aggregate quantities. Increased competition for means of production drives the upswing of the price level, but this involves shifting the inputs from established firms to the innovators and does not result in an immediate increase in output. There is also an increase in competition among outputs driving the downswing in the price level, but this is at least partially offset by the declining output of established producers in the perennial gale of creative destruction. It is only if and when declining profitability of established producers leads to panic and crisis that Schumpeter has prices and quantities falling together. Thus, Schumpeter has a theory of cyclical movements in the price level only weakly connected to the conventional interpretation of business cycle theory as explaining cyclical movements in the aggregates of output, employment and real incomes.

The driving force behind the movement of prices in Schumpeter's theory is the ebb and flow of innovations, which leads to discontinuous change in production, consumption and distribution. Innovations are generated by the endogenous process of economic evolution. Thus, I begin my critical review of Schumpeter's price theory in Chapter 2 with an exposition of his theory of economic development as a holistic process of economic evolution.

Chapter 3 addresses the role the business cycle plays in Schumpeter's analysis. Schumpeter argues the business cycle is a manifestation of the process of economic evolution, driven by the clustering of innovations. The ebb and flow of innovations impact on the movement over time of all economic magnitudes, including prices and quantities, in a long-wave pattern lasting somewhat more than half a century, which Schumpeter associates with the Kondratieff business cycle (named after the Russian economist who Schumpeter identifies as the pioneer in this field, see Kondratieff, 1935). The process is endogenous with the feedback mechanism between innovation and prices being particularly important. The chapter closes with a commentary section reviewing criticisms of Schumpeter's theory of the business cycle.

Chapter 4 reviews Schumpeter's explicit presentation of his price theory, which is given in Chapters VIII and X of *BC*. Chapter VIII explains how the clustering of innovations and their subsequent diffusion leads to movements in the price level with supporting data in the form of charts showing historical movements in price series for the UK (from the late 1700s), the US (from the early 1800s) and Germany (from the mid-1800s). Chapter X discusses impacts of the innovation process on prices of individual products, including those directly affected by innovations and those related to the innovations through their production process or as substitutes in demand. In a Commentary section, I introduce Sraffa's (1960) system of reproduction prices as a framework for analysing the implications of Schumpeter's theory for the movement of the prices of individual commodities and the price level over the course of the business cycle.

Chapter 5 critically examines Schumpeter's treatment of money, credit and banking along with implications for movements in the price level. Credit is an essential endogenous element in Schumpeter's process of development, expanding and contracting along with the increase and decline in innovations. Institutional arrangements are important to the way the business cycle progresses in Schumpeter's analysis and he acknowledges institutions evolve, but his analysis is specific to the institutional arrangements of his day. Arguably, the institutional arrangements behind the pattern of cycles that Schumpeter observed up to the early twentieth century are no longer in place. Further, changing institutional arrangements in banking, particularly national and international monetary authorities, labour markets, product markets and government policies have impacted on cyclical patterns. Thus, it not surprising that some of Schumpeter's hypotheses, particularly the declining result trend for the price level, are rejected by time-series data for the last half century or more.

Analytical difficulties with Schumpeter's treatment of common-sense, theoretical and statistical "norms" are the focus in Chapter 6. The basic difficulty is Schumpeter applies norms of a stationary economy to economies having experienced multiple cycles of development. The inconsistency between the concept of equilibrium and a process producing endogenous structural change is noted and used to justify the application of the concept of order as an alternative for determining norms in a developing economy. Also, arguments are presented for why a developing economy has different norms for determining cost than those of a stationary economy. Finally, Schumpeter's own writings are used to support rejecting perfect competition as characterising the norm in developing economies.

Following on from the argument for differentiating the norms of a developing economy from those of a stationary economy, Chapter 7 is devoted to the specification of norms for developing economies. With respect to the businessman's or common-sense norm, experience of obsolescence means higher returns from investments embodying current technology are required in a developing economy than in a stationary economy. For the theoretical norm of costs and prices, the threat of obsolescence means these are higher in a developing economy than in a stationary economy with the same technology and organisation. However, improvements in technology and organisation with innovation-driven growth mean that every cycle ends with a new normal that has a higher standard of living than the one before. With respect to statistical norms, the degree of heterogeneity across firms within industries is favoured as an indicator of stages of the business cycle instead of Schumpeter's reliance on the properties of time-series graphs in the neighbourhood of equilibrium. Finally, imperfect competition as Schumpeter recognises in *CSD* remains even at the end of the business cycle and influences common-sense, theoretical and statistical norms.

Chapter 8 addresses reconstructing Schumpeter's price theory, incorporating elements of post-Keynesian approaches to price determination and evolutionary analysis of differential firm growth as well as utilising the framework of reproduction prices from Sraffa (1960). The analysis follows the micro-meso-macro approach utilised in evolutionary economics. Post-Keynesian price theories are applied in the micro analysis to provide pricing rules for firms, while the meso analysis considers the impact of innovation and creative destruction on these pricing rules and on industrial structure both within industries and across the economy. Sraffa's framework of reproduction prices is used for linking prices across the economy. Finally, Schumpeter's macro analysis is combined with the micro and meso analyses to examine the trend and cycle in the price level as well as changes in the price system.

Chapter 9 concludes this volume by providing a summary of the fundamental ideas of the price theory introduced by Schumpeter. The strengths and weaknesses of his approach are summarised along with the suggestions for modification to provide a price theory suitable for application to a modern developing capitalist economy. By then the reader should have an appreciation for Schumpeter's argument that the traditional mainstream price theory is useless in understanding the process of economic evolution and that a different theory is required in its stead. While Schumpeter's theory is flawed, at least it addresses the right problem. Whether the suggested reconstruction sufficiently remedies the flaws is left for the reader to decide.

Notes

1 Schumpeter's understanding of the economic problem and his vision of how capitalism works differ not only from the current mainstream but also from most of his contemporaries. His background, education and career certainly influenced what he knew and arguably influenced his economic theorising. There are several excellent biographies of Schumpeter that provide insights into the connection between his life and work, which include works by Richard Swedberg (1991) and Thomas McGraw (2007).
2 The flexibility of traditional theory and the ingenuity of its practitioners is well demonstrated by further manipulation of the theory that demonstrates it is possible to have R&D expenditure exceeding the social optimum if the first discoverer is granted patent rights that provide a legal monopoly over exploitation of the results of the R&D and a race to obtain these rights ensues.

2   The theory of economic development

Schumpeter embeds his price theory in a holistic theory of economic development. Price changes, particularly the cyclical movement of prices, are but one aspect of the process of economic development that follows on from and contributes to the ebb and flow of innovations. A review of the main features of Schumpeter's theory of economic development is provided in this chapter and is followed in the next chapter by a corresponding treatment of his theory of the business cycle. Detailed discussion of Schumpeter's price theory is then taken up in Chapter 4.

I begin by discussing Schumpeter's rationale for departing from traditional theory. Most important is the sharp distinction that Schumpeter draws between the discontinuous change associated with innovation and the circular flow of the economy, which is characterised by a strong tendency towards equilibrium. Schumpeter argues that neglect of discontinuous change in the traditional theory points to the need for a theory of economic development that is distinct from, but builds on, traditional economic theory.

Preliminary to dealing with the causes and consequences of discontinuous change, Schumpeter argues that there are many forms of resistance to change in the economy. I review these obstacles to change, before discussing his treatment of entrepreneurship as representing the leadership required to overcome the obstacles. The penultimate section then discusses the institutions of development as they are deployed in Schumpeter's theory, namely, firms, markets, credit, banks and the state. I conclude with a summary and observations regarding relationships to the discussion in later chapters.

Schumpeter's point of departure

Schumpeter starts from the proposition that there is a qualitative distinction between the process of economic development and the circular flow of a stationary economy that is characterised by equilibrium. As qualitatively different phenomena, different explanations are required for their analysis. Schumpeter argues that traditional economic theory is appropriate to the analysis of the circular flow with equilibrium.

> However, where it is simply a question of making development or the historical outcome of it intelligible, of working out the elements which characterise

a situation or determine an issue, economic theory in the traditional sense contributes next to nothing.

(Schumpeter, 1961 [1934], p. 59)

Schumpeter is clearly aware that the sharp distinction he draws between the ordinary course of economic life and the disruptive changes associated with innovation is fundamental to the understanding of his theory. The distinction is explained at length towards the start of each of his two main theoretical treatises, *The Theory of Economic Development* (*TED*) and *Business Cycles* (*BC*). In *TED*, the distinction is between 'The Circular Flow of Economic Life' (Chapter I) and 'The Fundamental Phenomenon of Economic Development' (Chapter II). In *BC*, the distinction is between 'Equilibrium and the Theoretical Norm of Economic Quantities' (Chapter II) and 'How the Economic System Generates Evolution' (Chapter III). In each case, the qualitative difference in the phenomena under examination takes centre stage, which Schumpeter argues requires a different framework of analysis. Thus, the analysis of disruptive and discontinuous change (his own theory of economic development and of the business cycle) is distinguished from the analysis of inherently stable processes (traditional economic theory).

In *TED*, Schumpeter justifies the need for a separate treatment of disruptive change by contrasting the traditional treatment of small changes within a familiar framework to his object of treating discontinuous change by noting,

Economic life experiences such changes too, but it also experiences others which do not appear continuously and which change the framework, the traditional course itself. They cannot be understood by means of any analysis of the circular flow, although they are purely economic and although their explanation is obviously among the tasks of pure theory. Now such changes and the phenomena which appear in their train are the object of our investigation.

(op. cit., pp. 61–62)

In *BC*, he states,

we do not attack traditional theory, Walrasian or Marshallian, on its own ground. In particular, we do not take offense at its fundamental assumptions about business behaviour – at the picture of prompt recognition of the data of a situation and of rational action in response to them. . . . It breaks down as soon as we leave those precincts and allow the business community under study to be faced by – not simply new situations, which also occur as soon as external factors unexpectedly intrude but by – new possibilities of business action which are as yet untried and about which the most complete command of routine teaches nothing.

(Schumpeter, 1939, p. 98)

Two distinguishing elements can be identified in the above quotations, the magnitude of change and the divergence from experience. Schumpeter does not specify exactly how much change or divergence is required to constitute a situation of discontinuous change as opposed to a situation of small change in a familiar framework that could be handled by traditional theory. However, he does provide a brilliant example, 'Add successively as many mail coaches as you please, you will never get a railway thereby' (Schumpeter, 1961 [1934], p. 64, note 1). He repeats this example with added explanation to clarify the meaning of development in a paper written in 1932 but only recently published,

> This kind of "novelty" constitutes what we here understand as "development," which can now be exactly defined as: *transition from one norm of the economic system to another norm in such a way that this transition cannot be decomposed into infinitesimal steps*. In other words: Steps between which there is no strictly continuous path.
>
> (Schumpeter, 2005a, p. 115, quotation marks and italics in the original)[1]

Schumpeter's distinction between his theory of development and traditional theory is further clarified by his treatment of population growth and capital accumulation, the two elements that feature prominently as internal factors of development in the classical and neoclassical theory of economic growth.

> Nor will the mere growth of the economy, as shown by the growth of population and wealth, be designated here as a process of development. For it calls forth no qualitatively new phenomena, but only processes of adaptation of the same kind as the changes in the natural data. Since we wish to direct our attention to other phenomena, we shall regard such increases as changes in data.
>
> (Schumpeter, 1961 [1934], p. 63)

Population growth and capital accumulation are compatible with established routines generating a tendency towards equilibrium, so they can be accommodated by an adaptive response and don't constitute part of a distinct theory of development.[2]

The phenomena that are of particular interest to Schumpeter are new combinations in business because they represent creative responses affecting the working of the economy. The examples noted by Schumpeter (1961 [1934], p. 66) in *TED* are new products, new methods of production, opening of new markets, conquest of new sources of supply of inputs and new organisation of an industry, for example, creating or breaking a monopoly position. In *BC*, he introduces the term innovation to denote the class of phenomena and expands the list of examples to include changes in work practices, business organisation and distribution channels (Schumpeter, 1939, p. 84).

Schumpeter is careful to distinguish innovations from the antecedent inventions or discoveries, which are not necessarily internal to the economy. It is only turning inventions or discoveries into innovations in business practice that is inherently an economic process and, thus, the proper focus of the theory of economic development. In *TED*, Schumpeter explains the distinction in terms of the special form of economic leadership required to turn inventions into innovations,

> Economic leadership in particular must be distinguished from "invention." As long as they are not carried into practice, inventions are economically irrelevant. And to carry any improvement into effect is a task entirely different from the inventing of it, and a task, moreover, requiring entirely different kinds of aptitudes.
>
> (Schumpeter, 1961 [1934], p. 88, quotation marks in the original)

As a distinct factor of change, innovation is neither assured nor predictable in Schumpeter's analysis. At any point in time there are innumerable ideas that have not been implemented into innovations and this pool of unexploited innovations is growing indefinitely as human knowledge expands.

The key requirement for innovation according to Schumpeter is a creative response in the form of entrepreneurial action, which converts an idea into an innovation. These entrepreneurial actions are not automatic and instantaneous as implicitly assumed in neoclassical models with Olympian rationality leading to the continual optimisation with regard to all possible innovations. Rather, creative responses are exceptional so that entrepreneurial action only occasionally takes advantage of the available, but only imperfectly perceived, opportunities, or as Brian Loasby (1996, p. 17) puts it, 'The Imagined Deemed Possible'.

The emergent character of innovations leads Schumpeter to use economic evolution to describe the process brought about by innovation.

> The changes in the economic process brought about by innovation, together with all their effects, we shall designate by the term Economic Evolution. Although this term is objectionable on several counts, it comes nearer to expressing our meaning than does any other, and it has the advantage of avoiding the associations suggested by the cognate term Progress, particularly the complacency the latter seems to imply.
>
> (Schumpeter, 1939, p. 86)

Schumpeter's focus on economic evolution still leaves a role for the tendency towards equilibrium in his theory of economic development. Indeed, if one adopts Schumpeter's criterion for innovation of "doing things differently" to an extent that can't be accommodated by an adaptive response, innovations are rare and constitute a small portion of economic activity. Why bother breaking with traditional theory and argue for a theory focussed on such occasional and anomalous activity?

To Schumpeter, the tail wags the dog. Creative responses leading to new combinations in business are the driving force behind economic evolution, the process he holds responsible for the radical changes in technology that give rise to a generally rising living standard. Schumpeter insists that a complete theory of economic life, particularly under capitalism, must include an explanation of innovation and its consequences.

Schumpeter views his theory of development as an extension of traditional theory to cover the phenomenon of innovation. In *TED*, in referring to the analysis of the circular flow with which he begins the book, he states, 'the economic theory the nature of which was sufficiently expounded to the reader in the first chapter will simply be improved for its own purposes, by building on to it' (Schumpeter, 1961 [1934], p. 61). In *BC*, he accepts the widespread applicability of traditional theory and notes that even in circumstances where there is innovation through a creative response traditional theory still applies to those parts of the economy where firms aren't innovating (Schumpeter, 1939, p. 99). Thus, Schumpeter's theory of economic development is a theory in which innovation and the tendency towards equilibrium are clearly distinguished but coexist in a symbiotic relationship.[3]

Obstacles to change

Why are creative responses leading to innovation through entrepreneurial action so special? In *TED*, Schumpeter notes three difficulties encountered when doing things differently. The first is economic and concerns decision-making with incomplete or imprecise knowledge.

> First, outside these accustomed channels the individual is without those data for his decisions and those rules of conduct which are usually very accurately known to him within them. Of course he must still foresee and estimate on the basis of his experience. But many things are uncertain, still others are only ascertainable within wide limits, some can perhaps only be "guessed." . . . What has been done already has the sharp-edged reality of all the things which we have seen and experienced; the new is only the figment of our imagination. Carrying out a new plan and acting according to a customary one are things as different as making a road and walking along it.
>
> (Schumpeter, 1961 [1934], pp. 84–85,
> quotation marks in the original)

Schumpeter appeals here to common sense in terms of understanding the role of knowledge in decision-making. Creativity (imagination) enters the frame in lieu of precise calculation, in part because of 'the impossibility of surveying all the effects and counter-effects of the projected enterprise' (op. cit., p. 85). There leads to a reliance on 'intuition, the capacity of seeing things in a way which afterwards proves to be true' (ibid.). The discussion hints at modern treatments of decision-making under true uncertainty, such as bounded rationality. However, Schumpeter doesn't go far down this path and, indeed, uncertainty is not even specifically identified as a factor impeding creative responses in his later discussion of the subject in *BC*.[4]

The second difficulty noted by Schumpeter is psychological, namely that thought processes favour the familiar over the new. 'It is not only objectively more difficult to do something new than what is familiar and tested by experience, but the individual feels reluctance to it and would do so even if the objective difficulties did not exist' (op. cit., p. 86). Schumpeter argues that most people feel an inhibition when taking on something new. Again, Schumpeter's appeal is to common sense or introspection, emphasising the realism of his assumptions.

From psychology, Schumpeter turns to sociology for his third difficulty encountered when doing things differently.

> The third point consists in the reaction of the social environment against one who wishes to do something new. This reaction may manifest itself first of all in legal or political impediments. But neglecting this, any conduct by a member of a social group is condemned, though in greatly varying degrees according as the social group is used to such conduct or not.
>
> (op. cit., pp. 86–87)

Existing routines are generally accommodated into the traditions and social institutions operating at any time and place. Schumpeter notes that doing things differently can mean the innovator is subject to condemnation, ostracism or even outright attack. He notes that even though the experience of a period of turbulent development has helped accustom society to innovations, the difficulty remains.

Although Schumpeter doesn't include uncertainty or lack of knowledge in his list of obstacles to creative responses in treating the subject *BC*, he still notes three classes of obstacles. Resistance of the social environment and the businessman's psychological inhibitions are joined by a separate class of the lack of prerequisites, at least some of which are identified as part of resistance of the social environment in *TED*. Lack of prerequisites captures the need for complementary changes if an innovation is to be successful. Workers with the necessary skills and experience must be recruited, materials and intermediate inputs must be sourced and, often, new varieties of machinery are required. All of this requires cooperation from individuals and firms who may be highly sceptical of the success of the innovation. Customers need to be enticed to switch from previous suppliers or to try a, possibly radically, new product. Schumpeter also argues that innovators in general require external finance from banks, which means the entrepreneur must overcome reluctance to lend for untried projects (Schumpeter, 1939, pp. 99–100).

To bring their innovation to fruition the innovator is asked to overcome resistance in the social environment, the lack of prerequisites and personal inhibitions. This requires extraordinary character and ability, attributes that Schumpeter associates with leadership and identifies as the role of the entrepreneur.

Entrepreneurship

I label this section entrepreneurship rather than the entrepreneur to emphasise Schumpeter's treatment of entrepreneurship as a role rather than its embodiment in a person. In *TED*, the role aspect of entrepreneurship is contrasted to its embodiment in a person as follows: 'everyone is an entrepreneur only when he actually "carries out new combinations," and loses that character as soon as he has built up his business, when he settles down to running it as other people run their businesses' (Schumpeter, 1961 [1934], p. 78, quotation marks in the original). Similarly, in *BC*, he emphasises that no one is always an entrepreneur and that even a man carrying out new combinations will inevitably spend much time on more routine tasks (Schumpeter, 1939, p. 103).

Schumpeter explains his conception of entrepreneurship largely by way of exclusions. First, as implied above, entrepreneurship is distinguished from 'the Marshallian definition of the entrepreneur, which simply treats the entrepreneurial function as "management" in the widest meaning' (Schumpeter, 1961 [1934], p. 77, quotation marks in the original). Second, just as Schumpeter distinguishes innovation in terms of carrying out new combinations from invention, he notes that the entrepreneurial role is distinguished from that of the inventor. The entrepreneurial role is taking an invention or an idea to the stage of implementation. Finally, the entrepreneurial role is not that of capitalist and, hence, not that of risk taker. While ownership of property or money may make the introduction of a new combination easier, it is not necessary (Schumpeter, 1939, pp. 103–04). Indeed, the use of external finance by entrepreneurs plays a key role in Schumpeter's theory as is discussed in the next section on the role of institutions in development as well as in the next chapter on business cycles.

Exclusions help to distinguish Schumpeter's conception of entrepreneurship from uses of the term by others, but leave open the question of what specific activity is required for carrying out new combinations. Here, Schumpeter is clear that the required activity is leadership, 'every step outside the boundaries of routine has difficulties and involves a new element. It is this element that constitutes the phenomenon of leadership' (Schumpeter, 1961 [1934], p. 84). The difficulties referred to here are those identified in the above discussion of the obstacles to change, so the type of leadership that Schumpeter has in mind is the overcoming of the obstacles to change. For Schumpeter, the carrying out of new combinations is a type of economic leadership that is synonymous with entrepreneurship.

Associating leadership with entrepreneurship provides Schumpeter with a link between the function of carrying out new combinations and the personality characteristics of entrepreneurs. The discussion of personality characteristics of the entrepreneurial type in *TED* continues with the following passage on the rationality of the entrepreneur.

> he may indeed be called the most rational and egotistical of all. For, as we have seen, conscious rationality enters much more into the carrying out of new plans, which themselves have to be worked out before they can be acted upon, than the mere running of an established business, which is largely a matter of routine. And the typical entrepreneur is more self-centered than other types, because he relies less than they do on tradition and connection and because his characteristic task – theoretically as well as historically – consists precisely in breaking up old, and creating new, tradition.
>
> (op. cit. pp. 91–92)

Schumpeter then points to three heroic characteristics of the entrepreneurial type.

> First of all, there is the dream and will to found a private kingdom, usually, though not necessarily, also a dynasty. . . . Then there is the will to conquer: the impulse to fight, to prove oneself superior to others, to succeed for the sake, not of the fruits of success, but of success itself. . . . Finally, there is the joy of creating, of getting things done, or simply exercising one's energy and ingenuity.
>
> (op. cit., p. 93)

Schumpeter's stress on the exceptional personality characteristics of the entrepreneurial type is essential to his argument that traditional theory must be amended to include innovation as a process distinct from adaptive responses.[5] Even when there are obstacles to change, an abundant supply of entrepreneurs could provide the means for overcoming these obstacles and ensuring that inventions and discoveries quickly become innovations. In this case, there might be shocks to the economy from the introduction to innovations but Schumpeter's argument for innovation as a distinct internal factor of change would be substantially weakened. Further, as discussed in the next chapter, the swarming of innovations, which is at the heart of Schumpeter's theory of business cycles, depends on there being a large unexploited pool of potential innovations that are only tapped into once economic conditions are conducive and the path has been opened by a few pioneering entrepreneurs.

Institutions and development

Entrepreneurs provide leadership to overcome the resistance to change in the ways of doing things in Schumpeter's analysis. They normally operate outside the established system of production and so Schumpeter argues that 'new combinations are, as a rule, embodied, as it were, in new firms which generally do not arise out of old ones but start producing besides them' (op. cit., p. 66). The new firms need to obtain means of production. Schumpeter argues this involves the creation of credit by banks, which is then used to divert the means of production from existing firms. Markets are used for this purpose as well as to generate the revenues to repay loans with interest and yield profit. New firms, banks and markets are thus part of the institutional framework that supports innovation, as is the system of private ownership of property required for firms, banks and markets to play their respective roles in the innovation process.

The role of credit in diverting means of production is further explained in *TED*,

> The essential function of credit in our sense consists in enabling the entrepreneur to withdraw the producers' goods which he needs from their previous employments, by exercising a demand for them, and thereby to force the economic system into new channels.
>
> (op. cit., p. 106)

The entrepreneur's investment is offset by the reduction in production from existing business, which corresponds to savings when the reduced production is of consumer goods or to a decline in other investment when the reduced production is of producer goods. The extra purchasing power from the created credit drives up the prices of productive services and, as discussed in Chapter 4, the prices of final products.

In *BC*, Schumpeter elaborates on the functioning of a system in which innovations are the sole province of new firms using bank credit to secure their means of production in markets. There, Schumpeter assumes that credit is used exclusively for this purpose. He also assumes for simplicity that entrepreneurs never have their own funds, thereby emphasising that possessing funds is not necessary for carrying out new combinations. Finally, he assumes that old firms not only refrain from undertaking innovations, but also finance their current expenditures from their current receipts (Schumpeter, 1939, pp. 110–11).

These three propositions are meant to capture the essence of the process used for diverting productive resources from existing uses to the carrying out of new combinations under capitalism. Growth through saving and accumulation is treated as ancillary and largely due to profits or other incomes that would not exist in a stationary state. Causation according to Schumpeter runs from innovations to income flows of the types that are substantially saved. However, the income flows occur following the innovations, and so these innovations must be otherwise financed until the output from the carrying out of new combinations is available (Schumpeter, 1939, pp. 82–83).

Creating credit to finance innovations is generally the business of banks in Schumpeter's analysis. They issue either bank notes or deposit balances to entrepreneurs, allowing them to obtain means of production in competition with existing producers and thereby drive up prices. However, this process is limited by the requirement that the principal advanced be repaid with interest, which reduces outstanding credit and leads to autodeflation, driving prices back down below the initial level. In this sense banks can only succeed in their business of lending to entrepreneurs if there is a net deflationary impact on prices when the process is completed. The ups and downs of prices associated with credit creation and withdrawal are part of Schumpeter's theory of the business cycle that is discussed in the next chapter, while the implications in terms of the theory of banking, credit and money are discussed in Chapter 5.

Schumpeter portrays innovations as exclusively the domain of new firms in *TED*, but in *BC* he acknowledges a role for large firms with professional staff devoted to innovative activity (Schumpeter, 1939, p. 96). Still, he argues that the institutional changes from competitive capitalism to trustified capitalism that had occurred in the economy had not gone far enough to undermine his picture of disruptive innovations (op. cit., p. 97). It is only in *CSD* that Schumpeter emphasises the threat from large concerns to undermining the role of entrepreneurs in development.

> Since capitalist enterprise, by its very achievements, tends to automatize progress, we conclude that it tends to make itself superfluous – to break to

pieces under the pressure of its own success. The perfectly bureaucratized giant industrial unit not only ousts the small and medium-sized firm and "expropriates" its owners, but in the end it also ousts the entrepreneur and expropriates the bourgeoisie as a class which in the process stands to lose not only its income but also what is infinitely more important, its function.

(Schumpeter, 1976 [1950], p. 134, quotation marks in the original)

The decline of the entrepreneur is part of the process of undermining the institutional structure of capitalism, which Schumpeter goes on to argue in *CSD* threatens the continuation of capitalism as an economic system. Whether Schumpeter is right about the fate of capitalism as a system and whether it will be replaced by socialism are much debated (see, for example, the essays in Heertje, 1981). The important questions for the current and future applicability of the Schumpeter's theory of economic development, including his theory of prices, are whether a shift in innovation activity from new firms to giant industrial concerns has progressed sufficiently to alter the pattern of innovations entering the economy and whether such a shift would alter the impact of those innovations on prices. The first question is much debated in the empirical literature on innovation and firm size (see, for example, Acs and Audretsch, 1988a, 1988b), while the second question is a major focus of Chapter 8 of this volume.

Summary

Schumpeter sharply differentiates the process of economic development from that of the circular flow. He associates the circular flow with the stationary state of an economy, while economic development is solely concerned with the introduction of innovations into the economy. Intermediate processes, such as population growth or saving and accumulation, are dismissed as contingent on the gains derived from innovation and excluded from the basic analysis.

To further separate economic development from the circular flow, Schumpeter assumes that all innovations are sufficiently radical to face stiff resistance and require intervention of new men operating in new firms and needing newly created credit to dislodge means of production from established channels of the circular flow. Traditional economic theory is of no use in analysing the activity of innovation because it is based on the rational calculation associated with adaptive responses. Instead, a different theory is proposed by Schumpeter, which involves uneven impacts across time that are the subject of his theory of business cycles (the topic of the next chapter) and, in particular, to structural change within the economy that is the subject of his price theory (the topic of Chapter 4).

Notes

1 According to the authors of the introduction to the version of the paper published in English, the paper was included in a folder of papers presented to Emil Lederer on the occasion of his fiftieth birthday in 1932 (Schumpeter, 2005a, p. 108).

2 This provides the basis for Schumpeter's rejection of the treatments of economic development by the classical economists, most notably Ricardo and Mill, who put the issue of technical change outside the scope of explanation by their theory. Schumpeter comments more favourably on the approach of J. B. Clark, who separates statics and dynamics, and includes changes in techniques and in productive organisation among his dynamic factors (see Schumpeter, 1961 [1934], p. 59, note 1).

3 The connection between innovation and the tendency towards equilibrium is further developed in the next chapter as their interaction has a key role in Schumpeter's theory of the business cycle.

4 Uncertainty plays a secondary role in Schumpeter's analysis as without economic development there would only be the circular flow of repeated transactions and no uncertainty. Thus, without innovation acting according to routine is all that is necessary. This helps to explain the difference between Schumpeter, who ascribes profit to innovation, and Knight (1971 [1921]), who ascribes profit to uncertainty.

5 When Schumpeter discusses the crumbling walls of capitalism in *CSD*, he continues to argue for the scarcity of the entrepreneurial type. 'To act with confidence beyond the range of familiar beacons and to overcome that resistance requires aptitudes that are present in only a small fraction of the population and that define the entrepreneurial type as well as the entrepreneurial function' (Schumpeter, 1976 [1950], p. 132). However, he also argues that declining resistance to change will see entrepreneurship replaced by 'teams of trained specialists who turn out what is required and make it work in predictable ways' (ibid.).

3 Business cycle theory and statistical methods

Mainstream economics generally treats business cycles as arising from external shocks to the economy. These shocks disturb equilibrium, but only temporarily, as markets adjust to the shocks through a self-equilibrating process. For Schumpeter, business cycles are not aberrations, but rather an inherent part of the process of economic evolution associated with the introduction and absorption of innovations. Innovations lead to booms as entrepreneurs compete for means of production, such that, '*The recurring periods of prosperity of the cyclical movement are the form progress takes in capitalistic society*' (Schumpeter, 1927, p. 30, italics in the original). Recessions, in turn, are part of the process of adjustment to structural change required by the innovations, as old ways of doing things are replaced by the new.

Schumpeter's theory of the business cycle is an essential component of his theory of economic development starting from the first edition of *Theorie der wirtschaftlichen Entwicklung* (Schumpeter, 1926 [1912]), the precursor to the edition used for the English translation in the *Theory of Economic Development* (*TED*) (Schumpeter, 1961 [1934]). During the period from the mid-1920s to the mid-1930s, Schumpeter references this theory in a number of journal articles, both contrasting it to the contemporaneous theories of others (as in Schumpeter, 1927, 1930) and using it as the basis for explaining the unevenness of growth under capitalism (as in Schumpeter, 1928, 1935). In the process, he puts forward a number of arguments about the necessity of integrating theory, statistics and historical analysis to achieve a full understanding of business cycles.

The culmination of Schumpeter's research on business cycles is the two-volume *Business Cycles (BC)*, published in 1939. While the discussion of business cycles appears in the last chapter of *TED*, in *BC* the cyclical aspect of development takes centre stage. There is an extended discussion of each of the four cycle phases, prosperity, recession, depression and recovery, along with a discussion of a multiplicity of cycles of different lengths overlapping each other. *BC* also contains a discussion of the application of statistical method to the interpretation of cycles and trend in time-series data. Finally, the bulk of *BC* provides a detailed historical account of cyclical economic development, concentrating on the American, English and German experience since 1787.

In this chapter, I follow the structure of the argument as set out in *BC* and start with a discussion of Schumpeter's concept of the theoretical norm from Chapter II. Though economic evolution is driven by disruptive innovations and their diffusion through creative destruction, Schumpeter treats the theoretical norm of economic variables (prices, outputs and such) as determined by the conditions of the circular flow of a stationary economy with competitive general equilibrium. However, because the economy never reaches equilibrium, the concept of the theoretical norm is qualified and only becomes operational during those intervals of time when the economy is in the neighbourhood of equilibrium.

Chapter III of *BC* restates Schumpeter's theory of economic development from *TED*, although with minor differences as noted in my Chapter 2. The movement away from and toward equilibrium is then discussed in terms of the contours of economic evolution in Chapter IV. Here, Schumpeter lays out his argument using a series of approximations. The first approximation or Pure Model deals with the sequence of adjustments in economic variables following a wave of innovations that disturb the equilibrium of the circular flow. This includes the movement back toward a new equilibrium as the impact of the innovations dissipates, which produces a two-phase cycle of prosperity and recession. The second approximation covers the tendency for excessive investment in prosperity, which contributes to the downswing of the business cycle continuing beyond the neighbourhood of equilibrium. Recession leads into depression, which is followed by recovery, so that the two-phase cycle becomes a four-phase cycle. The third approximation deals with overlapping shorter cycles that arise from various aspects of the adjustment processes in the economy. Finally, there is a discussion of external factors as the source of complicating fluctuations in economic magnitudes.

Chapter V of *BC* develops the empirical implications of Schumpeter's business cycle theory with the title, 'Time Series and their Normal'. A key point is the difficulty of using statistical methods to discern the trend in a time series that has cyclical components of the variety implied by the analysis in Chapter IV, especially in view of the complicating effects of other influences. Schumpeter settles on the concept of a "result trend", which is given by the average growth between "normal points". The "normal points" are identified as the values of variables when the economy is in the neighbourhood of equilibrium with innovative activity at a low level. Finally, Schumpeter illustrates with the times-series graph for an idealised scenario in which a Kondratieff cycle of 57 years' length contains six intermediate cycles of nine-and-a-half years (Juglar cycles), each of which in turn contains three cycles of three and one-sixth years (Kitchin cycles).

The first section below presents an overview of Schumpeter's concept of the theoretical norm in the context of an economy undergoing development and, hence, subject to the disturbing influence of innovations. This is followed by a discussion of Schumpeter's exposition of his theory of the business cycle as a series of the approximations. Next is a section with discussion of the concepts of a "result trend" and "normal points" and their application to the interpretation of time-series data, ending with setting out Schumpeter's idealised scenario for the overlaying of Kitchin, Juglar and Kondratieff cycles. The penultimate section provides commentary, including criticisms of aspects of the business cycle theory, and identifies issues that require further consideration in building on the foundations of Schumpeter's theory. A final section summarises the key points made in the chapter.

Equilibrium and the theoretical normal of economic quantities

Schumpeter argues that the circular flow of a stationary economy, with economic activity repeated identically in each period, satisfies the conditions of competitive general equilibrium from traditional economic analysis. However, an economy organised with capitalist institutions inevitably generates innovations that disturb this circular flow. 'Capitalism, then, is by nature a form or method of economic change and not only never is but never can be stationary' (Schumpeter, 1976 [1950], p. 82). As a result, a fruitful analysis of the capitalist economy requires modification of the traditional analysis to incorporate innovations and their impact on economic magnitudes.

The particular modification suggested by Schumpeter is to treat innovations as causing movement away from equilibrium for a prolonged period required to diffuse these innovations and absorb their impact. However, he maintains that the flow of innovations eventually abates due to the disturbed economic conditions they create and that there is eventually a movement toward the neighbourhood of a new equilibrium. In this sense, Schumpeter's theory is an addendum rather than a replacement for traditional equilibrium theory.

Schumpeter acknowledges proving the existence of unique values of prices and quantities consistent with Walrasian equilibrium is not equivalent to demonstrating an adjustment process for moving to that equilibrium. Practical complications include the effects of lags, rigidities, expectations and imperfect competition. Each of these is shown to possibly impede movement toward equilibrium or to perpetuate disturbances, although examples are also given of circumstances in which each can help with constraining movement away from equilibrium or even encourage equilibration (Schumpeter, 1939, pp. 45–56).

In spite of the qualifications, Schumpeter maintains that concept of theoretically normal values is still useful. He argues actual values are attracted to the theoretically normal values as determined by Walrasian competitive general equilibrium, but only at the beginning and end of the business cycle. Further, the adjustment to equilibrium is not complete, so actual values can only be expected to be in the neighbourhood of this equilibrium. Recognising the speculative nature of his argument, Schumpeter acknowledges, 'our belief in the existence of an equilibrium tendency, which after every excursion draws the system back to a new state of equilibrium, will have to stand on trial to the last page of this book' (op. cit., p. 70).

As noted in the Commentary section of this chapter, Schumpeter's use of the Walrasian equilibrium from the circular flow as defining the theoretical norm of the values of economic magnitudes has been subjected to sharp criticism. In Chapter 6 below, I more closely examine Schumpeter's discussion of common sense, theoretical and statistical norms and the basis for his linkages among them. In the meantime, his conception of the theoretical norm as determined by Walrasian competitive general equilibrium is maintained for the purpose of explaining Schumpeter's business cycle theory in this chapter and explaining his price theory in the next chapter.

The contours of economic evolution

Analysis leading to identification of conditions holding when the economy is in the neighbourhood of equilibrium is a key part of Schumpeter's theory and is emphasised in his discussion of the contours of economic evolution. Schumpeter begins the theory of the business cycle with an economy in equilibrium of the circular flow. The economy is stationary with the same production and transactions occurring in each period. There is no innovation nor has there been any. Thus, the economy is expected to be fully adjusted to its theoretical norm (op. cit., p. 130).

Schumpeter then argues this state of the economy is unsustainable under the institutional arrangements of capitalism. Increased knowledge leads to ideas that can be exploited through innovations and there are entrepreneurs ready and able to carry them out. Further, the steadiness of the economy underpins reliable calculation of costs, prices and profits, with the prospect of a resulting profit motivating action to establish a new enterprise. Banks provide the requisite credit and the entrepreneur is able to acquire the means of production in the market by competing against established producers.

Innovation is endogenous in Schumpeter's theory. It also occurs unevenly over time as well as across sectors of the economy. While the unexploited opportunities for innovation expand with the spread of knowledge, leadership is required to overcome the resistance to change. Once one leader has shown the way, further innovation becomes easier. Resistance to change is eroded by the experience of change in a cumulative pattern (op. cit., p. 131).

Innovations have an uneven impact on prices and profits in various parts of the economy and move the economy away from the neighbourhood of equilibrium. Adjustments take time and lead to fluctuations and sequential responses to changing prices. The magnitudes associated with the theoretical norm no longer apply, which increases the risk of failure and undermines the conditions for further innovations, so entrepreneurial activity declines and eventually comes to a halt (op. cit., pp. 135–36).

Along with the decline in innovations, there is the repayment of loans by successful entrepreneurs. Overall, the amount of credit in the system falls, a process that Schumpeter refers to as autodeflation. This process leads to a new equilibrium, which compared to that at the start of the cycle has,

> a "greater" social product of a different pattern, new production functions, equal sum total of money incomes, a minimum (strictly zero) rate of interest, zero profits, zero loans, a different system of prices and a lower level of prices, the fundamental expression of the fact that all lasting achievements of

the particular spurt of innovation have been handed to consumers in the form of increased real incomes.

(op. cit., p. 137, quotation marks in the original)

The skeleton of the Pure Model or first approximation to explaining the business cycle is that a spurt of innovation generates prosperity followed by recession due solely to the economic evolution directly following from the innovations. The process begins with equilibrium of the circular flow and ends with the system in the neighbourhood of equilibrium, which is recognisable through the conditions in the quotation immediately above. The ups and downs of this approximation are a necessary accompaniment to progress through innovation. Schumpeter therefore objects to the view of traditional theory and public opinion, that progress and fluctuations are different and separable phenomena (op. cit., pp. 138–39).

Schumpeter acknowledges the demonstration that innovation could lead to fluctuations in the aggregate economy is not the same as showing historical business cycles are the outcome of this process. Yet, he then argues there are elements of the business cycle that well fit his explanation. First, his explanation provides a motive power by which one cycle follows on from another. Second, his explanation doesn't depend on errors of judgement of incorrect anticipations that are hard to accept as independent causes of repeated cycles. Finally, he claims his explanation is consistent with the observations of overproduction or underconsumption and the expansion and contraction of monetary time series (op. cit., pp. 139–42).

At the close of his discussion of the first approximation, Schumpeter brings the reader's attention to a few additional points about his Pure Model. First, his analysis doesn't imply business cycles have a constant duration or amplitude. Second, basing his theory of cycles, which are measured in terms of economic aggregates, on the phenomenon of innovation, which directly affects only part of the economy, should not be held against the theory. Finally, his model depends on the particular institutional structure of competitive capitalism, which may be evolving (op. cit., pp. 143–44).[1]

Schumpeter's second approximation extends his analysis to consider the impact of forces leading to a further propagation of the business cycle in a secondary wave that includes depression and recovery as well as prosperity and recession. The secondary wave involves expansion in sectors of the economy beyond those directly affected by innovations, as there is an extended restructuring of demand. There are also speculative expansions based on thinking the upswing is general in nature. The increase in production associated with this secondary wave is unsustainable as it is dependent on continuation of the boom conditions that fade with the decline in innovations. Innovations can lead to sustained increases in production in industries directly affected because they enhance productivity, but this not generally true of industries affected by the secondary expansions.

The nature of the secondary wave is such that the adjustment process of recession is propelled beyond the neighbourhood of equilibrium it would otherwise obtain. Schumpeter refers to this movement beyond the neighbourhood of equilibrium as depression. He then adds a fourth phase to the cycle, that of recovery, in which the economy is drawn back towards the neighbourhood of equilibrium (op. cit., pp. 148–50).

Schumpeter's mechanism for the turning point of the two-phase cycle at the end of recession is an upsurge of innovation spurred by having values that are in the neighbourhood of equilibrium. However, in the depths of a depression, conditions aren't ripe for an upsurge in innovation because there is no approach to equilibrium. After surveying various possible arguments for endogenous causes that might stop the downward spiral of a depression, Schumpeter has no sure-fire solution. Thus, he concludes there is a case for government action beyond reducing human misery and this case is stronger than it is in the case of the recession (op. cit., p. 155).

By replacing the two-phase cycle of prosperity and recession with a four-phase cycle that adds depression and recovery, the lower turning point for the cycle occurs between depression and recovery, rather than at the end of recession. Schumpeter recognises this means the line connecting theoretical norms no longer connects lower boundary points on the time-series graph. Rather, for the four-phase cycle, the line connecting theoretical normal values cuts through the time-series graph, which means the recovery phase is last of the four phases not the first phase of a new cycle (op. cit., p. 156). The upsurge of prosperity is driven by a new swarm of innovations and this is a feature Schumpeter associates with the beginning of a new cycle rather than the recovery from the bottom of a depression.

Schumpeter closes his discussion of the second approximation by adding other modifications to his Pure Model. First, he drops the assumption that the cycle is the first ever and begins from a stationary state and so is not affected by the results of previous evolution. Instead, he acknowledges that each neighbourhood of equilibrium, 'contains undigested elements of previous prosperities and depressions, innovations not fully worked out, results of faulty or otherwise adaptations, and so on' (op. cit., p. 157). Also, producers having become familiar with fluctuations in demand maintain capacity sufficient to deal with times of prosperity. As a result they will generally be operating below full capacity, which means that in prosperity output responds more easily and price rises less quickly than in the Pure Model. Corresponding to the unutilised capacity, there may be unemployment of labour associated with the uneven pattern of production as workers wait for a recovery that would lead to reemployment at their former job (op. cit., p. 158).

Other modifications introduced with the second approximation include, growth from saving, credit created for purposes other than financing innovation and investment not solely due to the direct effects of innovation. Further, there is explicit recognition of the possibility of imperfect competition and imperfect equilibrium even at the start of the cycle. All these modifications are acknowledged to create difficulties in both analysis and in interpretation of the observed pattern of business situations, but innovation remains the fundamental driving force behind both the primary and secondary waves of the cycle.

Schumpeter's third approximation starts by observing that with innovation as the driving force leading to cyclical movements there is no reason to expect a single periodicity. He then discusses statistical work on cycles, noting particularly the work of Clèment Juglar, N. D. Kondratieff and Joseph Kitchin on cycles having length of nine to ten years, 50 to 60 years and about 40 months, respectively (op. cit., pp. 162–65). With gestation and absorption periods differing across clusters of innovation, the choice of the number and duration of cyclical movements then is taken to be a matter for historical analysis. For descriptive purposes, Schumpeter adopts a three-cycle schema with long cycles of the sort used by Kondratieff overlaying shorter cycles of the type described by Juglar and even shorter cycles of the type described by Kitchin. He then pre-empts his own historical analysis, noting there is an exact fit in almost every case with six Juglars in each Kondratieff and three Kitchins in each Juglar (op. cit., pp. 173–74).

Schumpeter acknowledges sources of economic fluctuations other than economic evolution arising from innovation. First, any substantial disruption can cause a movement away from equilibrium that then stimulates equilibrating forces, much as occurs with a surge of innovation. Examples given include war and peace, variations in gold production and agricultural bounties and disasters. He treats these cases as special cycles, generated by exogenous events, which are superimposed on the cycles generated by the recurring clustering of innovations (op. cit., pp. 174–79).

Schumpeter then considers a variety of explanations for fluctuations producing repeated oscillations in the form of acoustic waves (op. cit., p. 179). He links these explanations to the overshooting followed by a return toward equilibrium explanation that features in the second approximation in his theory. Just as the second approximation does not deal with the fundamental force in his theory of the business cycle, so too with these other explanations (op. cit., p. 189). In Schumpeter's view they are not independent theories of the business cycle.

The last group of explanations of fluctuations considered by Schumpeter involves purchases of industrial equipment, especially replacement purchases. Schumpeter notes replacement purchases might fluctuate cyclically as owners are discouraged to make replacements when business is slack and encouraged to do so when business is brisk. He also notes there may be bunching in the age profile of existing equipment so the amount of equipment reaching retirement age is unevenly distributed over time. Finally, he considers the impact of a rise in desired production when equipment is already being used at full capacity. Schumpeter argues all these cases represent secondary phenomena. Some primary influence is required to explain the unevenness in the flow of demand or in the age distribution of existing equipment. As with the group of explanations of oscillations, they do not in themselves constitute theories of the business cycle (op. cit., pp. 189–92).

Time series and their normal

In Chapter V of *BC*, 'Time series and their normal', three types of variables are distinguished, namely theoretical, stochastic and historical. Theoretical variables are those that appear in law-like relationships within a system. The economic example given by Schumpeter is the relationship for determining the quantity demanded or price in the Walrasian system (op. cit., p. 194).

A theoretical variable becomes a stochastic variable when the value of that variable is subject to variation according to selection from a universe of possible values, which may be described by a distribution of relative frequencies. Schumpeter gives the example of price-quantity data that represent a Marshallian demand curve. The one "true" price for any quantity is a theoretical variable, but the observed price is a stochastic variable that might take on values deviating from the "true" price by the amount of random errors. If the theoretical law governing variables is unchanged, statistical methods can be applied to estimate the relationship of the law (op. cit., pp. 194–95).

Schumpeter then distinguishes a historic variable from a stochastic variable, 'by the fact that its theoretical law is in a process of change' (op. cit., p. 195). The example Schumpeter chooses to illustrate this distinction is the pattern over time for the price of a commodity starting from a position of Walrasian equilibrium, with the "true" price equal to its theoretical norm and with the stochastic norm given by a frequency distribution around this price. With economic evolution due to innovation, there is a shift from the old theoretical normal to the new as the system reaches the neighbourhood of a new equilibrium. Thus, the stochastic norm of a historic variable is changing over time.

A sequence of values of historic variables is a time series. Because the underlying the theoretical normal of the variable is changing over time, the laws of probability don't apply. Two specific problems are noted by Schumpeter in interpreting times-series data. First is the problem of the separation of cycles of different periodicity. Second is the problem that various different series are correlated, which requires examining the connection between series, which he denies can be done by formal methods due to the changing theoretical norms (op. cit., pp. 197–98).

Because time-series data represent observations from multiple theoretical norms and from periods in between, when no theoretical normal applies, they cannot in general be analysed as if they are observations on a stochastic variable. Instead, Schumpeter proposes to use his theory to provide economic meaning with which to interpret time-series data. This "principle of economic meaning" then provides the approach he applies in the historical analysis that comprises the bulk of *BC* (op. cit., pp. 199–200).

With regard to the division of a time series between trend and cyclical components, Schumpeter defines the descriptive trend for a time series as a smooth curve (most simply a line) fitted through the data by some statistical method, such as least squares. He then distinguishes descriptive trends from real trends and suggests that because the contour of economic evolution is cyclical, rather than steady, the underlying process is unlikely to be revealed by any process of curve fitting (op. cit., pp. 200–04).

A trend with economic meaning for time series is identified by Schumpeter from the proposition that innovations occur in swarms and that these swarms begin when the economy is in the neighbourhood of equilibrium after recovery from the preceding cycle. Thus, measuring a meaningful trend requires first identifying intervals of times-series that correspond to the neighbourhood of equilibrium. The trend fitted through such points in the times series corresponding to these intervals then provides a "result trend" that captures the various influences driving movement of the time series over the full length of the cycle, among which the structural changes associated with the cluster of innovations are of first importance (op. cit., pp. 206–07).

For the single two-phase cycle in Schumpeter's theory, the neighbourhood of equilibrium is approached only at the beginning and at the end of the cycle and the result trend forms a boundary to the movement of any time series. Once it is established that a given cycle has two phases and the points in between this cycle and the adjoining cycles fit the requirement of representing neighbourhoods of equilibrium, the result trend is given by a smooth curve that goes through the relevant extreme value of the time series. For each variable that rises relative to trend during the cycle, such as bank credit, profits and prices, the value is at a cyclical low in the neighbourhood of equilibrium, while for each variable that falls during the cycle, such as unemployment, the value is at a cyclical high. Of course, the influence of external factors distorts the result trend, so it is never solely a reflection of the cyclical process (op. cit., p. 207).

In the four-phase cycle of Schumpeter's second approximation, the system overshoots the neighbourhood of equilibrium due to secondary phenomena. Neither the peak nor the trough of a time series then lies in the neighbourhood of equilibrium. Instead, Schumpeter identifies the neighbourhoods of equilibrium by finding a characteristic behaviour that the time-series graphs can be expected to exhibit in the neighbourhood of equilibrium (op. cit., p. 208).

First, Schumpeter suggests smoothing or curve fitting in order to rid the series of miscellaneous noise factors associated with oscillations, vibrations and hesitations. While acknowledging the dangers of such operations, he argues that once this is done it is possible to examine the mathematical differentials of the smooth curves, both rates of change and higher derivatives. He does, however, warn that higher derivatives may be less reliable (ibid.).

Schumpeter then considers the method of "normal points", which he attributes to Ragnar Frisch (1931). This involves finding points of inflection from a smooth graph of a time series. Using the sine curve as an example of a smooth curve, Schumpeter notes this curve shows a characteristic behaviour of the second derivative vanishing at the point of inflection in the rising portion of the sine curve (the portion of the curve with a positive first derivative).

Schumpeter argues this vanishing second derivative indicates a point of equilibrium according to his "principle of economic meaning", which he illustrates using the example of the time series for employment. He suggests the rate of growth of employment is positive but falling in prosperity before falling at an increasing rate in recession. The rate of employment growth turns negative in depression, but falls at a decreasing rate and finally turns positive and grows at an increasing rate during recovery. The maximum growth rate of employment is reached at the inflection point of the upward sloping portion of the sine curve, which indicates equilibrium and the start of the next cycle (op. cit., p. 209).

This hypothetical example is qualified by acknowledging the rate of employment growth need not be related to the business cycle phases in precisely the manner described. However, Schumpeter still defends the principle of looking for economic meaning in the derivatives of smoothed curves of time series. As a general justification for having a point of inflection in the neighbourhood of equilibrium, Schumpeter relies on the pull of equilibrium growing as economic magnitudes move further away.

In spite of his favourable review of Frisch's method, Schumpeter worries about the practical difficulties of identifying inflection points, especially separating true points from the false. Also, the smoothing process may distort the location of the true points. Thus, he refrains from generally endorsing Frisch's method or directly adopting it in his interpretive work on time-series data.[2] Instead, he primarily relies on consideration of the historical circumstances together with visual inspection of graphs over periods for which data on relevant economic magnitudes are available.

To aid in visualising the implications of his theory for the interpretation of time series, Schumpeter graphically depicts the pattern of movement in a pro-cyclical economic variable as it would appear in an idealised cycle scenario. He assumes the idealised scenario consists of overlapping sine curve equations for three cycles of 38 months or three and-one-sixth years (Kitchin cycles), 114 months or nine-and-a-half years (Juglar cycles) and 684 months or 57 years (Kondratieff cycles). The amplitude of each cycle is proportional to its duration so that with the Kitchin cycles having amplitude standardised at one, the amplitude of the Juglar cycles is three and that of the Kondratieff cycle is 18. There is no trend in any of the cycles, each cycle consists of four equally long phases and the amplitudes are symmetric around zero. By overlapping and vertically cumulating movements from the three cycles, Schumpeter produces a graph that he notes is far from smooth even though it is constituted from very regular components (op. cit., p. 212).[3]

Schumpeter then uses the idealised cycle scenario as the basis for a discussion of statistical methods for identifying business cycles from time-series data. He devotes the bulk of this discussion to Frisch's method of normal points. After discussing the difficulties associated with cycles of different orders not being additively superimposed as assumed, he mentions that the problem of inflection points not being reliable is amplified by the overlapping cycles. Further, the Frisch method picks up other sources of fluctuations, such as seasonal, which Schumpeter illustrates in a graph of the time series of monthly freight car loadings in the US from 1917 to 1930 (Chart III, op. cit., p. 218). He concludes that while the Frisch method has advantages in terms of the principle of economic meaning, as a formal method it can only be a starting point for analysing time series. Theoretical and historical methods are then essential for correct analysis.

Commentary

Schumpeter constructs a dialectical relationship between equilibrium and innovation. Equilibrium stimulates innovation as actual prices move closer to their theoretical normal values, allowing entrepreneurs to make more reliable calculations of the short-run profitability of their potential innovations. However, a swarm of innovations disturbs equilibrium both for the narrow markets that they directly affect and for the broader economy. As disorder spreads through the economy, actual prices diverge by varying degrees from the preceding theoretical normal. This not only interferes with calculations of profitability of further innovations but creates, or at least appears to create, alternative profit opportunities of the sort to which Schumpeter refers in his discussion of the second approximation. Only as the wave of innovation subsides and its impact diffuses through the economy do conditions again become favourable to a new round of innovations, but this is generally delayed by the secondary phenomena that lead to depression and crisis followed by recovery. Thus, the business cycle is the form that growth takes under capitalism.

By stressing the role of equilibrium in defining the beginning and end of the business cycle, Schumpeter positions his theory of cyclical movement as a complement to the Walrasian theory of a stationary economy. Walrasian equilibrium provides the theoretical norms for the economy at the start and the close of the cycle, although the structural change wrought by innovation means the norms for the end of the cycle are different from those at the start. Schumpeter accepts Walrasian equilibrium not only as a logical construct but as a centre of gravity for the actual economy.

In the preface to 1937 Japanese edition of the *Theorie der wirtschaftlichen Entwicklung*, Schumpeter acknowledges, 'the Walrasian technique . . . is applicable only to a stationary process . . . a process which *actually* does not change of its own initiative' (Schumpeter, 1951, p. 159, italics in the original). Yet, in *BC* there is no substantive change to the use of Walrasian equilibrium as the anchor for the business cycle. In place of identifying the end of the business cycle with an 'a position approaching equilibrium' (Schumpeter, 1961 [1934], p. 244), Schumpeter qualifies the criterion to 'consider, instead of equilibrium points, ranges within which the system as a whole is more nearly in equilibrium than it is outside of them' (Schumpeter, 1939, p. 71). The neighbourhoods of equilibrium that constitute these ranges are still neighbourhoods of the Walrasian equilibrium as used in *TED*.

Schumpeter's insistence on the business cycle being the necessary form for capitalist growth, with innovation as the primary driving force, has never gained wide acceptance. Warning signs are clearly evident in reviews of *BC* that appeared in a wide array of leading journals in economics, history, statistics and business. The reviews are universally complimentary of Schumpeter's scholarship and congratulate him on producing a monumental and interesting two volumes. However, most contain at least some criticism, often reflecting the disciplinary or methodological interests of the reviewer. Overall, it is clear Schumpeter won respect but not many adherents to his approach to the analysis of capitalist development.

Reviews by economic historians applaud Schumpeter for his efforts to integrate history with economic theory, but suggest he overplays the role of the theory. Hans Rosenberg (1940, p. 99) writing in the *American Historical Review* suggests, 'The mutual cause-effect relationships of the "irregular regularities" of economic fluctuations as historical realities from the historian's viewpoint are

generated by the inseparable interplay of external and internal factors and, conse-
quently, cannot be treated realistically as "purely economic" phenomena.' Harold
Innis (1940, p. 92) writing in the *Canadian Journal of Economics and Political
Science* complains, 'the propensity to present graphs and to smooth out curves
tends to obscure the importance of discrete changes', which he follows with a plea
for a broader approach to economic history.

Simon Kuznets, perhaps the leading business cycle analyst of the time, writing
an influential review in the *American Economic Review*, comments unfavourably
on the relationship between the theoretical model and the empirical content in *BC*.
He opines,

> One cannot well escape the impression that Professor Schumpeter's theo-
> retical model in its present state cannot be linked directly and clearly with
> statistically observed realities; that the extreme paucity of statistical analysis
> in the treatise is an inevitable result of the type of theoretical model adopted;
> and that the great reliance upon historical outlines and qualitative discussion
> is a consequence of the difficulty of devising statistical procedures that would
> correspond to the theoretical model.
>
> (Kuznets, 1940, p. 266)

Kuznets also expresses serious doubts about the theoretical foundation for the
clustering of innovations and the regularity of business cycles.[4]

In contrast, Oscar Lange (1941), a theorist writing in the *Review of Economics and Statistics*, accepts Schumpeter's theory as explaining the clustering of
innovations based on the changing risk of failure. He writes, 'innovations will
be "bunched" at periods of neighborhood of equilibrium when the risk of failure
is smallest' and slacken 'as an intensification of the rate of innovation disequili-
brates the economy and increases the risk of failure' (op. cit., p. 192). However,
Lange goes on to fault Schumpeter for not having a theory of unemployment,
noting 'It is very difficult to locate the fluctuations of employment in Professor
Schumpeter's theory. In the Pure Model we encounter only a price cycle and an
output cycle' (ibid.).

The price and output cycles that Lange identifies in the first approximation
of Schumpeter's theory are non-synchronous. In the upswing of the price cycle,
entrepreneurs are taking productive resources away from established producers to
set up their own production, while output may decline or at best remain constant
given Schumpeter's assumption of continual full employment. In the downswing
of the price cycle, there is the extra output of entrepreneurs added to the social
product. As Lange (1941, p. 192) points out this provides a distinctive approach
to analysing the business cycle, 'For the unsophisticated observer the business
cycle is primarily an employment cycle', which is normally linked to changes
in output and capacity utilisation. Lange then suggests fluctuations in employment associated with entrepreneurial investment could lead to output rising in
the price upswing and falling in the downswing, but 'It is not at all clear how the

employment cycle can be tied up with Professor Schumpeter's theory: most probably in connection with the Secondary Wave, but Professor Schumpeter fails to do so explicitly' (op. cit., p. 193).

As early as in TED, Schumpeter clearly recognises the time displacement between the price impact of a surge in innovations, which occurs when entrepreneurs acquire of means of production, and the output impact, which occurs only after the entrepreneur's production process is implemented. Indeed, this time displacement is central to his argument that bank credit extended to entrepreneurs only creates the semblance of inflation and should not be confused with the impact of bank credit extended for consumption or speculative purposes (Schumpeter (1961 [1934], pp. 109–12). Yet, the theoretical and historical discussions in *BC* fail to clearly differentiate the phasing of cycles in price and output or other economic magnitudes, which creates confusion and contributes to at least some of the mixed reaction to *BC*. The relationship across time between movements in prices and movements in output is central to Schumpeter's defence of his credit theory of money and I discuss these issues in detail in Chapter 5, 'Money, Credit and the Price Level'.

Questions about the timing of cycles also feature in Erwin Rothbarth's (1942) review of *BC* for the *Economic Journal*. Notably, Rothbarth interprets Schumpeter's theory as implying that the risk of failure is the trigger for the cyclical pattern of innovation, with no specific reference to the role of prices or to the nuances of time displacement for movements in price and output in Schumpeter's first approximation to the theory of the business cycle. Not surprisingly, Rothbarth questions Schumpeter's timing of the upswing in innovations, even though he accepts the importance to the business cycle of increased entrepreneurial investment. He then suggests, 'It is, in fact, possible that the increase in innovation should occur during the slump as the decline in profits sharpens the wits of "old firms"' (op. cit., p. 227).

Using an approach related to Rothbarth's speculation about innovations increasing in the slump, Gerhard Mensch (1979) provides a theory of innovation in which basic and radical innovations peak in the trough of the business cycle (using the standard interpretation of the business cycle meaning a cycle in employment and output rather than prices). While he references Schumpeter on the link between innovation and business cycles, Mensch (1979, p. 7) attributes the upsurge of innovation to 'the degree of stagnation of the old technologies and the attractiveness of the new alternatives'. Furthermore, the indicator of the exhaustion of the old technologies is stagnation in investment and production. Thus, it is when the economy is stagnating that radical and basic innovations are most likely to be introduced, not in the neighbourhood of equilibrium as argued by Schumpeter.

Based on expanding the database on innovations and patenting used by Mensch, Alfred Kleinknecht (1987) finds that the pattern over time of radical innovations and patents supports Schumpeter's argument that innovations peak after the trough of the business cycle. He concludes there are 45- to 60-year cycles in both prices and output growth in major industrialised countries and for the world economy from at least the 1890s. However, he then states,[5]

> In Schumpeter's *Business Cycles* (1939), the bunching of innovations appears as the result of a swarm-like appearance of heroic entrepreneurs. The appearance of such entrepreneurs is not explained as a result of some socio-economic process, but as a kind of *deus ex machina*.
>
> (Kleinknecht, 1987, p. 200)

Clearly, Kleinknecht doesn't recognise or doesn't accept Schumpeter's argument that entrepreneurs are able to implement their innovations only under "normal" conditions, instead favouring an interpretation in which purely technological considerations interact with a socio-economic process to generate an upsurge in innovations.

Carlota Perez (2002, p. 27) also faults Schumpeter's explanation based on 'the bunching of entrepreneurial abilities' and argues 'that these bursts of entrepreneurship actually do occur, but they do so in response to opportunity explosions'. The opportunity explosions are associated with new techno-economic paradigms, which appear as revolutions rather than continuously because conditions are favourable for emergence only as the prior techno-economic paradigm nears exhaustion. The mechanism by which favourable conditions impact on innovations includes better access to financing for innovative firms, although not quite in the manner suggested by Schumpeter as I discuss further in Chapter 5.

Chris Freeman (2007, p. 137), a leading proponent of the technological interpretation of uneven development, summarises the developments from Schumpeter's insights, 'Since his death, while his theory of successive technological revolutions has been very influential, his attempt to defend the nature and periodicity of the Kondratieff cycle has encountered continuous strong criticism.' Long-wave theorists emphasise the cumulative nature of technological trajectories and, especially in more recent versions, the notion of general purpose technologies that have cumulative impact throughout broad areas of the economy.[6] Importantly, from the perspective of this volume, the emphasis on technological determinism moves away from Schumpeter's emphasis on the role of normal prices as a precondition for a new cluster of innovations, relying on the exogenous influence of technological opportunity rather than the endogenous influence of price adjustments.

A particular weakness in Schumpeter's business cycle theory, which I focus on in Chapter 6 is his argument that Walrasian equilibrium for an economy in a stationary state defines normal values of prices at the beginning and end of the cycle. As Freeman (1990, p. 27) notes, 'Both in *Theory of Economic Development* and in *Business Cycles* Schumpeter represents boom as a departure from equilibrium and recession as a return to equilibrium in largely Walrasian terms.' This means that Schumpeter's price theory relies implicitly on the Walrasian theory and its assumption of competitive general equilibrium, at least in so far as determining the theoretical norm to which prices converge at the end of the business cycle.

Oakley (1990) also questions Schumpeter's use of Walrasian equilibrium as the beginning and ending point of the cycle. Oakley (1990, p. 233) notes,

> It is readily apparent that this fiction, with its new entrepreneurs, new plants, new firms and new credit simply added into Schumpeter's perception of the circular-flow conditions, led him to grossly understate the complexity of the traverses that comprise economic development and the business cycle.

Yet, Oakley (op. cit., p. 240) supports Schumpeter on the argument that the economy in motion has a centre of gravity, given that 'it is clear that capitalism's motion has not been characterized by any continuous "explosion" into chaos over time.' Oakley then states, 'It follows that at least in some ill-defined sense, some empirical *centre of gravity* must exist. The extent to which it can be analytically defined and applied must remain a moot point' (ibid., italics in the original).

A different view of why capitalist motion has not exploded into chaos is provided by Gatti, et al. (1996). Starting from a Schumpeterian perspective, they emphasise the role of governments and central banks in constraining the tendency of capitalist motion toward incoherence. They build on earlier work by Minsky, which identifies financial fragility as a characteristic of modern capitalism arising from innovations in financing that react to the financing needs of innovators outside the financial sector. They then build a simulation model of the macro economy that emphasises the interaction between debts and profits, and use the model to show how central bank regulation of financing and government fiscal policy can offset movements toward incoherence due to the dynamic interaction of debts and profits. I return to the subject of financial fragility in the discussion of 'Financial Flows, Financial Innovations and Financial Instability' in Chapter 5.

Andersen (2012, p. 636), in his review of Schumpeter's main works, makes the following observations specifically on *Business Cycles*, 'In retrospect, the shortcomings of this book can be traced back to its depiction of macroevolution as a series of circular flows.' Andersen goes on to specifically point to the need for a theory of micro-evolutionary processes as the basis for macroevolution. He further suggests that hints about constructing such a theory can be found in Schumpeter's other works, particularly *CSD*.

Across all his works, Schumpeter associates successful entrepreneurship with profit, hence with price exceeding the cost of production. Cost for the entrepreneur may fall with price remaining constant, as in the case of process innovation, or price might rise with cost remaining constant, as can occur with product innovation that provides superior product characteristics, or there may be some combination of falling cost and rising price. However, in each case entrepreneurial profit is transitory and dissipates over time with expansion by the entrepreneur and imitation by other firms.

Schumpeter is clear in *TED* and *BC* that dynamic competition leads to dissipation of entrepreneurial profit, but he does not fully develop the analysis of the pattern of entrepreneurial behaviour and competitive response that leads to this dissipation. Instead, he maintains the separation where Walrasian theory determines theoretical normal prices toward which the economy gravitates at end of cycles, while entrepreneurial behaviour drives prices during the cycle. In *CSD*, Schumpeter seemingly retreats from the notion that monopoly and monopoly profits are completely eliminated from an economy in equilibrium, but he doesn't explain how this affects his earlier analysis. As Kurt Dopfer (2012) points out, Schumpeter makes important starts on the meso-level analysis of structural change associated with clusters of innovations but leaves out important linkages to micro-level behaviour of entrepreneurs and macro-level performance of the economy.

There are also difficulties with Schumpeter's analysis of the statistical norm for the economy. In arguing that the method of normal points helps in harnessing the concept of equilibrium, Schumpeter is referring to his graphs that depict four-phase cycles. However, with the two-phase cycle, the boundary of the graph, rather than its centre, determines normal conditions with the lower (higher) boundary being the appropriate boundary for a pro-cyclical (counter-cyclical) variable. Thus, for the two-phase cycle, the economy is in the neighbourhood of equilibrium when the time series is at an extreme value, which is not a normal point (point of inflection) using Frisch's method.

Schumpeter's interpretation of a vanishing second derivative for the time-series graphs is at odds with his own argument concerning the dynamics of innovation. The driving force of his cluster of innovations is gathering force in the upswing of a business cycle. If entrepreneurial success attracts followers and imitators, the rate of change of economic variables should be accelerating rather than decelerating at the start of the business cycle. Indeed, this is the case in the discussion in *BC* of how a cluster of innovations first starts from a stationary state. Yet, having the inflection point on the upward sloping portion of a time-series graph for an economic variable mark the beginning of the cycle means that the rate of change of the variable is at a maximum at the start of the cycle.

In his idealised depiction of time-series graphs in *BC* Schumpeter provides a single scenario applying to all economic magnitudes, but his analysis suggests differing patterns for the two key macroeconomic variables, the price level and aggregate output. Schumpeter identifies the upswing and downswing of the two-phase cycle with movements in the price level, but there is little movement in aggregate output in the upswing and rising aggregate output in the downswing. Only in the depression and revival phases associated with secondary phenomena do the price level and aggregate output move in tandem. If the idealised depiction of time-series graphs applies to the price level as indicated by Schumpeter in his discussion of the price level in Chapter VIII of *BC*, then a different shape and timing is implied for the idealised graph of aggregate output.

Schumpeter's idea that an environment with prices at some sort of normal level encourages innovation by enhancing the reliability of prediction of entrepreneurial profits is plausible if not proven. Yet, his analysis fails to convincingly link this general conception of norms with either the theoretical normal of Walrasian competitive general equilibrium or the statistical normal of Frisch's method of normal points. I provide a closer examination of Schumpeter's use of the multiple concepts of norms in Chapter 6, 'Norms, Equilibrium and Competition', and propose alternatives to his chosen concepts in Chapter 7, 'Norms for a Developing Economy'.

Summary

Innovation is at the heart of Schumpeter's theory of the business cycle, with the key proposition being that innovations come in swarms. A swarm of innovations is initiated when the economy is in the neighbourhood of equilibrium because entrepreneurs and their bankers can reliably calculate the potential profits from their innovations. The swarm then disturbs equilibrium through the competition for means of production financed by the creation of bank credit. Thus, the process of diffusion and absorption of the impacts of the swarm generates both the prosperity of the upswing and the recession of the downswing of the primary wave of a two-phase cycle. Prosperity and recession are inseparable in the process of capitalist motion.

Schumpeter recognises that secondary phenomena unleashed by the movement of the economy in the primary wave may lead to overshooting of the neighbourhood of equilibrium in the downswing, which leads to a four-phase cycle in which depression and recovery follow on from prosperity and recession. He also recognises that some innovations have more profound and widespread impact than others and so may take longer to diffuse and absorb, which means that overlapping cycles of different length may be part of the evolutionary process. Finally, he recognises that exogenous shocks, including those with oscillating or vibrating effects, are reflected in the time series of economic magnitudes. Clearly, the path for the time series of a historical variable is not determined by economic evolution alone.

The complications due to secondary phenomena, overlapping cycles of different lengths and the influence of factors outside the evolutionary process of innovation lead Schumpeter to conclude that the working of this process can't be revealed solely from the application of statistical methods to time-series data. Schumpeter notes that evolution means the theoretical normal for any historical variable is changing over time, so these variables can't properly be treated as stochastic variables subject to probability law. When Schumpeter moves on to his 'Historical Outlines', he states, 'It is obvious that only detailed historic knowledge can definitively answer most of the questions of individual causation and mechanism and that without it the study of time series must remain inconclusive, and theoretical analysis empty' (Schumpeter, 1939, p. 220).

Having made this point, Schumpeter moves on to a historical analysis of capitalist development over the period up to 1913 in Chapters VI and VII of *BC*. He then turns to the discussion of particular time series, starting with movements in the price level in Chapter VIII, 'The Price Level'. In the next chapter, I discuss Schumpeter's theory of the price level as presented in Chapter VIII and also his theory of the price system as presented in Chapter X, 'Prices and Quantities of Individual Commodities'. As noted in the discussion of criticisms of Schumpeter's business cycle theory, I further examine the relationship between price cycles and output cycles in Chapter 5 along with further consideration of the relationship between financial markets and entrepreneurial investments. Chapter 6 follows up on criticisms noted above of Schumpeter's use of the competitive Walrasian equilibrium for defining the theoretical norms for a developing economy, while Chapter 7 suggests an alternative approach to determining these norms. Chapter 8 then employs this alternative approach as the starting point in reconstructing Schumpeter's price theory in a manner appropriate to a modern developing capitalist economy.

Notes

1 Here, he alludes to the recent developments in the culture and structure of capitalism that are the focus of his later analysis in *CSD* (Schumpeter 1976 [1950]) on the inevitable replacement of capitalism with socialism.
2 As an exception, Schumpeter applies Frisch's method for determining normal points in a graph of the time series for US wholesale prices from 1790 to 1920 (see Chart IX, Schumpeter, 1939, p. 469). This application is discussed further in the next chapter.
3 The graph is depicted in Chart I (Schumpeter, 1939, p. 213) and the formulas used for deriving the values used in drawing the graphs are given in the Appendix (op. cit., p. 1051).
4 The influence of Kuznets's review is indicated by it being far and away the most cited in Google Scholar among all the reviews published after the appearance of *BC*. Recently, Foster (2015, p. 171) argues constructively, 'Kuznets and Schumpeter offered two distinct approaches to understanding economic growth and its fluctuations from a shared evolutionary economic perspective', and 'The challenge is to integrate the approaches of these highly distinguished economists into a powerful methodology that can compete with the prevailing one adopted in the endogenous growth literature.'
5 A similar view of Schumpeter's explanation of the clustering of innovations is expressed by Andrew Tylecote (1992, p. 15), 'But at no point does Schumpeter fill the crucial gap in his theory. If a new upswing is launched by basic innovations, what explains their arrival in clusters, every fifty years of [*sic*] so?'
6 According to Freeman, unevenness in economic growth is due to the nature of how radical innovations in technology spread (see Freeman, et al., 1982, Freeman and Louçã, 2001). The long wave resulting from introduction of a particular transformative technology has a duration and magnitude specific to that technology, making generalisations about its impact unsound other than recognising the common factors in the process of establishment and diffusion that ensure the impact is uneven over time. Lipsey, et al. (2005) refer to this long-wave process as the spread of a specific general purpose technology.

4 The price level and the price system

The theoretical structure set out by Schumpeter in Chapters I through V of *BC* deals holistically with the economy. He applies this theoretical structure in Chapters VI and VII when examining the historical experience of economic development through the end of the nineteenth century. Various economic magnitudes are then discussed separately in Chapters VIII through XIII, where he suggests that each magnitude has its own characteristic cyclical movement and trend. Schumpeter points to specific issues regarding measurement and meaning of each magnitude as well as to a particular history that reflects both the evolution of the system and the impact of external influences. In this chapter, I review the chapters that deal most directly with Schumpeter's price theory, Chapter VIII, 'The Price Level', and Chapter X, 'Prices and Quantities of Individual Commodities'.

Chapters VIII and X explain the distinction Schumpeter makes between the price level and the price system. This is particularly important as Schumpeter's theory of economic evolution driven by innovation implies uneven development and, hence, heterogeneous movement across prices of various commodities. Heterogeneity in movement of individual prices is so severe that Schumpeter abstains from any hypotheses regarding the movement of the price of any particular commodity. Yet, he has clear hypotheses about the price level in terms of both a result trend and the pattern of movement over the business cycle.

Schumpeter's theory of the price level is a monetary theory and, as such, is not derived from a microeconomic theory of the prices of individual commodities. As noted in the last chapter, credit expands with a swarm of innovations, which allows entrepreneurs to gain control of means of production. The extra credit adds to purchasing power in the economy and contributes to a general rise in prices (a rise in the price level or decline in the value of money). Later in the cycle, there is autodeflation in the price level as credit contracts when entrepreneurs use profits to repay their loans. Also, the value of output from innovators exceeds the value of output they displace, thereby absorbing purchasing power and putting downward pressure on prices in general. The combination of extra output and autodeflation leads to Schumpeter's conclusion that there is a downward result trend for the price level.

Acting alongside these monetary influences on the price level, there are declines in relative prices of at least some commodities directly affected by innovation and the creative destruction from innovative products and processes. A broad cluster of innovations means the price reductions resulting from the process of creative destruction can be widespread and lead to declines in aggregate price indices. However, such declines are not general through the economy and might occur in tandem with increases in prices elsewhere due to the structural change wrought by innovation. Therefore, the process of creative destruction is essential to justify Schumpeter's conclusion that the price system changes over the course of the business cycle, but the process is not necessary for his conclusion of a falling result trend for the price level.

This chapter examines Schumpeter's treatment of the price level and price system as presented in Chapter VIII and Chapter X of *BC*. A major objective is to disentangle Schumpeter's theory of the price level from his analysis of the process of creative destruction applied to the prices of individual commodities. The next section is devoted to Schumpeter's treatment in *BC* of the price level, while the following section has a corresponding discussion of the price system. In the third section I use a simple formal model of reproduction prices to provide commentary on the interrelated movements of the price level and the price system over the cycle. Discussion of Schumpeter's monetary theory and how it relates to movements of the price level is left to the next chapter.

The price level

Schumpeter starts Chapter VIII of *BC* by suggesting that while he discusses price-level movements first, the reader should not interpret this as meaning that they have special significance in terms of causation or symptoms. He reemphasises the holistic nature of his analysis, which implies no one element can be considered to operate independently of the others. He then points out the difficulty that his analysis of evolution driven by innovation poses in terms of heterogeneity of price movements for individual commodities or even composites of prices of related products. What then is the special role of the price level?

The price level has primacy in the discussion of economic magnitudes, at least in terms of sequencing, due to the use of money as a unit of account. Placing a value on the unit of account allows the determination of absolute prices as well as relative prices of individual commodities. More importantly, fixing the price level provides society with a standard against which to evaluate prices of individual commodities as well as for valuing their income and wealth in terms of purchasing power (Schumpeter, 1939, pp. 452–54).

Schumpeter is clear the price level derives its meaning from social context rather than from its relation to the prices of individual commodities. The value of a unit of currency is based on social habits that are historically conditioned. From this perspective, the money price of any particular commodity becomes definite only in terms of the social value of the unit of currency. Separation of the influence of the value of money (the inverse of the price level) from the influences specific to the commodity is required for proper interpretation of movement in prices of individual commodities.

Schumpeter notes that the separation is possible if there are no changes in commodity quantities while prices change. In this case, the change in expenditure measures the change in the price level regardless of changes in prices of individual commodities. After acknowledging that quantities do change, he discusses use of the total differential to provide an approximate decomposition of any change in total expenditure into price change and quantity change components. This leads him to the conclusion that the change in the price level can be approximated by the ratio of the price change component to original total expenditure, provided that the changes in price and quantity are small.

The formula Schumpeter (1939, p. 456) provides for calculating the change in the price level is:

$$\frac{\sum (p+dp)q}{\sum pq} = 1 + \frac{\sum qdp}{\sum pq} \tag{4.1}$$

where p is the original price of an individual commodity and dp is the corresponding change in price, while q is the original quantity of that commodity. Each term in the expression is summed over the full set of commodities deemed appropriate to the purpose, which for Schumpeter's theory is the set of final goods and services purchased by the household sector. The last term on the right hand side of the equation is an approximation to the proportional change in the price level, provided that price changes are measured over small intervals.[1]

Having set out the ideal measure of the price level implied by his theory, Schumpeter then considers the practical question of how to proceed given that he does not have a time series for this ideal measure. Here he relents and accepts the use of standard price indices, but stresses the importance of caution in their interpretation as measures of the price level. He then proceeds to discuss the use of indices based on wholesale price indices, which are more readily available, rather than the retail price indices suggested by his theory. After mentioning various advantages and disadvantages of using wholesale prices rather than retail prices, he suggests that the cyclical variation in wholesale prices is similar to that of the preferred retail price series. By this process of approximation, Schumpeter justifies use of time-series data on aggregate indices of wholesale prices, rather than retail prices, in comparing historical price data to his theoretical expectations (op. cit., pp. 458–61).

With regard to expectations from his theory, Schumpeter states,

> Price level should rise in prosperity – under the pressure of credit creation, which, under the conditions embodied in the pure model, would not be compensated either by an increase in output or by any fall in "velocity" – and fall in the downgrade – under the pressure of autodeflation and of increase in output – *more than it had risen in the preceding prosperity.*
>
> (op. cit., p. 462, quotations and italics in the original)

He modifies the pure model by the successive approximations discussed in Chapter IV of *BC*, especially the substitution for the two-phase cycle in the pure model by a four-phase cycle in the second approximation, which 'adds the expectation that the price level will go on falling in depression and that this fall should be corrected in recovery' (ibid.). As regards the third approximation, the complication is that with overlapping cycles of different durations the trend for any cycle is influenced by the phase of longer cycles. For example, a Kitchin cycle that overlaps with the upswing of a Juglar cycle has a more positive result trend than does a Kitchin cycle that overlaps with the downswing of the same Juglar.

The seemingly straightforward implications from the pure model are rendered increasingly complex by the successive approximations, even before accounting for the influence of external factors that Schumpeter recognises as exerting considerable influence at particular historical conjunctures. Nonetheless, there remain at least two definite hypotheses. First, is the expectation of considerable fluctuation in the price level, albeit with much irregularity reflecting the interacting influences of cycles with different periodicity. Second, for at least the cycle with the longest length, the price level at the end of the recovery (and start of the next cycle) is below the level obtaining at the start of the cycle, so that the result trend for the Kondratieff cycle is clearly a falling price level.

Schumpeter illustrates the working of cycles in the price level with time-series data for three countries, Germany, UK and US. The data for the UK start in 1779, for the US in 1797 and for Germany in 1851. Each of the series ends in 1913. The series are all for wholesale prices rather than retail prices, as broad composite series for retail prices are not generally available.

The first four charts are used by Schumpeter to discuss the result trends for the price level in the three countries. The first chart (Chart IV, op. cit., p. 464) shows the annual rate of change in the price level for all three countries, while the next three charts (Charts V, VI, VII, op. cit., pp. 465–67) are for each country separately and show the price-level series along with corresponding series for industrial production, money supply and interest rates on a logarithmic scale. Schumpeter notes the descriptive trend (the trend fitted through the historical data) for each country is falling. He then discusses external factors that could give rise to a difference between the descriptive trend and the result trend (the trend that excludes external factors and corresponds to the construct in Schumpeter's theory). He concludes that the result trend for each country is falling, which conforms to his theoretical expectation (op. cit., pp. 463–68).

Next, to show the presence of prolonged periods of rising and falling price level corresponding to Kondratieff cycles, Schumpeter uses a chart (Chart VIII, op. cit., p. 468) of the nine-year moving average of the price-level series in logarithmic scale for all three countries. The nine-year moving average is meant to remove the influence of price fluctuations associated with the Juglar cycle. He adds a further chart (Chart IX, op. cit., p. 469) for US data alone that shows, in addition to the raw price-level data, freehand curves drawn though the inflection points of 10-year, 22-year and 50-year cycles. This chart is meant to apply Frisch's method of normal points to the US data.

Schumpeter suggests Charts VIII and IX show two cycles of Kondratieff length and the start of a third such cycle. The first Kondratieff he associates with the Industrial Revolution, acknowledging some issues with the timing of the maxima. The second Kondratieff he associates with "railroadization", but notes the length of the downswing in price level was too long, extending well into the 1840s. After discussing the complicating influence of various external factors mentioned in his earlier historical discussion, particularly Chapter VII covering 1843 to 1913, Schumpeter concludes that his theory is not rejected by the time-series charts because major deviations from the pattern implied by his theory are sufficiently explained by historical evidence of the impact of specific external factors (op. cit., pp. 468–72).

After discussing price movements over the Kondratieff cycles, Schumpeter provides a brief discussion of the shorter Juglar and Kitchin cycles. This discussion is based on Chart X (op. cit., p. 474), which shows deviations from the nine-year moving average series depicted in Chart VIII. He suggests the fluctuations can be seen to have peaks and troughs that are each separated by nine or ten years for all three countries. Further, England and the US have six such cycles for the only complete Kondratieff covered by the data (Germany doesn't have data for the full cycle). As regards the Kitchin cycles, Schumpeter argues the data indicate reasonably well that each Juglar contains three Kitchin cycles. Thus, he takes the historical time series to provide support for his argument that there are overlapping cycles of different durations (op. cit., pp. 474–75).

The price system

The final section of Chapter VIII of *BC* deals with group prices, by which Schumpeter means price indices for broad composites of goods, such as consumer goods. He notes such composite indices differ from the price level in that they need not reflect forces impacting on the system as a whole. Further, if the groups are chosen to reflect common influences of demand, supply or stages of production, there might be systematic patterns of the movement of the price index for one group relative to others over the course of the business cycle. Thus, the discussion of group prices forms part of Schumpeter's discussion of the impact of the cyclical process on the price system (the structure of relative prices), rather than his discussion of impact on the price level as a social construct. Still, after presenting Chart XI (op. cit., p. 478) of selected group prices for the US from 1840 to 1913, Schumpeter concludes that the outstanding impression is the degree to which the various group indices move together, although with some variation in amplitude and period (op. cit., pp. 477–78).

Having noted the similarity of cyclical movement across various group prices, Schumpeter nonetheless goes on to consider the implications of his analysis of economic evolution for the structural relations within the system and how they might be reflected in differential movement of group prices. First, he considers the impact of innovation on the index for groups in which innovation is prevalent. After noting complications likely to blur the effect, he suggests the impact of innovation still shows through. He then points to a number of examples, including textiles at the beginning of the nineteenth century and power at the beginning of the twentieth, which illustrate the impact of innovation in terms of falling group prices relative to the price level. Thus, even at a high level of aggregation, the effects of innovation pushing down prices can be detected provided that the innovation is of sufficient breadth and magnitude (op. cit., pp. 478–79).

A second class of group prices considered by Schumpeter is prices of commodities sharing characteristics of organisation or marketing, such as monopolised industries. He suggests the cyclical behaviour of group prices in this class depends on the characteristics that are common to the group of products (op. cit., p. 479). Discussion of these effects is left to Chapter X, which deals with the prices and quantities of individual commodities.

The third class of group prices discussed by Schumpeter is prices of commodities separated by the stage of production, for example, raw materials, producer goods and consumer goods. Similar cyclical patterns are expected within each group, but deviations from any such pattern can still be important and interesting. His subsequent discussion takes aim at theories of the business cycle that are based on systematic differences across the class in the cyclical behaviour of group prices, although acknowledging there are implied differences for "endogenous" theories, including his own. He notes a particular implication of his own theory is that following an upswing in innovations and on through the cycle, non-innovative firms will be increasingly faced with rising prices for means of production, which might impact, along with other factors, on the relative movement of prices of producer and consumer goods (op. cit., pp. 479–82).

Schumpeter continues the discussion of the cyclical movement of relative prices in Chapter X of *BC*, 'Prices and Quantities of Individual Commodities'. He starts by noting the importance, when considering the price of an individual commodity, of taking account of corresponding movements in the quantity of the commodity. These movements in price-quantity pairs for individual commodities are the core of the process of cyclical development. Yet, because individual peculiarities become more important as the category of items included becomes narrower, the same cyclical process may have different impacts across individual price-quantity pairs (op. cit., pp. 520–21).

Schumpeter suggests the greatest regularity in cyclical behaviour of time series of price-quantity pairs can be expected in industries that don't have innovations occurring or aren't closely related to industries in which innovations are occurring, acknowledging this distinction is difficult to carry out in practice as innovations often permeate widely through the economy. In these non-innovating industries the impact of the cyclical process of evolution is felt, at least initially, only indirectly through the effect of the purchases of means of production by innovating firms. As noted above, such impacts are felt throughout the economy, but to differing degrees depending on the peculiarities of structure and behaviour in each industry (op. cit., p. 522).

In further discussing the common and differential impact of the cyclical process on different price-quantity pairs, Schumpeter distinguishes between nominal effects, which don't change relative prices, and real effects, which alter relative prices and tend to impact on quantities. Common effects that show up in inflation and deflation explain the greater similarity across commodities in price movements than in quantity movements. Differential effects show up in cyclical movements in deflated prices, which are given by the price index for a commodity divided by an aggregate price index.

In Chart XXI (op. cit., p. 523), Schumpeter depicts cyclical movements in deflated prices for several commodities for the case of the US from 1840 to 1913. These include raw materials, such as wheat, petroleum and coal, industrial materials, such as rubber, copper and pig iron, as well as steel rails as an example of a manufactured good. While there are clear differences in amplitude and timing across the individual time series, cycles are noticeable in each case and there is covariation. After discussing various qualifications, Schumpeter argues that under competitive conditions cycles are readily apparent in the prices of non-innovating commodities, but quantities tend to vary less with the exception of commodities whose use is inherently cyclical. He goes on to suggest that the statement is further verified by considering the cases of a number of constituents of indices of what he terms sensitive prices. Schumpeter identifies relatively strong pro-cyclical movement in time series of these sensitive prices, which remain pro-cyclical even after these prices are deflated by the common pro-cyclical influence of the aggregate price index (op. cit., pp. 525–28).

Schumpeter's discussion of the general impact of the cyclical process on price-quantity pairs is followed by noting special cases where the relationship between prices and quantities is complicated by the influence of past prices or the rate of change of prices. He points to technological lag as an influence that can cause fluctuations of price-quantity pairs to fall out of line with the general case. This influence is illustrated in an extended discussion of movements in coffee prices from 1870 to 1925, followed by a more general discussion of price cycles for animals, particularly the hog cycle. Schumpeter suggests some cycles in price-quantity pairs for coffee are due to innovation, while other cycles have been influenced by cycles in expenditures by consumers. He then downplays the importance of the propagation of waves through repetitions of lagged supply response for either coffee or animals, as he expects that producers would eventually learn the lesson in the absence of further innovations. Thus, he concludes that the true generating mechanism of the price cycle for hogs and other animals is, in fact, his own cyclical mechanism operating through fluctuations in consumer expenditure (op. cit., pp. 528–33).

Schumpeter goes on to consider the special case of shipbuilding, with Chart XXII (op. cit., p. 535) showing British time series from 1870 to 1934 for total tonnage (level and annual rate of change), shipbuilding (new construction), price of new steamer, freight rate index and interest rate. He considers a formalisation of the pattern of shipbuilding that embeds a self-perpetuating cycle, but dismisses the possibility because it requires, as above, that carriers fail to learn from previous experience, which is contrary to the assumed rationality of behaviour and not consistent with common sense. He goes on to conclude the cycles generated in the process of economic evolution driven by innovation still show through (op. cit., pp. 533–35).

This brings Schumpeter to the discussion of prices directly affected by innovation under the heading, 'Entrepreneurial Price Policies'. First, he discusses the case of an innovation in the production process of a commodity already produced under perfect competition, adding only clarification regarding the impact on price-quantity pairs to the discussion in the early chapters of *BC*. In particular, he notes that the process of adjustment in price and quantity may take substantial time as incumbent firms can be quite difficult to dislodge and may operate at a loss for many years (op. cit., pp. 535–36). The specifics of the adjustment process aren't discussed further, but subsequent discussion of the matter in *CSD* clearly indicates Schumpeter's awareness that, 'perfect competition is and always has been temporarily suspended whenever anything new is being introduced – automatically or by measures designed for the purpose – even in otherwise perfectly competitive conditions' (Schumpeter, 1976 [1950], p. 105).

Schumpeter continues the discussion in *BC* by acknowledging that the entrepreneur introducing a new commodity almost invariably faces imperfect competition. This brings him to add a discussion of price rigidity. First, Schumpeter discusses the occurrence of price stability without innovation. He identifies several circumstances in which such stability occurs, including traditionally sticky and authoritatively regulated prices, few-firm industries with a sluggishness of business spirit, irrational elements, cartels of the German kind and industries where capacity is maintained to meet cyclical peak demand. In all these cases, cyclical variation in prices may be missed, especially for the shorter Kitchin cycles. Further, the breakdown of stability doesn't imply a return to competitive behaviour, rather there is instability in which price movements become disconnected from movements in costs and also disconnected from the cyclical process (Schumpeter, 1939, pp. 539–41).

Schumpeter then suggests the analysis of price stability also applies when a new commodity is introduced, but the superiority of the new product means firms are on unequal terms. Nonetheless, price stability is expected to characterise the market for some time for two reasons. First, he notes that in the period in which the new commodity is vigorously gaining in the market, quantity sold is not sensitive to cyclical influences and the innovator need not reduce price to expand sales. Second, the entrepreneur in seeking to develop the market and protect themselves against imitators has an attractive strategy of choosing and maintaining a price that offers good value to customers and reduces potential profits to imitators (op. cit., pp. 541–43).

Schumpeter is clearly opposed to the view that price stability has serious dislocating effects on the economy in depression, both because genuine rigidity is rare and because the effect of rigidity is often overstated. He recognises the substantial effort firms put into obtaining and retaining monopolistic positions. However, his view is that, rather than enabling firms to engage in long-run restriction of output, the value of such efforts is more in allowing firms to survive through temporary difficulties and engage in long-run planning. He concludes his discussion of the price and quantities of individual commodities by noting that price rigidity and monopolistic positions are problematic for his theory predicting short-run movements of price-quantity pairs, but his theory still applies over the longer term. He also justifies a focus on studying movements of price-quantity pairs over the longer Juglar or Kondratieff cycles, rather than in the shorter Kitchins (op. cit., p. 543).[2]

Commentary

Schumpeter's price theory acquires a dynamic character from the theory of economic development of which it is part. In this section, I identify three elements of the overall theory that have particular importance in explaining price dynamics. I then develop a simplified formalisation to explain how each of the elements impacts on price dynamics.

The three elements of Schumpeter's theory of economic development to which I ascribe particular importance are (1) innovation, (2) credit creation and (3) competition. Innovation is important because of its discontinuous character, which imparts an uneven character to price-cost relationships across firms, commodities and time. Credit creation is important because, by providing the financing for entrepreneurs to divert means of production from established uses, it leads to a pattern of movement over time in the prices of means of production. Prices of means of production, in turn, impact on the price level. Competition is important because it is the primary process used by entrepreneurs with price-cost advantages to embed their position in a transformed industrial structure, implying a price system characterised by heterogeneity in price movements across firms and commodities.

Movements in the price level and heterogeneity in price movements for individual commodities are important in regulating Schumpeter's evolutionary process. Prices convey information to entrepreneurs on the potential profitability of their innovations. However, to encourage innovation the information needs to be reliable, meaning it needs to be indicative of both the current situation and the underlying structure that influences future outcomes. Schumpeter argues that innovations are stimulated by the economy being in the neighbourhood of equilibrium, when the information contained in each current price approximates the corresponding theoretical normal price. Stimulating innovation then moves the price level and the price system away from the neighbourhood of equilibrium and increasingly inhibits proper calculation of profit potential for further innovations, eventually leading to a decline in the flow of innovations.

In evolutionary terms, innovation, by creating variety, moves the economy away from the neighbourhood of equilibrium. Credit expansion enables and enhances the disturbance by allowing the innovations to rapidly permeate the economy. Competition then destroys variety. In particular, firms and products that can't achieve a price at least equal to production cost are eliminated in the process of creative destruction. All that remains at the end of this process are economically sustainable firms, which means firms operating without a loss given existing

technology, preferences and organisation. The reduction in variety aids in simpli-
fying and rendering more reliable the information entrepreneurs use to disrupt the
system through a new wave of innovations. This evolutionary process is clearly
endogenous. It is certainly not static, but it may be dynamically stable.

Having identified three basic elements affecting prices in the evolutionary process, my next step is to identify a simple formalisation for analysing the implied
dynamics affecting prices. In his only recently published *Treatise on Money* (*TM*)
Schumpeter (2014, p. 115, italics in original) gives a pointer of how to proceed
by noting, 'we gain a picture of an essentially stationary economic process, which
we describe as a circular flow because each of its phases leads back again to itself,
the image of a *purely self-replicating* economic process (Marx).'[3] In his seminal
contribution to formalising classical economics, Sraffa (1960) uses a system of
equations to determine prices that allow each production process to be replicated
by exactly covering the cost of replacement of produced means of production as
well as the wages of labour as original means of production (with or without the
addition of a profit on the cost of production).

I follow Kurz (2008) (also Kurz, 2013, Metcalfe and Steedman, 2013) and use
Sraffa's framework to discuss Schumpeter's treatment of the circular flow and
innovation. For simplicity, I start from Kurz's (2008) initial model and assume
that labour is the only non-produced means of production (no natural resource
inputs) and that all intermediate commodities are produced and consumed in the
current period (no durable capital).[4] In vector notation, the unit cost of production
is given as the sum of unit labour and unit intermediate input cost as follows:

$$\mathbf{c} = \mathbf{A}\mathbf{p} + \gamma\,\mathbf{w} \tag{4.2}$$

where $\mathbf{c}$ is the vector of unit production cost for all commodities (the ith element is
the unit cost of the ith commodity), $\mathbf{p}$ is the vector of commodity prices, γ is the
vector of labour requirements, $\mathbf{A}$ is the matrix of input-output coefficients and w is
the wage rate. The elements of the matrix $\mathbf{A}$ give the direct requirements of each
commodity for the production of one unit the commodity in that row, so a_{ij} gives
the direct requirements of commodity j used in producing one unit of commodity i.

Kurz starts with the economy, as does Schumpeter, with no profits and with
all firms that produce any particular commodity using identical technology.[5]
The price of each commodity is then equal to its cost of production. Under these
assumptions, Pasinetti (1977, p. 75) shows that the vector of commodity prices
can be solved from Equation (4.2) by setting $\mathbf{c} = \mathbf{p}$ to yield:

$$\mathbf{p} = ((\mathbf{I} - \mathbf{A})^{-1}\gamma)\mathbf{w} \tag{4.3}$$

where the elements of the matrix $(\mathbf{I} - \mathbf{A})^{-1}$ when multiplied by the vector of direct
labour requirements γ give the vector of total (direct and indirect) labour requirements. Multiplying this total labour requirement by the wage rate gives the cost
of production and this unit cost is equal to the product price. Here, the vector of
commodity prices is determined solely by technology, given by the input-output
coefficients and labour requirements, and by wage rates.

For the purpose of demonstrating how innovation affects prices under Schumpeter's evolutionary process, I choose the case of a process innovation at time t that reduces the amount of labour required to produce the ith commodity in future periods for the entrepreneurial firm (firm e) that introduces the innovation, $\gamma_{i,e,t+1} < \gamma_{i,e,t}$, while established firms (m for mature) have $\gamma_{i,m,t+1} = \gamma_{i,m,t}$. At current prices, this innovation is profitable because it reduces production cost at current wages and prices for intermediate inputs, which justifies banks providing credit to the entrepreneur to acquire means of production for the purpose of setting up the innovative production process.

Schumpeter argues that the credit extended to entrepreneurs increases the purchasing power chasing otherwise fully employed means of production. Assuming no other labour requirements or technical coefficients are affected, the demand for labour increases directly by the labour required by the entrepreneurial firm and indirectly through higher output of commodities used in producing the ith commodity.[6] More purchasing power chasing the same labour means that the wage rate rises as labour is shifted from established producers to the entrepreneur. The wage increase feeds through to the prices of all commodities in Equation (4.3). If the impact of the reduced labour requirements is ignored for the moment, the effect on the price vector is a proportional rise in the price of all commodities.[7]

A proportional rise in all prices conforms to Schumpeter's argument that increased innovation leads to a rise in the price level. As there is no immediate impact on the relative prices of commodities the price system is unaffected. Associating a rise in the price level with a system-wide increase in cost and price fits with Schumpeter's treatment of the price level as a social construct rather than as a mere aggregation of individual commodity prices.

How does the reduction in labour requirements from the process innovation directly affect pricing once output from the entrepreneurial firm comes to market? The assumption that all producers of commodity i use best-practice technology is no longer applicable. Suppose instead that the ith element of the vector of labour requirements is the weighted average of individual firm labour requirements, with the weights being the share of each firm in the total production of the commodity as follows:

$$\gamma_{i,t} = \sum_k \gamma_{i,k,t}(x_{i,k,t} / \sum_k x_{i,k,t}), \text{ for } k = e, m \quad (4.4)$$

where $x_{i,k,t}$ is the output of the kth firm and the term in parentheses is the firm's share in total output of the ith commodity. Assuming the entrepreneur starts small, most output still comes from established producers that utilise an outdated technology and the element of the labour input requirements vector corresponding to the ith commodity is reduced only slightly from its pre-innovation level.

Changing the labour requirements of the ith commodity without other adjustments, even by a small amount, would imply a change in the price system. However, the standard assumption in economics is that a homogenous product will sell at a uniform price regardless of any heterogeneity in production costs. This then raises the question of whether or not it is the weighted average of labour requirements that determines price. Here, Schumpeter is reasonably clear that the introduction of an innovation leads to profit for the system as a whole as well as for the entrepreneur. The existence of profits can be accommodated by pre-multiplying the unit cost vector from Equation (4.3) by a diagonal matrix of price-cost ratios, denoted by Ψ, as follows:

$$\mathbf{p} = \mathbf{\Psi c} = ((\mathbf{I} - \mathbf{\Psi A})^{-1}\mathbf{\Psi \gamma})\mathbf{w}, \text{ where } \mathbf{c} = \mathbf{Ap} + \gamma \mathbf{w} \qquad (4.5)$$

The ith diagonal element of Ψ is the weighted average price-cost ratio for the ith commodity, while the off-diagonal elements are each zero. There is profit in the system as a whole if the matrix of price-cost ratios is strictly larger than the identity matrix, $\Psi > \mathbf{I}$, which is satisfied if no element of the diagonal in the price-cost matrix is less than one and at least one element exceeds one.

If there are heterogeneous labour requirements for firms producing a commodity, then compensating differentials in the price-cost margins are required to ensure there is a single price in the market. In particular, each firm producing the ith commodity has the same price, p_{it}, at time t, if and only if, the price-cost ratio for each firm producing the commodity is given by:

$$\psi_{i,k,t} = p_{it} / c_{i,k,t} \qquad (4.6)$$

For consistency in aggregation from the individual firm values in Equation (4.6) to the industry relationship in Equation (4.5), the weighting scheme for calculating $c_{i,t}$ uses output shares for each firm, as shown in Equation (4.4) for calculating $\gamma_{i,t}$. The same weights are used for calculating $\Psi_{i,t}$, but here the industry average is the harmonic mean of individual firm values rather than the arithmetic mean.

Under what conditions will the example of a labour-saving innovation generate outcomes corresponding to Schumpeter's proposition that innovation results in profit for the entrepreneur and profit for the economy as a whole? One simple case is all non-innovating firms producing the ith commodity sell at the price equal to their common unit cost and the entrepreneurial firm also charges this price and earns a profit.[8] Price-cost ratios across the full set of firms in the economy are then given by:

$$\Psi_{i,e,t} = c_{i,k,t} / c_{i,e,t} > 1 \text{ and } \Psi_{j,k,t} = 1, \text{for all } j, k, \ k \neq e \qquad (4.7)$$

In this case, the weighted average price-cost ratio for commodity i exceeds one, while the corresponding ratio for all other commodities equals one. If the output share of the entrepreneurial firm is small, the weighted average price-cost ratio for the ith commodity is correspondingly close to one.

Suppose prices continue to be determined by the price-cost ratios in Equation (4.7) during the upswing of the business cycle. As the entrepreneurial firm expands, at first financed by credit and then increasingly by retained profits, the weighted average unit cost for the ith commodity drops while the corresponding price-cost ratio rises proportionally so there is no direct impact on the price system or the price level. However, without further increases in credit, there is no further rise in purchasing power according to Schumpeter and no further impetus to the price level.

The increased supply of the ith commodity from the entrepreneurial firm means total supply of that commodity can be expected to exceed demand at the price-cost ratios specified in Equation (4.7). Established firms might accept some reduction in output rather than cut price below their reproduction cost as is assumed by Metcalfe and Steedman (2013). If not and prices of the commodity remain uniform, then the price charged by all producers of the commodity falls relative to the price of other commodities.[9] Alternatively, if there is scope for heterogeneity of price for a single commodity, the entrepreneur's price falls relative to that of other producers of the commodity and the average industry price falls relative to the average price of commodities produced by other industries. Either way, the change in relative prices implies a fall in an aggregate price index under any scheme that gives weight to the entrepreneur's output, but doesn't readily meet Schumpeter's requirement for a fall of the price level as a decline in the value of money.[10]

If the entrepreneur's price falls below those of its competitors, they are likely to cede market share to the entrepreneur. If they match the price reduction, they are operating at a loss and come under pressure to shut down or switch to the new production technology with its reduced labour requirements. Both possibilities represent Schumpeter's process of creative destruction. One effect of this shift in production of the commodity from the old technology to the new is that less labour input is required for the same level of output. This conditional reduction in labour requirements is a factor contributing to a reduced aggregate demand for labour, weakening the forces that are driving wages and prices upwards in the business cycle upswing and contributing to the turning of the price-level cycle into a downswing.

In Schumpeter's analysis, the downswing of the price cycle occurs with the combination of creative destruction and autodeflation arising from the contraction of credit. Once they are well established, entrepreneurs turn to repaying the loans taken out for their establishment and early expansion. Without further innovations, this reduces the total outstanding amount of purchasing power available to buy commodities. In the formalisation of Schumpeter's analysis set out above, there would be a decline in labour demand and the wage rate.[11] With a decline in the wage rate, there is a fall in price across the board in Equation (4.7) that, because of its broad impact, clearly satisfies Schumpeter's requirements for being considered as a fall in the price level as opposed to just a decline in an aggregate index of prices.

In my example of innovation through labour-saving technical change, the diffusion of the innovation means an increasing share of output in the entrepreneur's industry coming from the new technology so that output can expand without additional labour. The expansion of output relative to labour employed continues until all production comes from the new technology. Thus, rising output is consistent with a falling price level during the downswing in the business cycle. Further, the rising real wage implied by aggregate prices falling faster than the wage rate, provides enough purchasing power to buy the increased output, even as credit is withdrawn from the economy.

Once the process of creative destruction is complete, all remaining producers of the entrepreneur's product are using the new technology. This is the end of the business cycle, at least the end of Schumpeter's two-phase cycle that returns to normal conditions after recession and excludes overshooting in depression. The wage rate and price level rise in the prosperity upswing (indeed, the rising price level defines the upswing), while the wage rate and price level fall in the recession downswing. Output continues to rise throughout the cycle after implementation of the innovation, driven by rising labour productivity even as product price falls and credit contracts. The relationship of the final price level to the original depends on changes in the wage rate, which I consider when examining Schumpeter's analysis of banking, credit and money supply in the next chapter.

A price vector equating price to unit production cost based on best-practice technology, as given by Equation (4.2), is a necessary, but not sufficient, condition for a Walrasian equilibrium of the type Schumpeter assumes prevails in the stationary state before innovation initiates a business cycle. Walrasian equilibrium also requires optimal individual behaviour, marginal cost pricing and market clearing for all commodities. As noted in the previous chapter, Schumpeter's reliance on Walrasian equilibrium as an anchor for the business cycle has been subject to strong criticism. It is thus reasonable to ask whether the extra assumptions required for Walrasian equilibrium are necessary for a price vector to satisfy the role Schumpeter posits for theoretically normal prices. I consider this question in depth in Chapter 6, 'Norms, Equilibrium and Competition', and argue that the extra assumptions are not only unnecessary but logically inconsistent with Schumpeter's characterisation of a developing economy.

The assumptions made in the simple formalisation of Schumpeterian evolution based on Equation (4.2) through Equation (4.7) are highly restrictive. Complications arise when the simple reproduction scheme is modified to allow for durable capital, as is explained in the discussion of obsolescence in Chapter 7, 'Norms for a Developing Economy'. In particular, new technology renders at least some old capital goods obsolete, which alters the calculation of reproduction cost. Having prices equal to these reproduction costs means production processes and the firms that utilise them are economically sustainable given current technology and the past experience of obsolescence. In this sense, such prices can be considered to be theoretically normal. Of course, when a future cluster of innovations impacts on reproduction costs and prices, the reliability of the original theoretically normal prices diminishes and a different approach to analysing prices is required.

Schumpeter presents his theory of the price level strictly in terms of macroeconomic or, more precisely, monetary phenomena. Changes in the price system are left to the vagaries of the specific innovations driving each cycle. In Chapter 8, 'Reconstructing Schumpeter's Price Theory', I propose using post-Keynesian price theories together with the reproduction price scheme as the basis for reconstructing Schumpeter's price theory in an integrated framework, which features firm pricing behaviour (micro analysis), competition between firms and industries through innovation and creative destruction (meso analysis), and movement in economic aggregates (macro analysis). The micro and meso components of the analysis draw on elements of the formalisation presented above, while the macro component draws on my review of Schumpeter's monetary theory as presented in the next chapter.

Summary

Schumpeter views his price theory as a supplement to the Walrasian theory of general equilibrium prices. Starting from an equilibrium position, entrepreneurs can reliably calculate the prospective profits to be earned from the introduction of an innovation. A swarm of disruptive innovations then moves both the price level and the price system away from the theoretical normal values associated with general equilibrium. This deters further innovation. There follows a process of diffusion of the swarm of innovations through the process of creative destruction that eventually returns the economy to the neighbourhood of a new equilibrium, albeit only after the working out of secondary phenomena that generate overshooting to depression, with possible panic, followed by recovery.

According to Schumpeter, the price level rises during the prosperity phase of the business cycle and falls during the recession phase. The fall continues into the depression phase and prices turn back upward in the recovery. At the end of the cycle, after the working of the process of creative destruction, the price level is lower than at the beginning. Innovation also leads to changes in the price system over the cycle, as relative prices are affected by innovation. However, Schumpeter refrains from any general characterisation of the direction of the changes in relative prices, even as between innovating and non-innovating commodities, as the movement of any particular price-quantity pair reflects the special circumstances and behaviour of the relevant industry.

My commentary in this chapter explains how Schumpeter's theory can be formalised in terms of a Sraffian framework of reproduction prices. I use the example of a labour-saving innovation in a competitive economy to illustrate movement of the price level that follows Schumpeter's two-phase cyclical pattern. The upswing is driven by a rising wage rate as competition from entrepreneurs for means of production increases the demand for labour, while wage rates fall in the downswing as repayment of loans by entrepreneurs combined with lower labour requirements from the innovation decrease labour demand.

The price system is also affected in the formalisation, as Schumpeter's analysis implies. Initially, the extra output from entrepreneurs is sold at a profit, with lower labour requirements not being reflected in price reduction. However, the process of creative destruction eventually ensures that profit dissipates and the price charged for the output of the innovative production process is equated with its unit costs of production, which implies a fall in price of this commodity relative to the prices of other commodities. If the commodity with lowered production costs is used in other production processes, the production costs and prices of these commodities tend to fall as well. At the aggregate level, falling prices of at least some commodities relative to wages are necessarily reflected in a higher real wage rate compared to the rate prior to the innovation.

Schumpeter explains movements in the price level primarily by the ups and downs in the amount of credit outstanding with entrepreneurs, which affects purchasing power in the economy. Linking this analysis to the formalisation in Equation (4.7) is most readily done through the nominal wage rate, as this is the only variable with a uniform impact on all prices. The next chapter examines Schumpeter's theory of banking, credit and money before considering how it can be linked to the determination of the wage rate under the institutional arrangements assumed in Schumpeter's analysis and also under the institutional arrangements as they have evolved since.

Notes

1 To deal with longer intervals, Schumpeter suggests the chain method for linking periods as advocated by Alfred Marshall. He also notes that his theory suggests using the Laspeyres price index method (with base period quantity weights), but that the Paasche index (with end period quantity weights) or Fisher's "ideal" index (the geometric mean of the Laspeyres and Paasche indices) are also acceptable, provided that changes are small (Schumpeter, 1939, pp. 456–57).
2 In *CSD*, Chapter VIII, 'Monopolistic Practices', Schumpeter (1976 [1950], p. 87) carries on this argument when he attacks 'criticisms of the profit economy which, directly or indirectly, rely on the absence of perfect competition'. He concludes the chapter pointing to the achievements of large-scale enterprise, even with temporarily restrictive practices, claiming that, with regard to progress and growth, 'perfect competition is not only impossible but inferior, and has no title to being set up as a model of ideal efficiency' (op. cit., p. 106).
3 The manuscript for this book is thought to date to before 1930, but was unpublished at the time of Schumpeter's death in 1950 and was only published as a transcription of the German language manuscript in 1970 with an introduction by Fritz Karl Mann (Schumpeter, 1970). The history of the publication of the book and a discussion of its content appears in the next chapter.
4 This complication is incorporated in the discussion of later chapters, particularly Chapter 6 that deals with the impact of obsolescence on costs.
5 Kurz (2013) suggests it would be appropriate to include a uniform rate of profit (normal profit) in the reproduction costs determining theoretical normal prices in a Schumpeterian system as this would bring the theory into line with both marginalist and classical theories of profit. This approach is not pursued here in the interests of keeping the analysis as simple as possible and consistent with Schumpeter's argument that profit exists only when there is innovation.
6 Technical coefficients are unaffected by changes in output if there are constant returns to scale in production.
7 The impact of alternative assumptions regarding labour and intermediate input coefficients in old versus new production processes is discussed in the context of a one-sector classical model by David Haas (2015).
8 Schumpeter (1939, pp. 535–36) argues that following entry the entrepreneur introducing a new method for producing a commodity for which the market is already perfectly competitive faces an infinitely elastic demand so they can capture at least some market share without lowering price. Metcalfe and Steedman (2013) assume that the innovator's price equals the price of the established firms as long as the established firms remain in the market. Otherwise, established firms would be operating at a loss. Pricing

behaviour of firms, entrepreneurial and otherwise, is further considered in Chapter 8 below.

9 To the extent that other commodities are used to produce the ith commodity, its cost of production and price are affected by increased cost of intermediate inputs, as is implied by the term, $(\mathbf{I} - \mathbf{\Psi A})^{-1}$, in Equation (4.5).

10 The distinction between changes in aggregate price indices and changes in the price level is clearly articulated by Schumpeter (1939, pp. 468–69) when, in discussing the problems of using aggregate price indices as measures of the price level, he states, 'mere shifts in the price *system*, though they do not per se influence our price level, do influence the indices we have. Hence individual prices may, beside their legitimate influence, acquire an illegitimate one as well.'

11 In his discussion of the historical evidence in Chapter X of *BC* Schumpeter acknowledges falling wage rates are not generally observed in the recession phase of Kondratieff cycles for which he has data. His explanation of this failure and its implications for the application of his price theory to the study of cyclical and trend movements in the price level are discussed in the 'Commentary on Money and the Price Level' section of the next chapter.

5 Money, credit and the price level

The analysis of the preceding chapters points to a key role for bank credit in Schumpeter's theory of economic development in general and in his theory of the price level in particular. Yet, money is not just a veil over the real economy for Schumpeter. Extension of credit by bankers to entrepreneurs is essential for them to acquire the means of production for the introduction of innovations into the economy. Expansion of the money supply is both a consequence and a facilitator of the entrepreneurial activity, which in turn is the primary driver of economic growth and structural change.

Schumpeter views the economy as a monetary production and exchange system. Money provides the social accounting system essential to the functioning of the complex social process of a modern economy, a point Schumpeter emphasises his *Treatise on Money* (*TM*) (Schumpeter, 2014) by stressing the need for a related social accounting process even in a socialist command economy. Institutional arrangements regulating banking, credit and money influence the evolution of the economy, which affects quantities produced and exchanged of individual commodities as well as their prices. The manner in which money and goods interact ensures prices and quantities have characteristically cyclical movement.

In emphasising the role of credit in enabling innovations to be introduced into the economy, Schumpeter establishes a connection between finance and innovation. While he makes note of innovations in finance supporting this connection, he doesn't directly consider the impact of financial innovations on the process of development. In particular, he neglects the potential impacts of such innovations for increasing financial instability and contributing to panics and crises, which have become a key focus in recent work on financial stabilisation.

My discussion of Schumpeter's analysis of banking, credit, money and the price level starts with a brief review of the historical record on movements in the price level, which serves to put the period examined by Schumpeter in *BC* within a longer historical context. I then discuss the key features of Schumpeter's theory of banking, credit and money, particularly as discussed in *TM*. These features include his conception of money as a social institution for account settling and his distinctive analysis of the role of bank credit in the time displacement between changes in prices and changes in output. This is followed by a discussion of the impact of financial innovations on financial stability and the implications for the role of governments and central banks in controlling instability. Changes since Schumpeter's time to institutional arrangements are then considered, with emphasis on changes to monetary institutions. The penultimate section consolidates implications for the relationship between money and the price level. A summary section closes the chapter.

The historical record

In Chapter VIII of *BC*, Schumpeter applies his cyclical theory of the price level to the historical record for the period up to 1913 as revealed in the 'Historical Outlines' of Chapters VI and VII. As discussed in the previous chapter, he includes interpretations of time-series charts of the price level for the United Kingdom, United States and Germany, concluding his theory is not rejected because major deviations in the time-series charts from the pattern implied by his theory are sufficiently explained by historical evidence regarding the impact of specific external factors (Schumpeter, 1939, pp. 468–72). In reaching this conclusion he concentrates his discussion on determining whether there is a downward result trend for the price level in each of the Kondratieff cycles for which he has data. He also examines whether there are substantial up and down movements over the course of each cycle.

Schumpeter addresses the argument that the price level is related to gold production (in an era when the major industrial countries still generally pegged their currencies to gold). First, he suggests it is the size of monetary gold stocks that matters for determining the money supply and the price level according to the quantity theory of the price level. He then argues the positive relationship between monetary gold stocks and the price level is due to the working of his process. Finally, he points out it would require exactly offsetting movements in monetary gold to completely wipe out the influence of his process on the time-series charts of the price level (Schumpeter, 1939, pp. 472–473).

The suggestion that monetary gold stocks, as opposed to total gold stocks, reflect the working of Schumpeter's process is central to understanding his position that the price level can be expected to show a declining result trend over the long cycle. Schumpeter is arguing the supply of monetary gold is endogenous and subservient to the working of the capitalist process he is analysing. Schumpeter holds a similar position with respect to the supply of fiat currency in discussing those historical periods where countries have moved away from the gold standard.[1]

The bulk of detailed data on prices given in *BC* are for the period from the 1800s through to the early 1930s. These data cover one full Kondratieff in Schumpeter's dating of cycles, the Kondratieff from 1842 to 1897. They also cover most of the preceding Kondratieff and a large part of the following one, including the initial upswing, the recession and the depression. Longer times series, such as those presented by David Fischer (1996, p. 4) covering English prices of consumables for the period from 1201 to 1993, show a pattern of price level movements for the nineteenth and early twentieth century that more or less fits the pattern of Schumpeter's cyclical and trend movements for the same period. However, it turns out that this pattern is not repeated over other periods.

Fischer (1996) notes prices in England were stable to declining throughout the nineteenth century, aside from an upswing around the middle of the century. He characterises this period as the Victorian equilibrium. He also notes two other long periods in which long-run inflation was absent, the Renaissance equilibrium (1400–1480) and the Enlightenment equilibrium (1660–1730). Before, after and in between were long periods of sustained inflation, which Fischer labels as price revolutions.

Alternating century-long periods of price equilibrium and price revolution are not consistent with Schumpeter's expected repeating pattern of cycle and downward trend. Fischer (1996, p. 9) specifically states, 'It should be understood clearly that movements we are studying are waves – not cycles. To repeat: not cycles, but waves.' The distinction is between cycles that 'are fixed and regular' and waves that 'differ in duration, magnitude, velocity, and momentum to' (ibid.). Fischer's data on price level movements from the thirteenth century onward provide clear evidence against Schumpeter's theory that the price level has a downward result trend, either over the full period or over the period starting from the Industrial Revolution. There are too many price revolutions exhibiting sustained inflation, including the revolution of the twentieth century.

Schumpeter's theory of the connection between credit and innovation may still be valid, especially for particular historical periods, but it is inadequate to explain movements in the price level over the full period of capitalist development. Implicit in Schumpeter's analysis is an assumption that the money supply is only affected by the expansion and contraction of credit in response to financing investments in innovation. Other factors, such as gold discoveries, are viewed as only having temporary impact. Fischer's data suggests there are systematic factors leading to price revolutions over extended periods. Later in this chapter I consider the possible systematic factors behind the price revolution of the twentieth century, but first it is important to further examine Schumpeter's distinctive theory of banking, credit and money.

The theory of banking, credit and money

Banks and their provision of credit to entrepreneurs are identified in the preceding chapters as having a particularly crucial role in Schumpeter's theory of economic development. While Schumpeter extensively discusses banking and credit in *TED* and *BC*, theoretical aspects are interwoven with the specific institutional arrangements observed by Schumpeter and embedded into his analysis. The focus in this section is on isolating Schumpeter's theory of banking, credit and money from specific institutional elements.

Schumpeter never published his treatise on money and currency for which he had plans from at least the early 1920s. An incomplete draft manuscript in German dating from around 1930 was found among his papers at the time of his death in 1950. According to Tichy (1984, p. 125), the draft treatise 'comprises almost everything that Schumpeter had written earlier on monetary theory', including a lengthy article, 'Das Sozialprodukt und die Rechenpfennige' (Schumpeter, 1917–18), which was translated into English by Arthur Marget and published as 'Money and the Social Product' (Schumpeter, 1956) by the International Economics Association in their series of translations of important foreign-language economics articles.

Shortly after the discovery of the unpublished money manuscript, a typescript in German was prepared under the direction of Marget, an ardent admirer of Schumpeter's monetary and price theory. A copy of the German typescript was given to Fritz Karl Mann, who edited the manuscript and eventually arranged its publication as *Das Wesen des Geldes* (*The Essence of Money*) (Schumpeter, 1970). Marget also started work on an English translation, but only managed the first two chapters and these were published long after his death as 'Money and Currency' (Schumpeter, 1991) in *Social Research*. An introduction to the two chapters by Richard Swedberg includes a discussion of why Schumpeter failed to publish the volume during his lifetime. In following years, an Italian translation appeared as *L'Essenza della Moneta* (Schumpeter, 1990) and a French translation including additional material appeared as *Théorie de la Monnaie et de la Banque* (Schumpeter, 2005b), while an English translation by Ruben Alvarado finally appeared in 2014 as *Treatise on Money* (*TM*) (Schumpeter, 2014).[2]

Marget (1951) provides a review of Schumpeter's monetary analysis in the issue of the *Review of Economics and Statistics* dedicated to Schumpeter soon after his death. In this review, Marget notes the advantage of having had access to the unpublished manuscripts for both *Das Wesen des Geldes* and *History of Economic Analysis* (HEA) as well as Schumpeter's published works in both English and German. Marget suggests Schumpeter follows the structure of 'the Quesnay-Walras concept of a "circular flow" of economic life conceived as a *system of flows of money expenditure directed towards objects sold against such expenditure*' (op. cit., p. 112, quotation marks and italics in the original). Further, he notes in Schumpeter's analysis, 'Money, in short, is the means whereby a link is established in *time* between the successive discretely realized events of the economic process' (op. cit., p. 113, italics in original).

The emphasis on flows of money expenditure subtly distinguishes Schumpeter's theory from those in which money is a medium of exchange for goods and services, while the emphasis on the time element points to the theory's distinctive character when dealing with credit extended to entrepreneurs to finance their innovations. As in theories in which money is only a veil, the extension of credit to entrepreneurs initially leads to a proportional rise in nominal expenditures without any increase in output, with current prices increasing to maintain proportionality between the money supply and nominal income without any change in the income velocity of money.[3] However, the analyses in *TED*, *TM* and *BC* point to qualitative and quantitative impacts of the monetary expansion on production processes that are contrary to the neutral-money approach.

With the credit provided to entrepreneurs by the banks, means of production are transferred from established producers to entrepreneurs. When entrepreneurs repay their loans, money supply and nominal income fall in tandem along with prices, which is the process Schumpeter calls autodeflation. Additional output from the entrepreneurs more than replaces the output lost from established producers, which adds to the downward pressure on prices and leads Schumpeter to expect a downward result trend for the price level over the full course of the cycle.

The two chapters of *Das Wesen des Geldes* translated by Marget and published as 'Money and Currency' (Schumpeter, 1991) help to clarify Schumpeter's position on the particularly social character of money. Chapter I is introductory and deals with currency policy, with Schumpeter discussing the impact of inflationary, deflationary and stable price policies on the economy and on different groups within society. While inflation favours debtors and deflation favours creditors, Schumpeter (1991, pp. 515–16) notes the broad attraction of stable prices, 'for scientific as well as practical purposes, to establish the comparability between sums of money at different places and at different times'. Importantly, he goes on to state, 'We shall develop our argument chiefly from the standpoint of this goal, without, however, identifying ourselves with it' (op. cit., p. 516).[4]

Schumpeter addresses the sociology of money in Chapter II of *TM*, identifying four functions of money in society, as a medium of exchange, a measure of value, a standard of deferred payment and a store of value. These functions are all now common in monetary theory, although the measure of value function is commonly referred to using the alternative terminology of money being a unit of account or a standard of value. Still, Schumpeter provides an early contribution by distinguishing these abstract functions from the particular historical and cultural circumstances in which certain forms of money emerge to perform each of these roles. Further, the emphasis on money being an institutional response to societal needs leads Schumpeter to focus on the logic of how these needs are met in capitalism, including an emphasis on the role played by banks and credit.[5]

Gunther Tichy (1984, p. 126) commenting on the original German version of *TM*, *Das Wesen des Geldes*, observes, 'Schumpeter emphasizes the function of money as a standard of value.' In a monetary production and exchange economy the value of money is generally understood and accepted by all participants across the full range of transactions in which they engage. This social understanding of the value of money is essential to the efficient functioning of the economy. While in primitive societies this standard of value might be tied to a particular commodity, in modern society the corresponding concept is generalised to purchasing power.[6] For Schumpeter purchasing power is a social concept more than a statistical measure, which leads him to refer to the price level as a social construct as opposed to an aggregate index of prices of individual commodities (see discussion in the Price Level section of Chapter 4 above).

In Chapter II of *TM* Schumpeter criticises those who believe that historical priority implies logical necessity when it comes to theorising about money (Schumpeter, 2014, pp. 17–19). In Chapter IX he further emphasises the logic of money does not require the declaration of money as legal tender (op. cit., pp. 218–21) or the emergence of money as a commodity used as a medium of exchange (op. cit., pp. 221–23). Thereby, he demonstrates, 'the complete logical autonomy of the unit of account vis-à-vis the idea of something "having value."

This demonstration likewise leads us to both the essence and the peculiarity of the institution of money' (op. cit., p. 223, quotation marks in original).

Noting that economic equilibrium determines only relative, and not absolute, prices, Schumpeter (op. cit., p. 226, italics in the original) argues, 'we can only proceed from price ratios to absolute prices or, in other words, procure the missing factor or missing equation by *equating any monetary economic variable to an arbitrarily chosen number.*' Further, 'Because our random number determines all monetary quantities of the area of study, we call it the *critical number* of the system' (op. cit., p. 227, italics in original). Finally, he suggests an expedient approach from a theoretical perspective is to equate the critical number to equilibrium consumption expenditure and to leave it at that level in discussing positions outside of equilibrium, which means deviations from equilibrium are reflected in differences in prices from equilibrium values.

In practice, the critical number is set socially, which could be done by a central bank or it could emerge from social practice (as in primitive use of metallic currency). Inherent uncertainty is introduced in either case as the critical number is determined with autonomy from the economic system. After discussing the practical problems encountered under both the paper money method (central bank) and the commodity money method, Schumpeter concludes,

> The result of the investigation of this chapter can now be expressed as follows: *this indirect and essentially nonsensical method makes up the essence of the social institution that we call money.* We take the fixing of the critical number to be also a kind of autonomous change of that number, i.e., a kind of continuous determination that in principle does not take the relations of the world of commodities into consideration, and now offer this definition: *the money method is that method of social account-settlement, according to which the critical number of the economic system changes autonomously.* Every such method creates tokens of account [Rechenpfennige] that exist as such – physically or on the books. *These tokens of account we call money.* Any such method subjects the economic variables to a new condition, to which they must adapt. We call *this* condition the *money tie* [Geldligamen].
>
> (op. cit., p. 233, italics in original)

Marcello Messori (1997, p. 669) suggests that one contribution of *TM* is,

> it shows that the macroeconomic importance of the coordination functions, carried out by money as a unit of account and as a means of payment, leads to the crucial role of banks as "social accountants", a role fully performed by banks' creation of means of payments.

Nicoló De Vecchi (1995, p. 64) explains Schumpeter's concept of banks as social accountants as follows,

> He presents money as a share certificate in production issued by a social accounting body and with debt-discharging effect. In other words, anyone who

has contributed to production does not directly receive goods in exchange, but is credited with a claim which can be used to purchase whatever commodity he likes from any other member of the community.

In this way, Schumpeter goes beyond the emphasis on money as a medium of exchange that bases the importance of money on its role as a substitute for barter in the exchange of goods, a role emphasised by those who treat money as a veil without lasting impact on the real economy.

The money connection to the real economy is a social process in which there is an ongoing battle by economic subjects to loosen the institutional restrictions that inhibit money creation, even though it is precisely these restrictions that make money useful. As De Vecchi (1995, p. 65) notes, 'the role of money in a market economy, why it is universally accepted in society, and how its value is determined are closely related for Schumpeter.' Tichy (1984, p. 130) observes that in *HEA* and in *Das Wesen des Geldes* Schumpeter's position is, 'it is impossible to determine generally what happens if additional money is created. The result depends on the purpose for which the new money is used.'

Agnès Festré and Eric Nasica (2009) emphasise the important role of banks in Schumpeter's analysis as the institution responsible for selecting which entrepreneurs receive credit. They note, 'Schumpeter views the bankers as the ephors of the capitalist economy that control and select what can be financed' (op. cit., p. 344), explaining that Schumpeter uses the term ephor referring to an elected official in ancient Sparta whose role was to exercise supervisory power over the king. If the banks properly do their job, entrepreneurs receiving credit are generally successful and the extension of credit to entrepreneurs is constructive in the sense that the economy expands with only temporary inflation. However, if banks engage in reckless finance, such as by extending credit to speculators, the effect is to unnecessarily enhance the destabilising secondary phenomena of prosperity and depression.

Tichy (1984, p. 137) opines Schumpeter never finished the draft of the treatise on money because 'a further chapter ("Interplay of money and goods market") was planned, which should have provided a genuine dynamic monetary theory.' With regard to this dynamic theory, Tichy (op. cit., p.130) suggests

> Comparing the monetary writings of Schumpeter, one has to conclude therefore that the content of the missing chapters of the posthumous draft cannot be found explicitely [*sic*] in Schumpeter's later work. Rather it can be found implicitly in his work on economic development.

Schumpeter's implicit dynamic theory of banking, credit and money follows on directly from having development as the distinguishing characteristic of capitalism. Schumpeter starts his discussion of credit in Chapter III ('Credit and Capital') of *TED* by mentioning that his theory of economic development, with its emphasis on structural change through entrepreneurship, leads him to a heretical position on the role of money and credit. In particular, he rejects the view that money is a veil with no real influence on the course of economic development. Instead, the creation of credit and, implicitly, the expansion of the money supply are necessary for entrepreneurs to acquire means of production, diverting them from established firms for use in innovative production activities.

Having started his analysis with the circular flow of an economy in a stationary state with full employment, Schumpeter (1961 [1934], p. 106, italics in the original) notes that

> in so far as credit cannot be given out of the results of past enterprise or in general out of reservoirs of purchasing power created by past development, it can only consist of credit means of payment created *ad hoc*, which can be backed neither by money in the strict sense nor by products already in existence.

Entrepreneurs use their newly created means of payment to acquire productive services. As there is no addition to the supply of such services, there is a rise in their prices that compresses the purchasing power of previously existing means of payment (op. cit., pp. 108–09).[7]

Schumpeter then argues that while the process above 'may be called credit inflation' (op. cit., p. 109), this would be misleading due to the subsequent production by the entrepreneur. Indeed the entrepreneur has 'if everything has gone according to expectations, enriched the social stream with goods whose total price is greater than the credit received and than the total price of the goods directly and indirectly used up by him' (op. cit., p. 110). Schumpeter suggests the process is better understood as 'a non-synchronous appearance of purchasing power and of the commodities corresponding to it, which temporarily produces the semblance of inflation' (ibid.).

Schumpeter's heresy regarding monetary theory extends to capital theory. Indeed, he has a monetary theory of capital, which derives from his theory of economic development. Schumpeter declares, '*Capital is nothing but the lever by which the entrepreneur subjects to his control the concrete goods which he needs, nothing but a means of diverting factors of production to new uses, or of dictating a new direction to production*' (op. cit., p. 116, italics in the original). The purchasing power created for entrepreneurs to acquire means of production represents additional capital for the economy from the time the loan is extended. After arguing that there would be no meaning to the concept of capital in the circular flow of a stationary economy, Schumpeter states, '*We shall define capital, then, as that sum of means of payment which is available at any moment for transference to entrepreneurs*' (op. cit., p. 122, italics in the original).

Schumpeter's theory of capital stands in sharp contrast to that of his former teacher Eugene von Böhm-Bawerk, who puts forward a theory of capital as goods used as aids in the production process. These aids increase the roundaboutness of the production process generating additional output, which constitutes the profit or interest of the capitalist. Profit and interest depend only on the productivity of capital and are independent of money or prices. Not surprisingly, Böhm-Bawerk reacted negatively to Schumpeter's theory of monetary capital and interest in *TED*.[8]

Schumpeter treats capital 'as an accounting concept – as measuring in terms of money the resources entrusted to a firm' (Schumpeter, 1939, p. 129). Bankers serve as social accountants through their granting of credit to entrepreneurs. Projects that are deemed able to return principal and interest are funded and become capital. A profitable innovation need not make production more roundabout as in Böhm-Bawerk's theory nor involve an expansion of the flow of commodities as in classical growth models. What is required is that revenues exceed operating and capital costs at current and foreseeable prices and output levels. Speeding up the production process without changing output can satisfy this requirement as can reducing the amount of commodities required to achieve a particular purpose (for example, passive solar design in houses to reduce energy consumption).

Schumpeter also defines interest in purely monetary terms, 'Interest is a premium on present over future means of payment' (Schumpeter, 1939, p. 123). He argues in both *TED* and *BC* that neither abstinence nor roundabout production is required to explain interest. Instead, entrepreneurial profits provide a logically sound, albeit transitory, source for the payment of interest. Interest is in a sense a tax paid by entrepreneurs to banks for the purpose of obtaining access to means of production in advance of owning a claim on society's resources. With innovation fully absorbed at the end of the business cycle, entrepreneurial profits are zero. Hence, there is nothing left with which to pay interest, so interest would logically equal zero in a stationary state.

Schumpeter's implicit dynamic theory of banking, credit and money as revealed in *TED* and *BC* has as its underlying framework the exchange equation from the quantity theory, which equates nominal income to the money supply times the income velocity of circulation. While Schumpeter's appraisal of the quantity theory of money in *HEA* clearly rejects the naïve version of the theory that requires proportionality between changes in money supply and price level (Schumpeter, 1954, pp. 1099–1106), he praises more sophisticated and flexible treatments. He concludes with the following comment on the controversies regarding the quantity theory,

> the chief progress of monetary theory in more recent times has been the result of a tendency to tear up the straitjackets and to introduce explicitly and directly all that the best presentations of the quantity theory relegated into the limbo of indirect influences. Lesson: in economics more than elsewhere, a good cause and one that will win out eventually may be so inadequately defended as to appear to be bad for decades together.
>
> (op. cit., p. 1106)

Schumpeter's use of the quantity equation together with his approval of sophisticated and flexible forms of the quantity theory has encouraged monetarist interpretations of his work. In an early example, Clark Warburton (1953) acknowledges Schumpeter's contribution to emphasising that innovations and entrepreneurial activity impart a distinctive cyclical character to the capitalist economy, but suggests Schumpeter overstates the importance of this mechanism relative to that of external shocks as an influence on business fluctuations. In particular, Warburton (op cit., p. 521) argues the Schumpeterian system should be altered to recognise that business depressions

> are the consequences of external factors associated with the banking and monetary system – or, more specifically, originate in shocks of monetary disequilibrium (failure to maintain the quantity of the circulating medium or events or actions expected or designed to contract the circulating medium).

Warburton's interpretation suggests causality from the money supply and to nominal income. In Schumpeter's theory the money supply increases with the extension of credit to entrepreneurs and decreases with the repayment of loans. Thus, it is real activity, investments in innovations, causing changes in the money supply. Odile Lakomski-Laguerre (2016, p. 508) argues that in Schumpeter's credit-based theory, 'the money supply has an endogenous nature that fundamentally undermines the validity of the quantity theory, especially the causal link between the money supply and nominal prices.'

Warburton's suggestion that depressions 'originate in shocks of monetary disequilibrium' ignores Schumpeter's treatment of such monetary disorder as a secondary, rather than primary, phenomenon. Schumpeter treats monetary disorders as repercussions of excesses of prosperity in the upswing of the cycle, rather than the result of exogenous shocks arising from the monetary sector. He makes this point clearly in *TED* with his critical comments on the monetary explanations of the business cycle that he associates with Keynes, Fisher, Hawtrey and the policy of the Federal Reserve Board (Schumpeter, 1961 [1934], pp. 252–53). As De Vecchi (1995, p. 52) explains, 'Schumpeter formulates a cycle theory which is part of a more general theory of capitalist motion and which cannot be likened either to monetary theories or real cycle theories.'

A monetarist interpretation of Schumpeter's treatise on money is also provided by Parth Shah and Leland Yeager (1994). They attribute to Schumpeter an analysis of the problem of monetary determinacy that is congruent with Patinkin's (1965 [1956]) analysis and suggest that, 'Although using different terminology, Schumpeter apparently envisaged the real-balance effect stressed by Patinkin' (Shah and Yeager, 1994, p. 443). In support of this congruency in analysis, Shah and Yeager point to Schumpeter's references to a "critical figure" for the money supply as being necessary to provide the economy with a nominal anchor if prices are to be determinate. They suggest that, 'while Schumpeter himself was not a monetarist of the Warburton-Friedman-Schwartz-Brunner-Melzer stripe, his historical observations and his theoretical points – especially the ones made in his 1970 book – do reconcile with a basically monetarist theory' (op. cit., p. 460).

Shah and Yeager ignore the apparent contradiction between the monetarist advocacy of a fixed rate of growth of the money supply and the requirement of Schumpeter's implicit dynamic theory of banking, credit and money, which is that the money supply expands unevenly over time due to the expansion and contraction of credit used to finance the flow of investments in innovation. As with Warburton, Shah and Yeager seem unwilling to admit Schumpeter's theory implies an endogenous money supply. They also ignore Schumpeter's explicit rejection of monetary theories of the business cycle noted above as well as his critical assessment of these theories in *HEA* (Schumpeter, 1954, pp. 1117–22). Nonetheless, these analyses do serve to highlight the centrality of money, credit and banking to Schumpeter's theory of capitalist motion, a feature that is obscured in most analyses of Schumpeter's contributions until recently.

A sharply contrasting interpretation of Schumpeter's monetary theory comes from Mathias Binswanger (1996), who interprets Schumpeter's theory in terms of Marx's analysis of the monetary circuit of capital. In Marx's circuit firms spend money (M) to acquire means of production and generate output of commodities (C) that are then sold for money (M'), which means making a profit requires that M' > M. Binswanger (1996, p. 431) writes, 'Schumpeter was one of the few economists who tried to link endogenous money creation to the expansion of the M-C-M' circuit and the evolution of capitalist economies in the long run.' Binswanger suggests the expansion of credit and the money supply in the upswing of the business cycle are consistent with firms earning profits sufficient to cover the interest on loans to the entrepreneurial firms and expand the aggregate monetary value of the capital of firms.

Binswanger acknowledges innovating firms are able to repay their bank loans from profits, but he doesn't work out the implications of these repayments for decreasing the amount of money in circulation. If the link he proposes between the monetary circuit and firm profits also applies in reverse, that contraction of the money supply would mean aggregate losses over firms. While losses are part of Schumpeter's analysis of the downswing of the cycle, they are generally restricted to established firms on the way to elimination through creative destruction. Aggregate profit remains positive through the recession phase of Schumpeter's business cycles. Only in crises and depressions are aggregate losses contemplated, and then they are attributed to secondary phenomena that are not a necessary part of Schumpeter's cyclical process of economic development.

Schumpeter works out the implications of declining credit and money supply in terms of a falling price level for goods, but he does not consider the implications for interest payments on debt or for the monetary value of the capital of firms. Binswanger's analysis suggests there is no problem in this regard during the upswing of the cycle, but extending his analysis to the downswing suggests firms in the aggregate may not be able to pay their interest bills and that the money value of firms' capital may contract. As is noted earlier, Tichy (1984) attributes Schumpeter's unwillingness to publish the treatise on money to his inability to complete a genuine dynamic monetary theory dealing with the interplay of money and goods markets. Some progress has been made in this direction in subsequent work on the flow of funds in finance, which is discussed in the following section.

Financial flows, financial innovations and financial instability

Schumpeter recognises the potential for monetary disorder in the second approximation of his theory of the business cycle. He notes that, 'the fact that entrepreneurial demand appears *en masse* signifies a very substantial increase in purchasing power all over the business sphere. This starts a secondary boom, which spreads over the whole economic system and is the vehicle of the phenomenon of general prosperity' (Schumpeter, 1961 [1934], p. 226, italics in original). Based on prosperity, banks extend credit to established firms on the expectation of profitable expansion of their business and also to speculators on the expectation of continued rises in asset prices.

Repayment of loans made to established firms and to speculators depends on continuation of the boom conditions. When the pace of innovations slows and the extra production from the entrepreneurial firms comes to market, price increases become price decreases and at least some established firms are driven to liquidation along with many speculators. In his discussion of the two-phase cycle in *TED*, Schumpeter treats the creative destruction of established firms directly impacted by competition from innovators as part of 'the "normal" process of resorption and liquidation;' but then adds, 'the course of events characterised by the outbreak of a crisis – panic, breakdown of the credit system, epidemics of bankruptcies, and its further consequences – we may call the "abnormal process of liquidation"' (op. cit., p. 236, quotation marks in original).

Schumpeter concentrates his remaining discussion of cycles in *TED* on explaining the "normal" process as it represents his central contribution to the analysis of cycles, while he considers that 'the abnormal presents no fundamental problems' (ibid.). In *BC*, Schumpeter adds discussion of the secondary phenomena that characterise the "abnormal" process beginning with the excesses of prosperity and ending in the depression phase of the four-phase cycle. He acknowledges that the secondary phenomena are generally quantitatively more important and cover a wider range of activity. However, he still insists on the primacy of innovations and points to their critical role in turning the cycle (Schumpeter, 1939, pp. 145–48).

Disentangling secondary phenomena from the primary impulse of innovation is complicated by their common foundation in the expansion of credit by banks, but there is a substantially different process for unwinding of the debts created by the expansion of credit. Entrepreneurs with successful innovations are able to repay their debts with profits that don't depend on continuation of prosperity, while loans to established businesses and speculators are susceptible to failure when there is a change in expectations going from prosperity to recession. Schumpeter argues the change from optimistic to pessimistic expectations is not the primary cause of debt deflation and the abnormal process of liquidation, rather they are a response to uncertainty in a period of rapidly changing relative prices as the economy adapts to structural change wrought by innovation.

Hyman Minsky (1986, p. 114) suggests that Schumpeter does not go far enough with his analysis of financial instability, 'Schumpeter may write of financial catastrophe, but he nowhere explains catastrophe. The significance of liability structures and the importance of business profits to banks as holders of business liabilities are only peripheral concerns in Schumpeter's analysis.'[9] Minsky further suggests that the explanation of financial catastrophe is to be found in the contribution of Keynes (1936), 'in identifying the two-price-system nature of capitalism: in a capitalist economy there is a price system for capital assets as well as the price system of current output' (op. cit., p. 115). The interaction of these two systems then explains the connection between the monetary sector and the real economy,

> Given that the money supply directly influences the price of capital assets, it cannot directly influence the price of current output. The price level of current output, however, is linked to the price level of capital assets through aggregate demand and supply. Given a price level of capital assets, the supply price of investment output and the financing conditions for investment, aggregate demand as well as the derived demand for labour are determined.
>
> (op. cit., p. 119)

Minsky goes on to ask, 'Why does the economy become financially fragile?' (op. cit., p. 120). His answer is,

> The Schumpeterian vision of the experimenting entrepreneur who innovates need but be extended to financial firms and their clients to explain why portfolios migrate to a brink at which a shortfall of cash flows or a rise in financing terms may lead to a marked revision of asset values and therefore of investment programmes.
>
> (ibid.)

According to Minsky, 'The task confronting economics today may be characterized as a need to integrate Schumpeter's vision of a resilient intertemporal capitalist process with Keynes' hard insights into the capitalist accumulation process by some inescapable properties of capitalist financial structures' (op. cit., p. 121).

The differences between Minsky and Schumpeter regarding the fragility of the financial system and the need for intervention are notable but matters of degree rather than reflecting fundamental differences in their understanding of the process of capitalist motion. In his discussion of banking and central banks in Chapter XIII of *BC*, Schumpeter mentions innovations in commercial and investment banking that serve to enhance the elasticity of the supply of credit with an acknowledgement that this also contributes to liquidation in recession and depression. As Frank Ülgen (2014, p. 271) comments, 'in his analysis of the 1929 Great Depression Schumpeter points to the inability of capitalism to police and to protect itself and maintains that the system's sustainability remains related to regulatory devices.'

Schumpeter is supportive of bank regulation to reinforce the private interest of banks in only making sound loans as well as to restrain irresponsibility and misconduct that are symptomatic of the excesses of prosperity. Charles Leathers and Patrick Raines (2004) point to Schumpeter's approval as expressed in *BC* of the regulations imposed with the Banking Acts of 1933 and 1935 in the United States. They go so far as to claim that in the modern environment, 'Schumpeter would take an equally negative view of the use of financial derivatives in financial speculation' (op. cit., p. 677).

Schumpeter also recognises the important stabilising role for central banks or what he terms bankers' banks to include institutional arrangements existing prior to the creation of central banking, such as the role of certain New York banks in the United States prior to the establishment of the Federal Reserve System. As Lakomski-Laguerre (2016, p. 508) observes, 'in Schumpeter's view, the main role of the central bank as a central institution of capitalism is to *preserve financial stability*.' Yet, Schumpeter sees clear limits to what bankers' banks can do beyond discouraging reckless lending in prosperity, noting the practical and political difficulties faced by bankers' banks. He specifically expresses caution concerning the use of expansionary policy during depressions. Aside from doubting the efficacy of monetary expansions when bank clients have no desire to borrow for investment in productive capacity, he worries that such actions are difficult to reverse against pressure from member banks and the public once better conditions return in revival and prosperity (Schumpeter, 1939, pp. 646–58).

In part, the differences between Minsky and Schumpeter can be attributed to evolution in financial institutions that were underway in Schumpeter's time and have continued apace since. Minsky (1990, p. 67) characterises the financial system in place when Schumpeter wrote *TED* as one of finance capitalism, with 'the emergence of financial organizations that could mobilize vast resources for projects such as railroads, utilities, mills and mines'. Under finance capitalism, during the great period of capitalist development from the Industrial Revolution up to the Great Depression, 'The business cycle became as marked a feature of economic life as progress' (ibid.).

In Minsky's scheme of financial evolution, the epoch following finance capitalism is one of managerial capitalism, which roughly corresponds to Schumpeter's period of trustified capitalism. Schumpeter recognises the emergence of trustified capitalism in *TED*, but the regime takes increasing prominence in *BC* and, especially, *CSD*. With managerial or trustified capitalism, large corporations have substantial market power and independence from commercial and investment banks. Minsky and Schumpeter agree that the characteristics of this epoch, particularly the bureaucratisation of decision-making in large corporations and the enhanced independence of managers of large corporations from banks, are in many ways favourable to stability of capitalist development.

Minsky (1990, p. 69) argues managerial capitalism in the era since the Second World War is in the process of being replaced by managed money capitalism, with vast accumulations in mutual funds, pension funds, bank trust funds and endowments of private institutions under the control of managers, and 'with the objective of maximizing the total portfolio return over each short period'.[10] The ownership of large portions of the stock of major corporations by these institutional funds reduces the financial independence of the corporate managers and results in frequent large block trades on stock exchanges. Minsky attributes the stock market crash of 19–20 October 1987 to difficulties in finding counter parties to large block sales from institutional funds, particularly mutual funds facing a flood of withdrawals from their retail customers. Since then, the dot.com bubble, Asian financial crisis and the global financial crisis have pointed further to the fragility of the financial system under managed money capitalism.

Institutional change and price level determination

In *BC* Schumpeter (1939, p. 144) acknowledges his theory of economic development and the business cycle is 'strongly institutional in character' and that 'it rests
on (abstractions from) historical facts which may turn out to belong to an epoch
that is rapidly passing.' Consideration of past and future changes in the capitalism, including the rise of trustified capitalism, is a main theme in *CSD*, but there
is little specific consideration of institutional change involving banks, credit and
money in *CSD*. Schumpeter does comment on the nationalisation of the Bank of
England in Chapter XXVIII ('The Consequences of the Second World War'), but
he dismisses the importance of this action.

> The nationalization of the Bank of England is, in particular, a highly sig-
> nificant symbol and may therefore stand out as a historical landmark. But its
> practical importance may well be equated to zero; the bank has practically
> been a department of the Treasury since 1914 and under modern conditions
> no central bank can be anything else.
>
> (Schumpeter, 1976 [1950], pp. 377–78)

The modern conditions Schumpeter refers to are those of the monetary production and exchange economy as outlined in his writings on the theory of money,
where banks have the role of enabling innovations and central banks have the
role of maintaining the system. Regardless of their degree of autonomy from the
government of the day, central banks are also subject to the influence of society at
large and usually follow policies consistent with the social and political fashion of
the times. As views change regarding the objectives of national economic policy,
central banks generally provide policies to accommodate.

That Schumpeter is well aware of the responsiveness of monetary policy to
social and political fashion is demonstrated in his Presidential Address to the
American Economic Association (Schumpeter, 1950), delivered just days before
his death. After acknowledging the use of a dose of controlled inflation as being a
reasonable accommodation to the difficulties of transiting from a war-time economy, he observes a longer term implication of employment policy,

> At a high level of employment (we seem, at long last, to be abandoning full
> employment slogans), whether "natural" or enforced by high-employment
> policies, wage demands or other demands that increase the money cost of
> employing labor become both inevitable and inflationary. They become
> inevitable because high-level employment removes the only reason why they
> should not be raised. And they become inflationary because, with high uti-
> lization of resources, borrowing from banks and upward revision of prices
> provides a perfectly easy method of satisfying them.
>
> (op. cit., p. 453)

Schumpeter goes on to suggest why corrective policies, such as credit ration-
ing, taxation or price controls, are unlikely to be used to combat the inflationary

pressure. Instead, he suggests inflation pressure will persist and become, 'an important part in the eventual conquest of the private-enterprise system by the bureaucracy – the resultant frictions and deadlocks being attributed to private enterprise and used as arguments for further restrictions and regulations' (op. cit., p. 455). Inflationary pressure has indeed persisted in most economies for most of the period since 1950, although far from uniformly across countries or time.[11] A key point in terms of applying Schumpeter's theory of the price level to recent experience is the importance of taking into account the interaction of institutional arrangements with social and political fashion.

Among the more important institutional changes since Schumpeter's time have been changes in international monetary institutions. The establishment of the International Monetary Fund (IMF) in 1944 as an international bankers' bank and supplier of international liquidity in the form of Special Drawing Rights moderated the impact of international monetary flows under the gold standard. The near universal abandonment of the gold standard followed in 1971 when the United States ceased conversion of US dollars into gold at a fixed price, with the ironic effect that the US dollar became the dominant international reserve currency.

The IMF frequently intervenes to help maintain convertibility of national currencies, but since 1971 the main mechanism for maintaining convertibility has been flexible foreign exchange rates replacing the very infrequent changes in gold points under the gold standard. Major currencies change in exchange value on a daily basis, although the changes rarely exceed more than a percentage point or two. Central banks can and do intervene in foreign exchange markets, but mostly in pursuit of maintaining orderly markets rather than to sustain a fixed value for their currency in terms of gold or other currencies.

Flexible exchange rates have released the constraints on domestic economic policy previously imposed by the need to prevent the loss of currency and gold reserves. With a flexible foreign exchange rate, a country's government and central bank have enhanced ability to pursue domestic policy objectives. Countries have varied in the way they have employed this freedom, some choosing to self-impose external constraints by fixing their foreign exchange rate in terms of the US dollar or joining a monetary union as in the case of the euro bloc. In most countries there has been a move towards labour-friendly policies, including unemployment relief, age pensions and minimum wages, all of which are explicitly or implicitly linked to the cost of living. These policies combined with the acceptance by governments and central banks of the need to limit unemployment have supported downward rigidity in nominal and inflation-adjusted wage rates. Explaining such rigidity in terms of loosening the constraints imposed by Schumpeter's money tie are explored in the next section.

Commentary on money and the price level

Schumpeter includes the exchange equation from the quantity theory of money as a condition that holds between aggregative magnitudes when the economy is in general equilibrium, referring to them 'as the *monetary ligamen*' (Schumpeter,

1939, p. 44, italics in original).[12] While he suggests that the quantity theory does not hold as an equality away from equilibrium, he nonetheless implicitly makes use of the relationship in analysing price movements over the full course of the business cycle. The form of the equation of exchange implied in most of his analysis relates money supply to the sum of household and producer income or expenditure, which is given by $MV = PY$, where M is money in circulation, V is the income velocity of money, P is the price level and Y is total income or expenditure as a "real" measure of the output of the economy (op. cit., pp. 544–52).

When banks extend credit to entrepreneurs to finance innovations, the money supply expands without any change in production or the income velocity of money and prices rise to offset the money supply changes. Schumpeter explains that the new purchasing power provided to entrepreneurs competes with the purchasing power of established producers for the fixed amounts of means of production, which Schumpeter assumes are generally fully employed. Competition drives up the prices for means of production, but how this translates into higher prices of finished goods is not clearly articulated. Also, the quantity theory equation need not hold exactly away from equilibrium, so proportionality between the credit or money expansion and the price level increase is not implied.

As is discussed in the Commentary section of the previous chapter, Sraffa's (1960) model of reproduction prices provides a framework for linking price movements to Schumpeter's theory of economic development. In Equation (4.7) the vector of prices of finished goods depends on technology as reflected in input-output coefficients and labour coefficients, on competition as reflected in the price-cost ratios for each commodity and on the wage rate. As explained in the text accompanying that equation, Schumpeter's theory of economic development involves all three of these influences. The first two influences are microeconomic in nature and only impact directly on specific parts of the economy, so are most directly related to Schumpeter's analysis of price system. Only the wage rate has an economy-wide impact, which identifies it as the influence most readily able to provide a link to Schumpeter's concept of the price level as a measure of the value of money.

Wage rate increases due to increased competition for means of production feature prominently in Schumpeter's review of the historical record of wage rates and wage bills in Chapter XI of *BC*. In terms of the relationship given in Equation (4.7), a rise in the nominal wage rate leads to a proportional rise in the prices of all commodities, which clearly satisfies Schumpeter's requirements for a rise in the price level (a decline in the value of money). An implication neglected in Schumpeter's discussion of historical data in *BC* is that there is no rise in real wage rates when nominal wage rates and the price level rise proportionally.

Schumpeter (1939, pp. 568–71) shows real wage data for the United Kingdom, United States, Germany from around 1850 to the early 1900s in Charts XXVIII through XXX, respectively. Slow real wage growth appears in each chart during the period from the start of data to 1857 and the period from 1898 to 1912, which represent the first quarter of the second and third Kondratieff, respectively, based on Schumpeter's dating of the Kondratieff cycles. Schumpeter makes no direct comment on the slow real wage growth of the prosperity phase of the second Kondratieff and suggests the German data for the prosperity phase of the third Kondratieff match expectations from his theory but 'in England they rose rather less than we should have expected' (op. cit., p. 569).

Autodeflation during the recession phase of the business cycle can also be explained in terms of Equation (4.7), but this requires a decline in the nominal wage rate as purchasing power is withdrawn from the economy with the repayment of loans to entrepreneurs. However, Schumpeter observes a tendency for the wage rate to stay constant or even to rise in recession and often in depression. He refers to the impact of external factors in explaining exceptional rises in wage rates in the United States and the United Kingdom during the recession phase of the second Kondratieff, which covers the period of 1856 to 1873. For the United States, Schumpeter attributes the exception to the external factor of the Civil War, while for the United Kingdom he suggests, 'it must be attributed to gold' (op. cit., p. 568). He also acknowledges the general failure of wage rates to fall in recession or even depression, explaining that 'autodeflation never does full work' (op. cit., p. 572). Instead, the money supply tends to stay up in recession and support a constant or even rising wage rate and wage bill (op. cit., pp. 572–74).

Schumpeter's linking of historical experiences of downward rigidity of money wages with the money supply staying up in recession and depression opens the way to using his theory to explain the price inflation of the period since the Second World War. Indeed, his commentaries noted above on early post-war inflation in *CSD* and 'March into Socialism' (Schumpeter, 1950) are good examples of such explanations. Of course, assigning a leading role to the behaviour of wage rates in influencing movements in the money supply and price level implies an endogenous process of money supply determination different from the process implied in Schumpeter's theory of the business cycle. This suggests the need to reconsider Schumpeter's theory in the context of evolving social, cultural and political conditions as well as the changed institutional arrangements impacting on monetary policy, a topic taken up in Chapter 8, 'Reconstructing Schumpeter's Price Theory'.

Summary

Essential to understanding Schumpeter's theory of money is that he views money as part of a social process. The key role he identifies for money in this process is as a standard of value, noting that the understanding of the value of money in society is essential to the efficient functioning of a capitalist economy. Management of money is the responsibility of the banks, which leads to Schumpeter putting banks in the role of social accountants. Banks in turn are overseen by the bankers' banks (central banks).

Banks evaluate entrepreneurial projects and, if deemed profitable, provide credit allowing the entrepreneurs to compete with established firms for means of production. This is social accountancy in action, as credit from the bank gives the entrepreneur a claim on society's resources without any prior production or wealth. Firms not qualifying for credit have their claims on society's resources invalidated and are restricted in their participation in the production process. Even firms with established businesses may be unable to continue in production without access to credit.

Expansion of credit to entrepreneurs and competition from entrepreneurs for means of production leads to inflation, but the inflation is only temporary as the profitable output from the innovation allows the entrepreneur to repay the loan and withdraw the extra purchasing power from the economy. In *TED* and *BC* Schumpeter expects the net impact on the price level to be negative over the full course of the longest business cycle (the result trend is downward for the Kondratieff cycle), but in his later writings he acknowledges the persistence of inflationary pressure due to high employment policies accommodated by banks and monetary authorities.

In accepting that inflationary pressure has increased with the changing social, cultural and political conditions of the time, Schumpeter is true to his vision that such conditions and the institutional arrangements accompanying them are outcomes from an ongoing evolutionary process. Further changes, especially the establishment of the International Monetary Fund as the central bankers' bank and international agreements on bank regulation, have served to bolster the resilience of the international financial system. However, entrepreneurial innovations in finance of the sort pointed to by Minsky have worked in the opposite direction and the adoption of flexible foreign exchange rates has loosened the constraints of the money tie on individual countries (sometimes with good and sometimes with bad outcomes). All of this supports the need to revise Schumpeter's monetary analysis if it is to be applied to modern conditions and institutions, as is done in reconstructing his price theory in Chapter 8.

Notes

1 See, for example, his discussion of the movements of the American price level during the long wave of 1787 to 1842, an era of free banking (Schumpeter, 1939, pp. 292–96).
2 Messori (1997) provides an extensive discussion of the history of the publication of *Das Wesen des Geldes* and the discovery in the Harvard University Archives of further material identified as drafts of additional chapters of the treatise manuscript, which are included with the French translation (Schumpeter, 2005b) and as a second instalment to the Italian translation (Schumpeter, 1996).
3 Marget (1951, p. 112, n. 3) credits Schumpeter with, 'priority, among contemporary economists, in the formulation of the concept of "income velocity"'.
4 The translation of these passages in *TM* differs slightly, but the substance is the same (see Schumpeter, 2014, p. 9).
5 Schumpeter's journey from viewing money as a part of pure economics in his early work to emphasising its institutional nature in *Das Wesen des Geldes* is the focus of discussion in Dangel-Hagnauer (2013).
6 Schumpeter (2014, p. 36) gives the example of cattle being used as a measure of value in primitive societies, but notes that cattle very infrequently changed hands given their importance to the owner. Schumpeter thereby emphasises the difference between the function of money as a measure of value and its use as a medium of exchange.

7 A formal link between prices of the means of production and prices of finished goods is provided in the Commentary section of Chapter 4 by applying Sraffa's (1960) framework of the production of commodities by means of commodities.

8 Swedberg (1991, p. 39) comments on the exchange of views between Böhm-Bawerk and Schumpeter in a series of articles commencing with Böhm-Bawerk's review of *TED*, noting, 'Böhm-Bawerk's verdict: Schumpeter's theory was useless and a disservice to economic science.'

9 While Minsky is often critical of aspects of Schumpeter's analysis, he also professes great admiration for Schumpeter's vision and scholarship. Minsky started his PhD thesis under Schumpeter's supervision in 1949 but switched to supervision by Leontief after Schumpeter's death. Details of the relationship between Minsky and Schumpeter are given in Knell (2015), which also contains a discussion of how Minsky blends the work of Schumpeter and Keynes in developing an analysis of the financial fragility of the capitalist process.

10 Ülgen (2014, p. 265) suggests there has been a shift in bank strategies since the 1980s, with 'banking activities turned away from the financing of productive activities to focus more upon speculative operations with high short-term returns.' Schumpeter's theory provides for a shift in financing from the financing of entrepreneurs to financing speculative activity as part of the shift from prosperity to recession phases of the business cycle.

11 Whether this has led to the full conquest of the private-enterprise system by the bureaucracy is left for the reader to decide.

12 Schumpeter seems to be using monetary ligamen to refer to a flexible connection that connects the money supply to aggregate nominal income and aggregate nominal expenditure. In the quotation from *TM* (Schumpeter, 2014, p. 233) earlier in this chapter, Ruben Alvarado translates Geldligamen as money tie, which suggests ligamen is a possible misspelling of ligament. However, Schumpeter is usually very precise in his use of English and the word is emphasised in italics and the term monetary ligamen is included in the index of *BC*.

6   Norms, equilibrium and
       competition

In the Commentary section of Chapter 3, I review several criticisms levelled at Schumpeter's theory, especially his use of perfectly competitive general equilibrium for a stationary state as defining the theoretical norm for an economy experiencing development. Also criticised is his analysis of statistical norms, particularly using Frisch's method of inflection points to identify result trends from the time-series graphs of economic variables. In this chapter, I expand on these criticisms and discuss alternative approaches to determining common-sense, theoretical and statistical norms for a developing economy.

In Chapter 3, I stress the dialectical relationship between innovation and equilibrium in Schumpeter's theory of economic development. Schumpeter argues having prices at equilibrium levels encourages innovation as potential entrepreneurial profits can be reliably calculated, but innovation disrupts equilibrium and starts a process of transformation. With transformation, the calculation of potential profits from further innovation becomes perilous and innovative activity subsides. Only when the innovations are generally absorbed and the economy moves back towards equilibrium are conditions conducive to a new spurt of innovations.

Schumpeter treats entrepreneurship as an emergent property of capitalism. There are always ideas and inventions awaiting exploitation. Potential entrepreneurs come into contact with these ideas and inventions stochastically but not infrequently. They then require the will to overcome their own psychological adherence to the status quo as well as leadership to overcome social resistance to change. They also require access to means of production, which depends on the provision of credit from banks. The proposition that satisfying these requirements is encouraged by achieving the businessman's norm of "normal" business conditions is plausible if not proven. However, this alone does not provide a basis for associating "normal" business conditions with any particular statistical or theoretical norm.

Schumpeter's insistence on discontinuity between development and equilibrium deprives his analysis of norms of any connection to evolutionary processes. Even though he draws parallels between his norms and those of Marshall's long-period equilibrium, he rejects Marshall's evolutionary mantra, *natura non facit saltum* (nature doesn't leap). He therefore refuses to follow Marshall's method of linking short-period and long-period equilibria through the working of evolutionary processes.

Modern evolutionary economics analyses industry evolution in terms of a process of variation, retention and selection. Schumpeter's theory of development is characterised in terms of innovation introducing variety, growth of entrepreneurial firms retaining successful innovations and creative destruction selecting entrepreneurial firms over established firms. The process of innovation and creative destruction for an industry reduces heterogeneity around dominant processes and products, creating a condition better described as order than as equilibrium.

As early as *TED*, Schumpeter clearly recognises the historical shift from competitive capitalism to "trustified" capitalism. However, he goes further in *CSD* and other later writings, recognising the positive role of the large corporation as an engine of economic progress and growth. In spite of his recognition of imperfect competition and the impact it has on price determination in both *TED* and *BC*, perfect competition remains the foundation for his analysis of price cycles and structural change in the price system. Yet, imperfect competition provides a reason for expecting prices to remain above reproduction costs at the end of the process of innovation and creative destruction.

The section below critically examines Schumpeter's treatment of the three concepts of "normal" along with the relationships among them. I then consider the apparent contradiction between evolution and equilibrium and the resolution attempted by Marshall with his distinction between short- and long-period time horizons, which leads to distinguishing between disrupted and orderly industries. Schumpeter's treatment of imperfect competition is discussed in the fourth section before closing the chapter with a summary.

Schumpeter's three concepts of "normal"

Schumpeter discusses three concepts of "normal" in *BC*, the common-sense or businessman's concept of normal business conditions, the values associated with a theoretical norm and the values associated with a statistical norm. Schumpeter starts *BC* by suggesting that a business is having a "normal" year if its revenues cover its costs and there is no incentive to increase or decrease investment. Further, the general business situation is "normal" if this same condition applies to all firms aside from those working under special advantages or disadvantages (Schumpeter, 1939, p. 4).

Essentially, Schumpeter is associating "normal" conditions from the businessman's perspective with the economic concept of normal profits. Normal profit (zero economic profit) is the long-run outcome of free competition in classical economics, so Schumpeter starts with a definition of the businessman's norm that fits a long history of economic theorising. It is then only a short, but not uncontroversial, step to substitute for the classical conception of normal profits, the more modern and restrictive Walrasian concept of competitive general equilibrium.

Opting for the Walrasian equilibrium as defining the theoretical norm provides Schumpeter with the advantages of a theoretical system that has a unique and stable solution under standard assumptions. This is not true of the classical system represented in Sraffa's reproduction scheme, which I describe in Chapter 4. That system is underdetermined and can be solved with a range of profit rates corresponding to different wage rates. Further, there are no stability properties for the Sraffian system interpreted as a set of accounting relationships. It also lacks the underpinning of rational (optimising) behaviour by households and firms that is a distinguishing feature of the Walrasian equilibrium.

Schumpeter clearly recognises the usefulness of the Walrasian equilibrium concept for analysing business cycles depends on the economic system having an equilibrating mechanism. However, he also recognises that lags, frictions, expectations and imperfect competition impair the equilibrating mechanism, which means equilibrium will at best be approached rather than exactly achieved (op. cit., pp. 47–68). Further, even at the end of the cycle, when innovation is low, some evolutionary potential remains from the continuing diffusion of prior innovations. There are still firms using processes and producing products that disappear from the economy with complete diffusion. All this leads Schumpeter to claim that the theoretical norm is given by ranges of values in the neighbourhood of equilibrium, rather than the specific values at an equilibrium point, and this theoretical norm only applies when '*the system approaches a state which would, if reached, fulfil equilibrium conditions*' (op. cit., p. 71, italics in original).

Two key issues arise in appraising Schumpeter's argument concerning convergence to equilibrium conditions. First, there needs to be some mechanism by which actual prices are drawn towards the long-period values along a dynamic path. Second, the long-period values for a developing economy can diverge from those associated with the competitive general equilibrium for a stationary state. These issues are addressed in the remainder of this chapter, but first I comment on Schumpeter's treatment of the statistical norm.

As noted in Chapter 3 above, Schumpeter distinguishes among theoretical, stochastic and historical variables, with a historical variable being a variable whose stochastic norm changes with changes in its theoretical norm. Time-series data are observations on historical variables, so the stochastic norm is changing in a developing economy. Yet, inference from time series, such as estimating a trend, generally assumes that all observations relate to the same stochastic norm. This may be an appropriate assumption for an economy without development, but Schumpeter argues it is clearly inappropriate in a developing economy.

Schumpeter's solution to dealing with the changing theoretical norm between business cycles is to use result trend for aggregate time series of data plotted between the neighbourhoods of equilibrium that occur in the transition between business cycles. In these intervals, the statistical normal value of each variable corresponds to its theoretical normal value so the result trend provides an approximation to the true trend between the two theoretical normal values. Schumpeter then suggests following Frisch's method of normal points and using the inflection point in a smoothed graph of the time series for an economic variable to identify the neighbourhood of equilibrium. However, substantial qualifications and cautions are added to this suggestion.

Reluctance to fully accept Frisch's method leaves Schumpeter open to the criticism levelled by Simon Kuznets (1940, p. 268) in his review at the time of publication of *BC*, which is,

> One searches in vain for a definite formulation of the criterion by which historical evidence is analyzed to distinguish the Kondratieff cycles from the Juglars and used to establish for the former the terminal dates and also those of the four phases.

It is not surprising that in the many studies following Schumpeter's lead in examining the impact of innovations on cycles or waves in economic development, historical evidence is abundantly used but the method of using points of inflection to identify the neighbourhood of equilibrium is ignored.[1]

Schumpeter's focus in discussing historical data is on the behaviour of time series of aggregate data. Even his discussion of prices and quantities of individual commodities is devoted to broadly defined categories, such as wheat, petroleum and pig iron, generally at a national aggregate level. Prices for individual products or specific producers are not considered. Aside from an occasional side comment in the historical analysis, he shows no particular interest in the examining movements within the individual components of these series.

By ignoring movements within the individual components of aggregate series, Schumpeter disregards his own warnings regarding the difficulties associated with combining data from different series into what he calls synthetic series, such as the series for total output. In particular, he argues that combining time series into synthetic series hides differences in individual movements, which obscures the impact of structural change (Schumpeter, 1939, p. 18). His macro perspective on development neglects heterogeneity within the aggregates and obscures the impact of structural change on individual components of the aggregate.

As Metcalfe (2012, p. 26) notes, 'Evolution is not a product of average behaviours but a product of the outliers that are distant from the prevailing averages.' Heterogeneity is an essential component of any evolutionary analysis. Schumpeter is quite clear about innovation creating heterogeneity between entrepreneurial firms and their established counterparts. He is also clear that, in addition to replacement of the old by the new, innovation leads to expansion of the market through lower prices, better products and other developments that attract demand. However, in spite of some powerful hints in *CSD*, he is less clear on the mechanics linking innovation through competitive selection to market expansion.

In Walrasian equilibrium there is no variation in characteristics across firms as all producers operate optimally. By positing this equilibrium as determining the norms for a developing economy at the transition between cycles, Schumpeter's analysis is deprived of connection to the evolutionary process that is occurring within aggregates. I examine the implications of this missing connection for determining the statistical norm for a developing economy in the next chapter.

Equilibrium, evolution and order

In *HEA*, Schumpeter provides the following definition of equilibrium:

> If the relations which are derived from our survey of the 'meaning' of a phenomenon are such as to determine a set of values of the variables that will have no tendency to vary *under the sole influence of the facts included in the relations per se*, we speak of equilibrium: we say that those relations define equilibrium conditions or the equilibrium position of the system and that *there exists* a set of values of the variables that *satisfies* equilibrium conditions.
>
> (Schumpeter, 1954, p. 969, quotation marks and italics in the original)

This strict definition sets a standard that Schumpeter goes on to argue applies without qualification to the general equilibrium of the Walrasian system with perfect competition.

According to Schumpeter in *TED* and *BC*, the economy develops from within. At the start of the business cycle, prices are at levels considered by businessmen to be "normal". Entrepreneurs creatively react to these prices and generate a cluster of innovation. The creative reaction of entrepreneurs to the prices associated with the businessman's "normal" is a process purely internal to the economy and thus constitutes endogenous development. However, the development from within contradicts Schumpeter's requirements for beginning the process from a position of equilibrium.

In Chapter II of *BC*, Schumpeter acknowledges the developing economy under capitalism never quite reaches a state that satisfies the conditions for a perfectly competitive general equilibrium. His way of dealing with the non-occurrence in practice of the equilibrium state is to resort to a modification, the neighbourhood of equilibrium, rather than a point of equilibrium. In the neighbourhood of equilibrium, values of economic variables are in a range around their theoretical equilibrium values. Having thus freed himself from the straightjacket of the logical purity of the Walrasian analysis, Schumpeter has an operational form for his realistic analysis of the history of business cycles. However, a consequence is to call into question the relevance of Walrasian equilibrium to his business cycle theory and to open the theory to criticisms, such as that expressed by Kuznets (1940), of there being no quantitative test of the correspondence between his empirical analysis (historical and statistical) and his theory.

Schumpeter comes close to addressing the contradiction between evolution and equilibrium when he discusses the role of time in connection with his theoretical norm. Here, he suggests that his concept of a theoretical norm corresponds to Marshall's concept of normal values, which are those that Marshall associates with long-period equilibrium (Schumpeter, 1939, p. 45).[2] Marshall (1920, V, V, pp. 363–78) uses the distinction between short-period and long-period equilibrium as part of a structure for introducing evolutionary notions of internal and external economies occurring through time. However, Schumpeter's interpretation of

Marshall's analysis removes its evolutionary intent and replaces this with a static equilibrium along Walrasian lines.

Shackle (1965, p. 36) claims, 'Marshall's peculiar triumph is his creation of a unity out of the conceptions of equilibrium and of evolution.' According to Shackle, Marshall is able to combine equilibrium and evolution because,

> Equilibrium is a state of adjustment to circumstances, but it is a fiction, Marshall's own and declared fiction, for it is adjustment that *would* be attained if every endeavour to reach it did not reveal fresh possibilities, give fresh command of resources, and prepare the way for inevitable, natural, organic further change.
>
> (ibid., italics in the original)

Marshall's long-period equilibrium is a conceptual device for incorporating into supply and demand analysis those adjustments of supply that take time (Marshall, 1920, V, V, VII, pp. 377–78), which opens the door to incorporating evolutionary processes.

Marshall utilises this opening when he goes on to consider the case of industries with increasing returns, industries in which rising demand is associated with falling prices in the long run. Here, Marshall distinguishes not only between short-period and long-period supply, but also between the individual firm and the industry as a whole. To deal with the heterogeneity of firms that is a basic feature of his analysis, Marshall relies on his concept of a representative firm. Marshall suggests it is the marginal cost of this representative firm that determines the supply price of the industry and that 'we also expect a gradual increase in demand to increase gradually the size and the efficiency of this representative firm; and to increase the economies both internal and external which are at its disposal' (Marshall, 1920, V, XII, p. 460). This leads him to state that, 'when making lists of supply prices (supply schedules) for these industries, we set down a diminished supply price against an increased amount of the flow of the goods' (ibid.).

Modern commentators on Marshall's evolutionary intent, such as Raffaelli (2003), Metcalfe (2007) and Hart (2013), discuss how this intent all but disappears in the subsequent development of his ideas (Shackle being among a few exceptions). Much of the responsibility is attributed to Marshall's followers, especially Pigou who replaces Marshall's representative firm with the logically consistent alternative of the equilibrium firm in Pigou (1928). Subsequently, the equilibrium firm develops into the optimising and uniform firm, at which point all heterogeneity and evolutionary content is lost from the analysis of firm behaviour and from the relation between internal and external economies as an influence on the relationship between unit cost and output over time.

Schumpeter is clearly amongst those who favour purging any evolutionary intent from Marshall's long-period equilibrium. In 'The Instability of Capitalism' (Schumpeter, 1928), Schumpeter first asserts the equivalence between Marshallian and Walrasian theory and then goes on to argue the only logical possibility in these theories is that statically stable competitive equilibrium requires increasing costs (supply price increasing with the quantity supplied) at any time horizon. Finally, Schumpeter concludes this section of the article claiming,

> We are merely clinching, on the one hand, what seems to us to be both the true real-cost-phenomenon, and, on the other hand, what seems to be both the meaning of economic "statics" and the nature of equilibrium. That this is perfectly in keeping with the fundamental drift of Marshallian analysis, I will try to show in a footnote.
>
> (op. cit., p. 368, quotation marks in the original)

The footnote mentioned in the above quotation covers almost a full page in small print. Schumpeter begins by acknowledging that, 'Marshall, indeed, repeatedly protests against the limits of the static apparatus' (op. cit., p. 368, note 2), but then suggests that much of the analysis in *Principles* rests on static analysis and that, 'in fact, in one decisive point, when dealing with refinements calling for rigour of analysis, he has confined his argument to increasing cost' (ibid.). The note continues by attacking Marshall's declining supply curve, pointing to misgivings by Mr. Keynes, successful challenge by Professor Sraffa, and apparent repudiation by Professors Pigou and Young. The note also argues that 'causation runs from improvement to expansion and cannot adequately be dealt with by static analysis alone' (op. cit., p. 369, n.2 continued).

As Raffaelli observes in regard to the comments on Marshall in Schumpeter (1928),

> This biased reading of Marshall stems from Schumpeter's dislike of Marshall's evolutionary philosophy. The ways in which the pair *routine/innovation* works in the two systems are noticeably different: whereas Marshall had in mind their continuous interaction, Schumpeter placed them into non-communicating tool-boxes.
>
> (Raffaelli, 2003, p. 119)

Raffaelli further attributes rejection of Marshall's view of improvement being continuous and organic due to its incompatibility with Schumpeter's own view of innovation as being discontinuous and outside the domain of static analysis.[3]

Schumpeter's biased reading of Marshall gives context to his suggestion in *BC* that there is correspondence between his own theoretical norm based on Walrasian equilibrium and the normal values in Marshall's long-period analysis (Schumpeter, 1939, p. 45). Schumpeter is referring to his own reconstruction of Marshall's analysis, which removes elements inconsistent with a perfect Walrasian general equilibrium. In doing this, Schumpeter recognises a role only for logical time in the sense of a planning horizon based on current technology.

Schumpeter thus resolves the contradiction between equilibrium and evolution by demanding their total separation. Yet, he also treats economic development as endogenous to capitalism, meaning no external mechanism is required to generate development. This implies the impulse to innovation is external to the relations among economic variables but is internal to capitalism as a system. While in *BC* and *TED* the entrepreneurial role is exercised independently of any other economic function, this fiction is abandoned in *CSD* when the industrial research laboratory features as a primary source of innovations. Also abandoned in *CSD* is the notion that perfect competition is the normal state towards which any industry moves in the process of development.

Metcalfe (2008) argues the use of the equilibrium concept by Schumpeter, and also by Marshall, is inconsistent with an evolutionary approach to the analysis of the economy. The essential difficulty is the emergent nature of innovation. While Schumpeter recognises the effects of innovation and insists that innovation comes from within the system, he excludes any consideration of the development process in determining the theoretical norm. Yet, 'If some system is in equilibrium it has reached a balancing state from which no escape is possible without the intervention of external forces, forces that of necessity cannot be part of the specification of the system' (Metcalfe, 2008, p. 138).

In place of equilibrium, Metcalfe suggests Hayek's concept of order as constituting the appropriate balancing state for a developing economy. 'All evolutionary change presupposes a substrate of order, of organization on which the processes of variation, adaptation and development can operate, the system is restless but it is not chaotic' (ibid.). Importantly, the concept of order does not represent the stationary state as part of an evolutionary process, avoiding the logical contradiction between equilibrium for a stationary state and evolution.

Nelson (2013) suggests a specific form of order, namely market order, as defining the balancing state for a developing economy to replace the concept of the perfectly competitive Walrasian general equilibrium of a stationary state. According to Nelson (2013, p. 29),

> An orderly market is characterized by a set of routines established over time that when employed by potential buyer and potential sellers are tuned to each other and generally result in transactions that are satisfactory for most parties on both sides of the market.

With market order a rough balance between supply and demand is achieved as in Schumpeter's neighbourhood of equilibrium, but without consistency with perfectly competitive Walrasian general equilibrium.

Nelson uses the concept of market order for developing a price theory in which supply and demand changes influence prices and quantities, much as in theory based on Walrasian equilibrium. However, this is done in a form compatible with evolutionary analysis, by allowing for routine-based behaviour with bounded rationality, such as firms using price-setting routines, rather than assuming optimisation by individual economic agents and perfect information to all market participants. Nelson (op. cit., p. 37) recognises that this is just a starting point,

> when the analysis is of long run change, the characterization of how markets work, of the nature of the relevant economic order, like the analysis of supply

and demand conditions, cannot be static, or comparative static. Economic orders, like technologies, and ways of living in a society, evolve.

Evolution of order in Schumpeter's theory occurs through the disruption of innovation, which is distinct from equilibrium and also from order. Here, evolutionary analysis of variation and selection overlays any balancing of supply and demand. Theories of differential firm growth provide one approach to working out the implications for industry evolution, while industry life cycle theories provide an alternative. In each of these theories there is a tendency for heterogeneity in the industry to rise as variation is introduced and the industry is disrupted, while variation falls as the industry matures and order is restored. These theories and their implications for the "norms" of a developing economy are analysed in the next chapter prior to reconstructing Schumpeter's price theory in Chapter 8.[4]

Schumpeter on imperfect competition and monopolistic pricing practices

In both *TED* and *BC*, Schumpeter builds his price theory from the starting position of the perfectly competitive general equilibrium of a stationary state. Yet, with his original formulation in *TED* he is clearly aware of the historical shift towards large-scale enterprise and emergence of an era of "trustified capitalism". He gives as an example of an innovation in business organisation, 'the introduction of large-scale manufacturing businesses into an economic system in which they were previously unknown' (Schumpeter, 1961 [1934], p. 133).

There is extensive discussion of the implications of imperfect competition for his business cycle theory in Section F of Chapter II of *BC* (Schumpeter, 1939, pp. 56–68) and a further discussion of the impact of imperfect competition on price rigidity in markets with entrepreneurial activity in Section D of Chapter X (op. cit. pp. 535–43). A few years later in *CSD* he writes, 'The introduction of new methods of production and new commodities is hardly conceivable with perfect – and perfectly prompt – competition from the start' (Schumpeter, 1976 [1950], p. 105). Yet, at no point does Schumpeter deviate from the use of perfectly competitive general equilibrium as determining the theoretical norm for developing economies as well as for stationary economies.

In the preface to the 1937 Japanese edition of the *Theorie der wirtschaftlichen Entwicklung*, Schumpeter writes, 'it might be asked how I should deal with the new theory of imperfect competition. The answer is that this theory proves particularly useful in working out the details of the process that this book attempts to describe' (Schumpeter, 1951, pp. 161–62). Yet, when Schumpeter comes to discuss imperfect competition in Chapter II of *BC* published in 1939, he only considers the possibility that imperfect competition interferes with the tendency towards equilibrium in the economic system, as such interference would impede the process of economic development. Potential difficulties in achieving equilibrium are noted in each of the cases of bilateral monopoly, oligopoly and monopolistic competition. Further, in discussing entrepreneurial price policies in Chapter X of *BC*,

Schumpeter readily acknowledges that the introduction of an innovation is very likely to occur in imperfectly competitive situations that encourage price rigidity and other restrictive practices. However, at no point does Schumpeter show the usefulness of theory of imperfect competition in working out the details of the process of economic development.

A positive role for imperfect competition in the process of economic development only comes to prominence in *CSD*, first published in 1942. Here, Schumpeter not only treats imperfect competition as an essential part of the process of innovation-driven development, but extols its role in promoting the process. In Chapter VIII, he discusses the role of the large-scale firm and the monopolistic practices it employs, and concludes,

> What we have got to accept is that it has come to be the most powerful engine of that progress and in particular of the long-run expansion of output not only in spite of, but to a considerable extent through, this strategy which looks so restrictive when viewed in the individual case and from the individual point of time. In this respect, perfect competition is not only impossible, but inferior, and has no title to being set up as a model of ideal efficiency.
>
> (Schumpeter, 1976 [1950], p. 106)[5]

Schumpeter's discussion of historical developments in *BC* contains extensive commentary on the role of specific businesses in introducing new processes and new products, pointing both to the rise of dominant firms as a result of innovation and entrepreneurial efforts to organise industries through central management of a trust.[6] This historical work seems to have influenced the further evolution of Schumpeter's view of the connection between imperfect competition and innovation. In one of his last presentations, he concludes with the following statement about the role of imperfect competition in the historical approach to business cycles,

> Also, it should not be forgotten, that there are many individual problems of business cycles which can only be solved on the basis of such understanding. An instance is the question of the effects of given degrees of monopoly in an economy upon the processes of prosperity and depression. Without the kind of experience that industrial history supplies, all we have to say about this question reduces to reckless assertions or trivial speculations.
>
> (Schumpeter, 1949, p. 315)

In reviewing Schumpeter's main works, Andersen (2012) points to the transition from a Mark I evolutionary model in both *TED* and *BC* to a Mark II model in *CSD*. Andersen follows the common distinction among Schumpeterians, characterising the Mark I model as one in which individual entrepreneurs innovate through the establishment of new firms and the Mark II model as one in which innovations are primarily made by established large-scale firms. He then adds a further distinction, pointing out that the Mark I model has a macroscopic focus on evolution of the economy as whole while the Mark II model has a microscopic focus on oligopolistic competition within individual industries. According to Andersen, both microscopic and macroscopic analyses are required for a complete theory of economic evolution.

Andersen also points to the need for meso-level analysis, as in Dopfer and Potts (2008), to deal with the linkage between microscopic and macroscopic analyses, commenting that when Nelson and Winter (1982) use their Mark II modelling of micro-evolutionary processes to analyse economic growth, they are providing a micro-evolutionary model for the whole economy. Providing a more general analysis at the macro level requires a meso-level analysis of the feedback from macro developments to the transformation of the complex system of evolving populations at the micro level. As an example of such transformation, Andersen (2012, p. 642) refers to 'Schumpeter's (1928, pp. 384–85) idea that there has been a real historical transition from the firms and mechanisms of the Mark I model to the firms and mechanisms of Mark II.'

The macroscopic focus of Schumpeter's Mark I model is reflected in the very limited development of firm pricing behaviour in *TED* and *BC*. The upswing in prices following a cluster of innovations is attributed to competition for means of production. Prices of finished goods rise due to higher wages and raw material prices, suggesting a type of supply and demand equilibrium even though disruptive innovation is meant to be a disequilibrium process. Also, we are told innovators earn profits and these profits have macro implications, but not given much analysis of how innovative firms initially set prices relative to their own costs or relative to the prices of established competitors. Likewise, in the downswing of the cycle, prices and profits decline under the pressure of imitation and diffusion, but there are no details of the pricing processes that lead to these outcomes.

Specific practices extensively discussed by Schumpeter in Chapter VIII in *CSD* are price rigidity (Schumpeter, 1976 [1950], pp. 92–96) and the conservation of capital (acting to protect capital values, particularly by not immediately investing in new cost-reducing machinery) (op. cit., pp. 96–98). These practices and monopoly behaviour in general are viewed as protective devices against the uncertainty and disruption experienced in the process of economic development.[7]

Schumpeter points to the need to account for strategies to deal with the uncertainty inherent in an economy undergoing economic development driven by innovation.

> Thus it is true that there is or may be an element of genuine monopoly gain in those entrepreneurial profits which are the prizes offered by capitalist society to the successful innovator. But the quantitative importance of that element, its volatile nature and its function in the process in which it emerges put it in a class by itself. The main value to a concern of a single seller position that is secured by patent or monopolistic strategy does not consist so much in the opportunity to behave temporarily according to the monopolistic schema, as in the protection it affords against temporary disorganization of the market and the space it secures for long-range planning.
>
> (op. cit., pp. 102–03)

The final section of Schumpeter's discussion of the price system in Chapter X of *BC* is devoted to entrepreneurial price policies. Here, Schumpeter distinguishes the situation faced by entrepreneurs developing new production methods for an established product and entrepreneurs who introduce a new product. In the first case, Schumpeter suggests that the entrepreneur is a price taker and faces an infinitely elastic demand, while in the second the entrepreneur almost certainly faces imperfect competition (Schumpeter, 1939, pp. 535–36). This leads to a general discussion of price rigidity and the reasons for its prevalence in oligopolistic and monopolistic industries (op. cit., pp. 536–43). Yet, Schumpeter does not suggest any pricing theory to displace or supplement the perfectly competitive pricing of the Walrasian model of perfectly competitive equilibrium. In this sense, his price theory remains incomplete.

Two articles containing seminal contributions to the theory of price rigidity, Sweezy (1939) and Hall and Hitch (1939), appeared in the same year, 1939, that *BC* was published. The articles independently introduce the concept of a kinked perceived demand curve to explain why oligopolistic firms don't change price in response to a change in demand or production costs. In each case the kink in the demand curve is rationalised by reference to uncertainty about the reactions of rivals that face businesses when making decisions to change price. The rationalisations bear many overlaps with the reasoning used by Schumpeter in his discussion of the prevalence of price rigidity in both *BC* and *CSD*.

It is understandable that Schumpeter makes no reference to Sweezy (1939) or Hall and Hitch (1939) in *BC*, given the close timing of their publication. However, there are other indications Schumpeter rejected the kinked demand curve as a theoretical advance. Most specifically, he comments negatively (Schumpeter, 1939, pp. 839–40, n. 1) on an earlier contribution by Sweezy (Graham, et al., 1938) that employs the concept of a kinked demand curve to explain why a decrease in wage rates might not lead to an increase in employment by oligopolistic firms. In particular, he rejects the implication that firms would not react to a rise in costs due to higher wages, acknowledging that the implication is logically correct but suggesting it has little claim to being realistic. Instead, he suggests that a firm raising prices following an increase in wages would find its competitors doing the same.

Schumpeter doesn't mention models of price rigidity based on kinked demand curves in either *CSD* or *HEA*, which were published in 1942 and after his death, respectively. He clearly would have been aware of Sweezy's article, given his interest in Sweezy's earlier analysis and the fact that they were colleagues and close friends at Harvard.[8] He was also probably aware of the Hall and Hitch article as in the closing chapters of *HEA* he cites the article by Harrod (1939) that precedes and introduces the Hall and Hitch (1939) article in the May 1939 issue of *Oxford Economic Papers* (Schumpeter, 1954, p. 1152, n. 7 cont.). It seems Schumpeter did not find the kinked demand curve as either important or useful in further developing economic analysis in general or the analysis of capitalist development in particular.

Schumpeter's brief discussion of modern developments in the Marshall-Wicksteed apparatus in the closing chapters of *HEA* also ignores or dismisses other developments in the analysis of pricing behaviour that emerged in the late

1930s and into the 1940s. There is no mention of the analysis of full-cost pricing that is the main theme in the 1939 *Oxford Economic Papers* articles by Harrod and by Hall and Hitch. Further, Schumpeter is dismissive towards the measure of the degree of monopoly introduced by Lerner (1934), which he refers to as a gadget (op. cit., p. 1149, n. 2). In the text preceding the comment on the degree of monopoly concept, Schumpeter uses gadget to refer to theoretical development that adds nothing fundamentally new.

In Chapter 8 I follow up on Schumpeter's suggestion from the preface to the Japanese edition of *Theorie der wirtschaftlichen Entwicklung*, namely that the theory of imperfect competition can be useful in working out the details of the process of economic development. However, it is not the theory of imperfectly competitive equilibrium as discussed by Schumpeter in *BC* and *HEA* that I find useful for this purpose. Rather, it is post-Keynesian theories building on the full-cost principle of Hall and Hitch (1939) and the mark-up pricing model of Kalecki (1938) that serve as the starting point for the analysis.

Summary

Schumpeter argues the actual values of economic variables converge on values given by their respective common-sense, theoretical and statistical norms at the interval in the transition between business cycles. The common-sense norm is that the firm's revenues cover its costs and there is no incentive to increase or decrease investment. The theoretical norm is given by perfectly competitive general equilibrium, characterised by 'values of the variables that will have no tendency to vary *under the sole influence of the facts included in the relations per se*' (Schumpeter, 1954, p. 969, italics in the original). Finally, the statistical norm is given by the point of inflection in the smoothed time-series graph of values of each economic variable.

In this chapter, Schumpeter's methods for determining theoretical and statistical norms are rejected as applicable to developing economies. The discussion focuses on analytical differences between a developing economy at the nadir of innovative activity and an economy in a stationary state. A fundamental reason for rejecting Walrasian equilibrium as determining the theoretical norm for a developing economy is that this type of equilibrium is inconsistent with evolution.

Schumpeter insists on an analytical separation between the analysis of the economy at rest and the analysis of economic development. Yet, he also treats economic development as endogenous to capitalism, meaning that no external mechanism is required to generate development. In *BC* and *TED*, the entrepreneurial role is exercised independently of any other economic function, but this fiction is abandoned in *CSD* when the industrial research laboratory features as a primary source of innovations. If the requirement for equilibrium, Walrasian or otherwise, is abandoned, evolutionary theory can then be applied both to the process of development and to the determination of norms.

Replacing the concept of equilibrium with that of order allows continuity in the analysis of innovation and order, while recognising that, at least in the case of radical innovation, they involve distinct processes. Also, important is recognising that perfect competition is implausible for a developing economy, even at rest. Schumpeter admits as much, especially in his later writings. However, he never revises the norms that apply to the developing economy, which is the focus of the next chapter.

Notes

1 See, for example, Mensch (1979), Perez (1983), Tylecote (1992), Freeman and Louçã (2001), Perez (2002) and Lipsey, et al. (2005).
2 At this point, Schumpeter (1939, p. 45, italics in the original) acknowledges 'the danger in associating a certain *state of the system* with a *lapse of time* during which changes will unavoidably occur'. These changes are due to the difference in prices and quantities that are required to satisfy the different equilibrium conditions before and after the cluster of innovations driving the business cycle.
3 Support for this view is given in Schumpeter's semi-centennial appraisal of Marshall's work, 'I do not think that the theory of evolution at the back of them was satisfactory. No schema can be that does not go beyond an automatic expansion of markets – an expansion not otherwise motivated than by increase of population and by saving – which then induces internal and external economies of scale that are in turn to account for further expansion' (Schumpeter, 1941, p. 243).
4 This analysis falls into the category of appreciative theorising, which has been a hallmark of evolutionary economics in the tradition of Schumpeter since the seminal work of Nelson and Winter (1982). They suggest that 'The adherents of a broad theoretical structure share a way of looking at phenomena, a framework of appreciation. A theory defines the economic variables and the relationships that are important to understand, gives a language for discussing these, and provides a mode of acceptable explanation' (op. cit., p. 46). This is the spirit in which obsolescence, firm heterogeneity and differential firm growth are examined in the next chapter.
5 Although not generally given to hyperbole, Schumpeter here loses all restraint and ignores the difficulty of making comparisons of desirability when one of the alternatives is supposedly impossible.
6 For an example of the rise to dominance based on innovation see the discussion of the Ford Motor Company (Schumpeter, 1939, pp. 415–17) and for an example of organising an industry into a trust see the discussion of Standard Oil (op. cit., p. 385).
7 These views don't differ substantially from those expressed by Schumpeter in his discussion of entrepreneurial price practices in Section D of Chapter X of *BC*, but the emphasis shifts from arguing that the practices are 'not sufficient to upset the working of our process' (Schumpeter, 1939, p. 543) to his above quoted conclusion in Chapter VIII of *CSD* that such restrictive practices are part of the strategy by large-scale enterprises that contributes to the long-run expansion of output.
8 Paul Samuelson (2015, p. 32) writes of the close relationship between Schumpeter and Sweezy, who worked for two years as Schumpeter's official assistant lecturer in the first course in economic theory for postgraduate students at Harvard.

7   Norms for a developing economy

Schumpeter argues Walrasian equilibrium prices provide the theoretical normal prices in a stationary economy, but when an economy is developing prices are subject to the disruptive influence of clusters of innovation. He also argues prices approach new equilibrium values at the end of the business cycles of the longest duration, thereby establishing a new set of theoretical normal prices. Furthermore, the rate of change of the price level slows when the economy is in the neighbour-hood of equilibrium, so the inflection point in the rising section of the time-series graphs of the price level occurs in this neighbourhood and identifies the statistical norm for the price level. Finally, an economy in the neighbourhood of equilibrium conforms to the businessman's or common-sense norm in terms of "normal" busi-ness conditions. Thus, when the economy is in the neighbourhood of equilibrium at the end of the business cycle, theoretical, statistical and common-sense norms all apply and normal values for prices and other economic variables are each approximately reflected in current values, while otherwise disruption prevails.

The concept of normal prices is critical to Schumpeter's explanation of growth and development under capitalism. Innovative activity is dialectically connected to the deviation of prices from their normal values. As prices move away from normal values, innovation activity is suppressed because the calculation of profit from potential innovations becomes increasingly unreliable under these circum-stances. Only when prices approach the theoretical, statistical and common-sense normal values can potential profits be reliably calculated from current price infor-mation, which allows innovation to once again blossom. Thus, for Schumpeter innovation-driven growth under capitalism is endogenous and necessarily takes the form of cycles in the price level and structural change in the price system.

I argue in Chapter 6 that general equilibrium and perfect competition should be rejected as providing norms for a developing economy. In this chapter, I argue market order and imperfect competition provide the starting points for determin-ing theoretical and statistical norms for a developing economy. Replacing the concept of equilibrium with that of order and allowing for imperfect competition provides continuity in the theoretical and statistical analysis of the process of the introduction and absorption of disruptive innovations.

One feature of a developing economy that any determination of theoretical and common-sense norms needs to take into account is the impact of creative

destruction on obsolescence. Schumpeter emphasises the obstacles faced by entrepreneurs in obtaining finance for introducing their innovations into the economy.
He also recognises that once development is underway these difficulties spread
across the economy. While the entrepreneur faces uncertainty the innovation will
generate sufficient revenue to cover production costs and repay creditors with
interest, all businesses face the prospect that revenues or costs will be impacted by
innovations. In a developing economy, the threat of obsolescence due to innovations is ubiquitous, even though the extent of impact is uncertain. Investors and
creditors in any business reasonably expect to receive a surplus of revenues over
the operating and depreciation cost of any investment in embodied technology,
which provides a buffer against the threat of obsolescence.

Uncertainty associated with innovations impedes the external financing of investment as there are inherent differences across individuals and firms in assessing
the prospects for particular investments, with incumbents having more information and often more optimism than outsiders. This encourages reliance on internal
financing of firm growth through retained earnings where possible. As innovation
creates heterogeneity in firm costs and revenues, the ability to grow through internal financing is unevenly distributed across firms. Theories of differential firm
growth are used to examine the evolution of industry structure by both evolutionary and post-Keynesian economists. These theories suggest the process of adjustment of prices to innovation and creative destruction generally stops well short of
yielding zero profits, providing yet another reason for expecting prices in a developing economy to remain well above unit operating and depreciation cost when the
economy is not experiencing substantial disruption from innovations.

In the Commentary section of Chapter 4, the theoretical normal prices in a stationary economy are determined by setting price equal to reproduction cost using
Sraffa's system of production of commodities by means of commodities. Imperfect competition, obsolescence and differential firm growth suggest the theoretical
normal prices for a developing economy are greater than reproduction cost. The
determination of the theoretical normal prices in this chapter builds on the Sraffian
system of reproduction prices, but with allowance for price exceeding reproduction
cost in each industry by an amount that reflects the impact of imperfect competition,
the threat of obsolescence and the requirements for financing capacity expansion.

With regard to statistical norms, the basic difficulty in identifying the statistical
norm for a developing economy is taking account of structural change. Schumpeter's analysis in *CSD* recognises the process of creative destruction reduces
heterogeneity across firms through selection, while innovation increases heterogeneity. The theory of industry life cycles builds on this observation and associates first increasing and then decreasing firm heterogeneity with the passage of
new industries through shakeout and maturity following their creation through
major innovations. Theories of differential firm growth based on internal financing of investment also yield a pattern of increasing and then decreasing firm heterogeneity as innovations spread.

Low firm heterogeneity at the end of an industry life cycle or the process of
differential firm growth mean firm-specific measures, such as price, unit cost and

productivity, converge across firms. Only at this point does the average of values across firms provide an unbiased estimate of the attractor value toward which firms are converging. Across the whole economy actual values approach their corresponding attractor values when a cluster of innovations reaches its fullest diffusion. Thus, the statistical norm for a developing economy is identified by a minimum rate of structural change across industries and a minimum variation in characteristics across firms within each industry, which are well short of the stationary-state outcomes of uniform firms and no structural change.

The next section deals with the impact of creative destruction and the threat of obsolescence on theoretical and common-sense norms in a developing economy, while the following section discusses using measures of firm heterogeneity for identifying the corresponding statistical norm. The fourth section continues the discussion of firm heterogeneity emphasising the impact of differential firm growth on pricing and suggests interpreting theoretical normal prices as being attractors for the evolution of prices in the selection process driven by differential firm growth. The various influences on theoretical normal prices in a developing economy are then brought together in an adaptation of the Sraffian system of reproduction prices. I conclude with a summary pointing to implications for reconstructing Schumpeter's price theory, which is the subject of the next chapter.

Creative destruction, obsolescence and norms for prices

For Schumpeter creative destruction is the process by which new ways of doing things replace the old, with the consequence that equipment, skills and organisation used in the old ways become obsolete. There is no allowance for such obsolescence in the Walrasian equilibrium of a stationary economy, which is appropriate when technology is unchanging. The argument developed below is that the theoretical norm (as well as the common-sense or businessman's norm) for the developing economy requires adjustment for the threat of obsolescence.

Schumpeter makes the case for obsolescence being part of the normal conditions in a developing economy. As early as in *TED*, in discussing the transitory nature of profits from established business he observes with respect to depreciation charges that, 'Quite rightly, therefore, much more than wear and tear is frequently written off and many companies strive to write off the whole of capital as soon as possible' (Schumpeter, 1961 [1934], p. 209). In *BC*, he emphasises that innovation involves more than the rearrangement of this capital equipment as is often assumed in neoclassical analyses of technical change. Rather, innovations are generally embodied in plant and equipment, so that new machines and even new plants are necessary (Schumpeter, 1939, pp. 93–96).

Writing later in *CSD*, Schumpeter goes further and recognises the prospect of further changes in technology as a factor delaying investment in the latest technology.

> A new type of machine is in general but a link in a chain of improvements and may presently become obsolete. In a case like this it would obviously not

be rational to follow the chain link by link regardless of the capital loss to be suffered each time. The real question is at which link the concern should take action. The answer must be in the nature of a compromise between considerations that rest largely on guesses.

(Schumpeter, 1976 [1950], p. 98)

Here, Schumpeter recognises a developing economy differs from a stationary economy in terms of factors affecting investment decisions, but he gives no consideration to how basing investment decisions on guesses about the future course of technology might influence his analysis of economic development in general or the theoretical norm for determining prices in particular.

What are the theoretical implications for the norms of an economy arising from obsolescence? Whenever products from new technology are more attractive to buyers because they have lower price or better features, the change in technology means reduced revenues or higher costs to owners of plant and equipment that embody the old technology. In the extreme, the investments in plant and equipment embodying the old technology have zero value and are obsolete. As Schumpeter recognises, this makes it less attractive to invest in any equipment that embodies a particular current technology.

To reduce the prospect of losses from "following the chain of improvements", expected revenues from making investments in new embodied technology need to exceed the level of expected costs calculated by assuming that the investments never become obsolete. Thus, in a developing economy the prices of outputs from investments with embodied technology should exceed the equilibrium prices for the products from using the same technology in Schumpeter's stationary economy, which means the prospect of further economic development increases theoretical and common-sense normal prices.[1]

It may seem surprising that a developing economy would be characterised by higher theoretical and common-sense normal prices than a stationary economy with the same technology. However, there is an option value to uncommitted productive inputs in the developing economy that is not present in the stationary economy. The option value is lost once these inputs are committed to the technology embodied in a machine. This is the loss Schumpeter associates with "following the chain of improvements". There is no loss of option value in the stationary economy because the technology never changes.

Of course, comparison of prices between the developing economy and the stationary economy misses the importance of technical progress to improvements in living standards. An economy undergoing development has rising productivity, so that the economy has cost and price reduction over time. Schumpeter makes this point forcefully in the related context of explaining the impact of imperfection of competition that he considers an inherent corollary of innovation. 'In this respect, perfect competition is not only impossible but inferior, and has no title to being set up as a model of ideal efficiency' (Schumpeter, 1976 [1950], p. 106)).

Obsolescence can be incorporated into the theory of prices by modifying the version of Sraffa's (1960) model of reproduction prices introduced in the

Commentary section of Chapter 4. There, a vector of reproduction prices for all commodities is determined by the wage rate for labour and the technical requirements of production in terms of labour used directly and indirectly (through the use of intermediate products). Fixed capital is excluded from the model, which necessarily precludes consideration of the prospect of obsolescence.

To consider the impact of the threat of obsolescence, the model is modified to include fixed capital following the joint-production approach of Sraffa. Each production process using a machine is treated as having an extra output, namely a machine one year older than the machine used as input. In the last year of the machine's life, the machine is an intermediate input and there is no extra output of a year-older machine. If a machine lasts for n years, there are n separate production processes, one for machines of each age.

The simplest case for considering the impact of the threat of obsolescence involves the "one-hoss shay" model, where a machine has constant productivity over its finite lifetime. In every year, this machine uses the same amount of labour and other intermediate inputs to produce one unit of the same product along with a year-older machine (until the last year when there is no older machine). The price of machines of all ages then can be solved from the series of n price equations for production processes with machines of various ages. The revenue in each equation is the price of the finished product plus the price of a one-year-older machine, while the cost is the price of a current machine plus the wage cost for direct and indirect labour. The price of the product and the wage cost are identical across the n production processes. When there is no interest cost associated with holding machines, the depreciation charge allocated to each year of the machine's life is just $1/n$ times the original price of the machine.[2]

Suppose the machine becomes obsolete in year m, with $m < n$. There are then only m processes over which the machine is used, which means that the depreciation charge required to recover the machine's cost over its economic lifetime is then $1/m$ times the price of the machine. To yield zero profits from each of the production processes utilising the machine over its economic life, the theoretical normal for reproduction cost and price of products utilising the machine includes a depreciation charge of $1/m$ times the price of the machine. The depreciation charge applied using the $1/n$ rule understates the value of machine inputs used in production by a proportion m/n.

At the time of investment, the economic lifetime of a machine or any other tangible or intangible asset that embodies current technology is unknown. It is only after the asset can no longer be profitably employed in a production process due to deterioration or obsolescence that the pattern of depreciation charges consistent with recovering the full cost of the asset is determined. The particular pattern of depreciation charges to determine reproduction prices using Sraffa's method is therefore only known *ex post*.

It is extremely unlikely that the prices actually received in any year for the outputs from the production process exactly match the unit reproduction cost including depreciation charges, with or without allowance for obsolescence, during the asset's economic life.[3] Looking backwards provides the information necessary to calculate the correct pattern of depreciation charges, unit reproduction cost and price from applying Sraffa's method over the revealed economic lifetime of all fixed assets. These depreciation charges can be considered "normal" in the sense of providing an amount just sufficient to cover reproduction cost of each fixed asset based on equal contributions to production cost during each year of the asset's economic life, but provide only an imperfect guide for setting prices that equal reproduction cost over the future lifetime of newly acquired machines of the same type.

Because of uncertainty and differing knowledge of each firm, there is undoubtedly divergence across firms in their estimation of the impact of future technological change on obsolescence of existing equipment, even where the firms use similar processes to produce highly substitutable products. As Schumpeter recognises, the common-sense or businessmen's concept of normal cost is thus somewhat ill-defined. Depreciation charges based on physical lifetimes and engineered patterns of productivity constitute a particularly optimistic extreme (no threat of obsolescence), while higher charges that make some allowance for obsolescence represent a middle ground. Immediate expensing of the full cost of equipment constitutes a particularly pessimistic extreme that eventuates only if the equipment becomes obsolete at the end of the first production period.

Accounting methods occasionally recognise the potential loss to the value of fixed assets from obsolescence by using depreciation charges that exceed the rate of physical deterioration. The expected useful life in these cases is based on the guess about the length of time for which the asset will remain profitable to operate rather than the time at which it wears out. As an example, computer equipment is assigned a useful life of three years rather than the five or more years for which the physical components of the equipment are expected to keep functioning.

Allowances for potential obsolescence are the exception rather than the rule in accounting because of uncertainty. At the time of investment, the impact of creative destruction is unknown so the proper allocation over time of the cost of the investment is undetermined. All that is reasonably certain is, in at least some cases, assets with embodied technology will prematurely cease being profitable to operate due to competition from new technology. Accelerating the depreciation of inputs committed to embedded technology is thus reasonable *ex ante*, but the amount of depreciation that would recover the cost of the inputs is only known *ex post*.[4]

Rather than make decisions based on accounting statements incorporating the threat of obsolescence, businesses often adopt other procedures for recognising the threat. This is particularly the case when it comes to evaluating investment projects. One common practice is the use of maximum payback periods. Here, the requirement is that the cost of the investment must be recouped within a maximum number of years regardless of the lifespan of the assets acquired to carry out the investment. For example, a maximum payback period of three years is used, even though the physical lifetime of the investment is five years.

Another common practice for evaluating investment decisions that embody technology is to include a large risk factor in the discounting of expected future returns from the investment. For example, instead of discounting future returns at a risk-free rate of 5% per annum, an investor adds a 15% risk premium and discounts at 20% per annum. To yield the same discounted net revenue, a five-year project would then have to generate 1.67 times the annual net revenue using a 20% discount rate compared to using a 5% discount rate. In terms of generating enough discounted net revenue to match the investment cost, this is roughly equivalent to shortening the payback period from five years to three years without applying discounting to any expected revenues. More generally, there is an equivalence relationship between shortening the payback period and raising the risk premium in terms of having a negative impact on the project generating sufficient revenue after truncation or discounting to exceed its investment cost.

Accelerated depreciation, imposing maximum payback periods and adding risk premiums are each business practices used to reflect the threat of obsolescence in evaluating of investments that might be negatively impacted by technological change. Without some adjustment to the expected costs or revenues for the investment, the evaluation process would eventually lead to losses of the type Schumpeter associates with "following the chain of improvements". Thus, normal business practice incorporates adjustments for the threat of obsolescence, and so should the theoretical normal price incorporate adjusted depreciation charges reflecting the expectation of obsolescence on the realised economic lifespan of assets.

Various adjustments included in normal business practice and those in the calculation of a modified reproduction cost differ in method and generally produce different outcomes in terms of values of costs and prices. However, parallels exist and conditions can be derived under which the methods yield similar or identical outcomes. The parallel is closest with practice of using maximum payback periods. The adjustment to reproduction cost has depreciation charges allocated over the m years of economic operation rather than n years of physical lifetime, with $m < n$. Thus, there is exact correspondence between using a maximum payback period and amending the reproduction cost to account for obsolescence in the simplest case with no interest, provided there is equality between the number of years in the maximum payback period and that over which obsolescence is calculated.

Correspondence in outcomes to those with the adjustment of reproduction cost can also be derived for rates of accelerated depreciation and additional risk premiums. However, in each case, the outcome is identical, or even approximate, only under particular parameter values. This raises the question of when, if ever, forces are at work that result in approximate equality between the outcomes from the adjusted reproduction cost and the calculations under business practices that take account of the threat of obsolescence. Following Schumpeter's suggestion, the end of the business cycle might well be conducive to such convergence, particularly if it is associated with a standardisation of business practices and a convergence of estimates regarding the number of years to obsolescence. Thus, as in Schumpeter's analysis, conditions prevailing the end of the business cycle are most appropriate as reflecting theoretical and common-sense normal values for a developing economy.

Firm heterogeneity, industry maturity and the business cycle

Firm heterogeneity is a standard feature of a developing economy and merits consideration as leading to differences between the norms for developing and stationary economies. In a stationary economy with free competition, it reasonable to expect all firms have adjusted to the way of doing things that yields maximum profits. This way of doing things is generally considered to be unique, which leads to uniformity among the many firms engaged in the same activity within a competitive market. Homogeneity is thus the norm for firms engaged in any particular activity in a stationary state.

Schumpeter only implicitly deals with firm heterogeneity when he discusses the introduction and diffusion of innovations. His discussion of creative destruction in *CSD* is suggestive of an expansion and then reduction in variety following a cluster of innovations, but he does not further pursue this evolutionary perspective. This section and the following section discuss the impact of innovation in theories of firm growth and the evolution of industry structure.

Innovation leads to differences among firms, in products, processes, organisation, markets, etc. Schumpeter distinguishes the entrepreneurial firm from its established rivals in terms of these characteristics. Also, the embodiment of changing technology in investments means firms are in general distinguished by the vintage of their plant and equipment. Likewise, development and branding of new products is a form of intangible capital that is distinct and reversible only at substantial loss in the value of the asset, as is the choice of physical location for a manufacturing, wholesale or retail business.

When technologies change over time in a developing economy, it is still conceivable for all firms to follow the same, or at least a similar, patterns of investment in tangible and intangible capital. Indeed, if all firms had the same objective of maximising profit and had access to complete information there would be a universally optimal course of action. Indivisibilities in the production process would no doubt lead to some differences across firms, but there is a more fundamental source of firm heterogeneity in a developing economy. As discussed by Bloch and Metcalfe (2011), firms are different because differences in their knowledge lead them to take different actions when the future is uncertain, particularly in regard to investments that involve commitments to irreversible technology.

As noted in the previous section, a firm considering an investment requiring commitment to an embodied technology makes guesses about the future, including the prospects of the development and implementation of superior technologies. These guesses are informed by the firm's knowledge of the technological trajectory for its business, its understanding of the behaviour of current and potential rivals, and its thinking about the development of the broader economic environment. The modern "capabilities" literature links a firm's knowledge to the organisation of the knowledge of the individuals within the firm as well as their connections to external networks (see, for example, Barney, 1991, Dosi, et al., 2002, Ramazzotti, 2004).

Bloch and Metcalfe (2015) argue that specialisation of knowledge across individuals is ubiquitous in modern economies and the successful coordination of such knowledge within the firm is central to the firm's competitiveness. Coordination of specialised knowledge has been particularly important to large firms, but variation of knowledge across individuals implies firms of all sizes differ in their collective knowledge and that the knowledge of smaller firms is even more specialised and distinct. Given the influence of these differences in knowledge on investment decisions subject to uncertainty, heterogeneity is generated in the use of technologies across firms. Similar considerations apply to other irreversible investments, such as in organisational structure, product characteristics, branding and location.

If firms are necessarily heterogeneous in a developing economy, how does this affect the norms of the economy? Here, it is useful to distinguish between two possible meanings of normal, as average versus as an attractor or end state. While normal as an average is by far the more common meaning, Schumpeter clearly has in mind the latter meaning when he qualifies the Walrasian equilibrium as determining theoretical normal prices only at the end of the business cycle. As I argue in discussing the logical contradiction between equilibrium and evolution in the previous chapter, Schumpeter chooses poorly in nominating the Walrasian equilibrium as the end state for the business cycle in a developing economy. Nonetheless, his intuition of using the end of the business cycle as a focal point in defining norms has merit, particularly in regard to heterogeneity across firms.

Schumpeter's argument that the business cycle is the form development takes under capitalism identifies the business cycle with the ebb and flow of innovative activity. Innovative activity is low at the end of the business cycle because of the high degree of adjustment to the disturbance caused by preceding innovations. This allows the reliable calculation of returns to innovations, so innovative activity resumes and gains strength through the cumulative process I describe in Chapters 2 and 3. Schumpeter clearly has in mind disturbances in terms of his macro orientation on evolution, but he recognises that firms constitute the essential micro units of the meso-level evolution of the structure of the economy. A correspondence at the meso level to the macro-level disturbance caused by clusters of innovation is increased heterogeneity across firms.

Heterogeneity within a population of firms is impacted by the evolutionary process of variation, selection and replication. Variation introduced by innovation tends to increase the heterogeneity of firms measured by the amount of variation in the characteristics of firms or, where relevant, the range of individual characteristics along a quantitative scale. Selection through competition has the opposite impact, tending to reduce the amount or range of variation. Replication when analysed in the form of differential growth associated with characteristics of firm performance, eventually concentrates the population around best-performance characteristics and, thereby, reduces the variation in firm characteristics across an industry.

A business cycle driven by the rise and fall of innovative activity, as in Schumpeter's pure model with two phases, would thus be expected to have increasing heterogeneity of firms and increasing variance of firm characteristics in its upswing, followed by decreasing heterogeneity and variance in the downswing. The end of the cycle would then be associated with low heterogeneity across firms and low variance of firm performance characteristics. While low heterogeneity of firms is neither the average nor the usual outcome over the course of the business cycle, it does have a claim as providing a norm in the sense of being the attractor or (temporary) end state to Schumpeter's cyclical process of development. Also, low heterogeneity also makes the average more reflective of individual outcomes, thereby increasing consensus among firms on costs and other magnitudes.

Schumpeter's broad conception of innovation creates difficulties in dealing with firm heterogeneity for purposes of measurement. Much of Schumpeter's discussion in *BC* deals with national aggregates, but the discussion in Chapter X, 'Prices and Quantities of Individual Commodities', makes use of the classification of activity by industry, such as shipbuilding. Grouping activity by industry has become standard in both theoretical and empirical research in evolutionary economics, although theoretical work often assumes a single homogenous product for the industry as a simplification. There is a consensus view that the whole economy is too broad for considering how firms interact in the process of economic development, but the individual product is too narrow by excluding product competition within a group of related firms. Classifying firms by industry comes closest to capturing the group of firms that are interrelated for purposes of analysis of structural change and is widely adopted in meso-level empirical analysis of innovation.

One strand of evolutionary analysis of the relationship among firms is the theory of industry life cycles, which is explained as follows:

> Three stages of evolution are distinguished. In the initial, exploratory or embryonic stage, market volume is low, uncertainty is high, the product design is primitive, and unspecialized machinery is used to manufacture the product. Many firms enter and competition based on product innovation is intense. In the second, intermediate or growth stage, output growth is high, the design of the product begins to stabilize, product innovation declines, and the production process becomes more refined as specialized machinery is substituted for labor. Entry slows and a shakeout of producers occurs. Stage three, the mature stage, corresponds to a mature market. Output growth slows, entry declines further, market shares stabilize, innovations are less significant, and management, marketing, and manufacturing techniques become more refined.
>
> (Klepper, 1997, p. 148)

According to the life cycle theory, heterogeneity across firm characteristics within an industry is high during the first stage of industry development, falls with a decline in innovation and entry as well as a shakeout of producers in the second stage and stabilises in the third stage.

Klepper (1997) goes on to note the above pattern does not fit the evolution of all industries and specialisation seems to play a key role in many of the non-conforming industries. In particular, specialisation of firms in the critical areas of process and product innovation seems to limit the shakeout of firms to those operating in that particular area, with large numbers of firms and entry of new firms continuing in the other areas. This suggests a moderate residual level of firm heterogeneity when industries characterised by specialisation reach maturity.

Maturity is perhaps the closest concept to providing a businessman's idea of a norm in a developing economy. In a mature industry there are established products, production processes and distribution channels. Many variations in ways of doing things are eliminated through creative destruction on the way to maturity. However, as noted above, the standardisation of ways of doing things associated with maturity sometimes encourages specialisation, with differences across firms in their characteristics corresponding to their different roles in product design, production, marketing and distribution. Thus, heterogeneity remains in a mature industry, but the heterogeneity is of a qualitatively different type from that associated with the earlier stages of evolution towards industry maturity.

Depression and recovery are secondary phenomena in Schumpeter's theory that cause the economic variables to move away and then back towards their normal (long-period) values. Measures of firm heterogeneity, in contrast, can be expected to continue to decrease towards their mature low values. Whenever firms react to downturns by further efforts to lower costs by adopting best-practice techniques, there is a further impetus to standardisation. Thus, firm heterogeneity always has a two-phase cycle and, after major technological breakthroughs and the establishment of new industries, a sustained low value of a measure of heterogeneity across each industry heavily impacted by the innovations indicates of the end of the Kondratieff cycle.

At the end of the business cycle driven by a cluster of innovations, most new industries are mature and firm heterogeneity within the industries is low. Also, each firm has values close to the industry average value for each firm characteristic susceptible to measurement on a linear scale and close to the most common, median, variety for other characteristics. Thus, at the end of the Kondratieff cycle, the statistical norm of the average or median value of each firm characteristic converges on the corresponding norm for the businessman and also converges on the theoretical norm given by the attractor value of that characteristic.

As an indicator of the end of the Kondratieff cycle, using low values of measures of firm heterogeneity has advantages over the method advocated by Schumpeter. First, there is no need to have separate procedures for two- and four-phase cycles and, second, there is no need to rely on the difficult identification of inflection points when dealing with four-phase cycles. Rising levels of firm heterogeneity indicate the upswing of the business cycle and falling levels indicate the downswing, with the end of the cycle occurring when firm heterogeneity is at or near a minimum. However, there are both conceptual and practical difficulties with using measures of firm heterogeneity for timing the phases of the business cycle.

On a conceptual level, the key difficulty is aggregation, specifically determining how to use the measures of firm heterogeneity at the industry level to form an indicator of the business cycle, which is a macroeconomic phenomenon. A cluster of innovations likely affects many industries directly, but the rate at which the innovations spread and are fully digested is unlikely to be identical. Focussing on leading industries provides a possible approach if the leading industries for a wave of innovations are clearly identifiable. Otherwise, some sort of average or median measure might be used. Ignoring industry classifications and using a measure of heterogeneity across all firms in the economy provides an aggregate measure, but runs the risk of spurious influences from changes in the relative importance of industries when firm characteristics vary substantially across industries.[5]

Limitations on data are an obvious practical problem with the use of measures of firm heterogeneity for dating phases of business cycles. Many countries still don't provide comprehensive firm-level data. Even where data are provided, they are generally only annual data and are often released with a substantial lag. Finally, confidentiality requirements often restrict the type of data provided. Thus, for the foreseeable future the use of data on firm heterogeneity to identify cycle phases is likely to be limited to historical studies of those economies where reasonable data on firm heterogeneity have been available for a considerable period.

So far, the discussion of the impact of cyclical development on firm heterogeneity is in the mode of appreciative theorising. Formalisation requires specification of how firms behave and interact as well as specification of institutional context and household behaviour in input and output markets. Formal modelling of differential firm growth is considered in the next section for the purpose of demonstrating the potential, as well as the limitations, of applying evolutionary analysis to determining norms for a developing economy.

Differential firm growth and industry evolution

Examples of modelling of industry evolution as a replicator process with differential firm growth are Metcalfe (1994, 1998, 2007), Andersen (2004) and Markey-Towler (2016). Firm growth in these models increases with prior profitability, so the most profitable firms tend to grow the fastest and increase their share of the market. With an assumption of competitive market clearing, there is a tendency in the basic model for increasing industry concentration with only the lowest cost firms remaining in the long run and for price to move to the cost level of these firms.

Modifications to the basic model that allow for industry growth, economies of scale and continued innovation activity impede the long-run tendency for unit cost to approach the lowest obtainable level as well as the tendency for profit to be completely eroded. A model with similar firm growth dynamics by Steindl (1976 [1952]) also has industry output concentrating in the hands of the low-cost firms, but Steindl argues that increased concentration alters the pricing behaviour of the remaining firms as they recognise their interdependence. As a result, price remains well above lowest obtainable unit cost and low-cost firms cease growing relative to the industry.

The setup of the Metcalfe and Andersen basic models is that firms differ only in their unit cost for producing a single homogenous product, with each firm's unit cost fixed in perpetuity and constant with respect to output.[6] Further, the output of each firm is equal to its production capacity and total industry demand is constant. Product price is set to clear the market (quantity produced equals quantity demanded at that price). Firms then expand (contract) their production capacity in the next period by an amount equal to their current profits (losses).

In this basic model the evolution of the industry follows the Fisher Principle from evolutionary biology where the change in average behaviour is related to the variance of behaviour across the population. Metcalfe (1994, p. 332) shows with the assumptions of the basic model, the weighted average unit cost across firms in the industry decreases at a rate proportional to variance of unit cost across the firms. With low-cost firms expanding their share at the expense of high-cost firms, the industry weighted average unit cost eventually converges on the lowest unit cost among the firms. Convergence is at a decreasing rate because the variance of unit cost is decreasing.

Along with the decline in weighted average cost, there is a decline in product price. This reflects the fact that production capacity expands by the amount of profit earned by firms in the industry. If average cost is falling, average profit would rise with a constant price. This would expand capacity growth and drive down price whether demand is constant or a decreasing function of price. As unit cost converges on the lowest level among firms, the price change approaches zero and price approaches lowest unit cost.

Notably, the dynamics of the basic model of differential firm growth lead toward values of cost and price that satisfy the conditions for a Walrasian equilibrium. In the Walrasian model, outcomes are derived by imposing equilibrium (no tendency to change without external disturbance). In contrast, the differential firm growth model incorporates a process of adjustment and yields a price equal to lowest unit cost as an attractor. Because the variance of unit cost decreases as the attractor is approached, the approach is asymptotic and only reached at the infinite horizon. This limits the meaning of price equal to lowest obtainable unit cost as a norm for the economy.

More fundamentally, it is the special nature of the assumptions of the basic model of differential firm growth model that yields the long-run outcome satisfying the conditions for Walrasian equilibrium. These assumptions essentially yield a stationary state once the adjustment to cost differentials is complete with no variation remaining in unit cost and no growth in output, so it is hardly surprising to find the outcome is consistent with Walrasian equilibrium. More important is that alternative specifications of the model affect the process of convergence and the value of the attractor.

Metcalfe (1994, p. 333) shows altering the basic model to include output growth implies price remains above unit cost by an amount sufficient to generate profits to finance an increase in production capacity equal to the increase in demand. Further, firms with unit cost above the lowest unit cost price remain in operation indefinitely, even though they continue to lose market share. The meaning of price equal lowest obtainable unit cost as a norm for the economy is thereby undermined.

The growth of market demand impedes the working of the Fisher Principle by weakening the link between cost performance and growth of market share across firms. Metcalfe (1994, pp. 334–42) shows modifying the basic model of differential firm growth to consider economies of scale of the various types Marshall (1920) introduces in *Principles of Economics* means the working of the Fisher Principle is further impeded. Under some assumptions Metcalfe shows the weighted average unit cost for an industry rises over some intervals in the process of long-run adjustment and the lowest obtainable unit cost may not act as the attractor for either the weighted average cost or price in the long run. Metcalfe (2007) further shows that if firms differ in their investment strategies the force of the Fisher Principle is impeded whenever higher cost firms have more aggressive investment strategies than their low-cost rivals.

Andersen (2004) extends the differential firm growth model beyond the selection process to consider the impact of the innovation process, which involves using the generalisation of the Fisher Principle due to Price (1972). Rather than modelling the variation in unit cost across firms, Andersen simplifies by abstracting from the use of capital equipment and models differences in labour productivity across firms. The change in weighted average labour productivity thus becomes the measure of population fitness and Andersen decomposes this measure into a selection effect due to the Fisher Principle and an innovation effect due to Price. The selection effect depends positively on the variance of productivity across firms, while the innovation effect depends positively on the covariance between labour productivity and the change in labour productivity across firms. If firm productivity is constant, we have only a selection effect as assumed in Metcalfe's (1994) basic model.

Andersen examines the how innovation impacts on average labour productivity growth by having firms allocate their labour between production and research. The labour allocated to innovative activity generates improvements in the firm's productivity equal to a stochastic variable times the number of research workers. No assumption is made that workers are optimally allocated between production and research. Instead, as in the seminal work of Nelson and Winter (1982), the focus is on seeing the difference in performance between firms using different allocations. Simulations show that one firm achieves sufficiently greater profits (a combination of high productivity and low research expenses) at some point, such that its expansion means all other firms incur losses and are driven from the market. Thus, concentration of production at lowest obtainable unit cost among operating firms is a clear outcome, but there is no guarantee of continuing research effort driving further reductions in unit cost. Also, the industry is left as a monopoly.[7]

In all the models of differential firm growth reviewed above price is determined to clear the market. All producers sell their capacity output regardless of the impact on market price. Yet, in each model the selection process operates to concentrate production among a small number of producers or even a single producer. In a related model that doesn't explicitly use evolutionary principles, Steindl (1976 [1952]) assumes firms change behaviour as industry production becomes concentrated through the relative expansion of low-cost producers and the elimination of high-cost producers.[8]

By linking the change in behaviour (pricing and investment rules) to changing market structure, Steindl adds a rule-changing (meso) dimension to his micro analysis. At some point in the process of concentration surviving firms come to recognise their common interests and desist from further expanding capacity beyond what is required to maintain their desired capacity utilisation ratios. This allows the firms to maintain a price well above their unit operating cost and accommodate demand fluctuations through variations in capacity utilisation rather than changing price. The process of concentration stops before all firms with unit cost higher than the lowest obtainable are driven from the market even in the long run. Price is kept well above the lowest obtainable unit cost and even above the weighted average unit cost including the higher cost producers.

Overall, the formal modelling of differential firm growth undermines Schumpeter's argument that the values of variables associated with Walrasian equilibrium provide theoretical normal values for a developing economy. The basic model of differential firm growth can yield a long-run tendency toward the removal of all firms not operating at lowest obtainable unit cost and yield a market price close to this cost. However, this result is shown to depend on highly restrictive assumptions not appropriate for a developing economy. As Metcalfe (2014, p. 31) puts it, 'Evolutionary competition, as sketched above, defines an open-ended process in which output of the industry would concentrate in the "fittest" firm only if all other influences remain constant. But other things rarely remain constant.'

The assumptions of the basic model of differential firm growth are consistent with a stationary state in the long run. However, when these assumptions are altered to allow for conditions appropriate to a developing economy, such as a positive rate of output growth or a shift away from competitive behaviour in concentrated industries, having price equal to lowest obtainable unit cost is no longer the attractor for actual unit cost and price. Thus, in a developing economy the theoretical norm in terms of the eventual outcome of the evolutionary process of differential firm growth is not likely to be the ideal of Walrasian equilibrium, rather it contains elements of production above lowest cost as well as prices that exceed this cost level.

Theoretical normal prices for a developing economy

In this section I incorporate the norms for a developing economy from the discussion in the earlier sections of this chapter into the Sraffian framework for determining theoretical normal prices. In Chapter 4, theoretical normal prices for a stationary economy are determined by setting price equal to reproduction cost for each product as shown in Equation (4.3), which is reproduced here as

$$\mathbf{p} = \mathbf{c} = ((\mathbf{I} - \mathbf{A})^{-1}\gamma)w \tag{7.1}$$

where $\mathbf{p}$ is a vector of product prices, $\mathbf{A}$ is a matrix of input-output coefficients, γ is a vector of labour requirements and w is a wage rate. The inverted matrix,

$(\mathbf{I} - \mathbf{A})^{-1}$, when multiplied by the vector of direct labour requirements, γ, gives the vector of total (direct and indirect) labour requirements. As in Schumpeter's analysis, there is no profit element included in the determination of theoretical normal prices for a stationary economy.

Innovation and creative destruction are incorporated into the pricing analysis in Chapter 4 by allowing price to exceed unit cost. This gives rise to the relationship in Equation (4.5), reproduced here as

$$\mathbf{p} = \psi\mathbf{c} = ((\mathbf{I} - \psi\mathbf{A})^{-1}\psi\gamma)\mathbf{w}, \tag{7.2}$$

The ith diagonal element of $\mathbf{\Psi}$ is the weighted average price-cost ratio for the ith commodity, while the off-diagonal elements are each zero. If the innovation involves the ith product at time t+1, then the immediate impact of the innovation is $\mathbf{\Psi}_{i,t+1} > 1$ and $\mathbf{\Psi}_{j,t+1} = 1$ for all j $\neq$ i. Having price exceed unit cost in industries with innovation and equal to unit cost in industries without innovation guarantees $\mathbf{\Psi} > \mathbf{I}$, which means there is profit in the economy as a whole as long as there is any output of the innovative product. Prices beyond the industry with innovation are affected whenever the product of this industry is used as an input in the production processes of other industries.

The contrast between the theoretical normal prices for a stationary economy as determined by Equation (7.1) and prices in an economy undergoing development as determined in Equation (7.2) provides the analytical framework for my commentary on Schumpeter's price theory in Chapter 4. However, the discussion earlier in this chapter suggests that theoretical normal prices in a developing economy are raised above reproduction costs (calculated based on physical lifetimes of equipment) by the threat of obsolescence and by the financing requirements for expansion of productive capacity. In addition, as Schumpeter recognises, especially in his later writings, imperfect competition is a necessary feature of a developing economy that may further increase price above reproduction cost.

Revising theoretical normal prices for a developing economy starts with recognising that price exceeding reproduction cost is a characteristic of the developing economy that doesn't disappear under "normal" conditions. Thus, at least some elements of the diagonal of the $\mathbf{\Psi}$ matrix exceed the value of one when determining theoretical normal prices for a developing economy. Further, the analysis earlier in this chapter suggests using attractor values in defining norms of technical coefficients of production the elements of the $\mathbf{A}$ matrix and the γ vector, with the attractor values being the average or median values obtaining at the end of the Kondratieff cycle. These attractor values normally exceed those for the best-practice technology.[9] Finally, for the purpose of incorporating Schumpeter's arguments on cyclical variation in the price of means of production (including the wage rate), the wage associated with normal conditions is distinguished from values over the course of the cycle.

If the particular values of all the parameters of Equation (7.2) associated with the theoretical norm for a developing economy are denoted with subscript N to indicate normal values, then the vector of theoretical normal prices is given by

$$\mathbf{P_N} = \psi_N \mathbf{c_N} = ((\mathbf{I} - \psi_N \mathbf{A_N})^{-1} \psi_N \gamma_N) \mathbf{w_N}, \qquad \psi_N > \mathbf{I} \qquad (7.3)$$

As noted in the previous two sections, norms are defined by conditions achieved with the extensive, but generally less than complete, diffusion of a cluster of innovations at the end of the Kondratieff cycle. Each cycle has its own norms with the relationship between norms of consecutive cycles being a major topic in the next chapter.

Andrews (2015) uses the difference between reproduction prices and normal prices in distinguishing Smith's concept of natural prices from Marshall's concept of long-run normal prices. According to Andrews, Smith considers natural prices to be determined by the costs of reproduction, while for Marshall the long-run normal price is the price that persists in the absence of disturbance and after sufficient time for adjustments to all elements of the production process. Importantly, there is no presumption in Marshall's concept that competitive forces would drive price to the level of unit cost in any particular industry even in the long run, whereas Smith identifies monopoly as one of the reasons why market prices might remain above the natural price of a commodity in the long run.

The difference between theoretical normal prices for a stationary economy given by the reproduction prices in Equation (7.1) and theoretical normal prices for a developing economy given by Equation (7.3) is due to factors that keep prices above reproduction cost levels based on best-practice technology. Developing economies are characterised by obsolescence, expansion of productive capacity and imperfect competition that each contribute to a margin, $\pi_{i,N}$, by which price for the ith commodity exceeds its reproduction cost, where $\Psi_{i,N} = 1 + \pi_{i,N}$ is the ith diagonal element of the Ψ_N matrix in Equation (7.3). The contribution of each factor to this margin is now discussed in turn, followed by a discussion of their connections.

Innovation-driven development introduces new technologies into the production and distribution process, which offer lower production cost and/or better products and lead to obsolescence of machines and organisations that employ old technologies. Examples of obsolescence abound, including horse-drawn carts and carriages, clipper ships, electronic calculators, phonograph records and computer cards. As noted in the discussion of Chapter 6, using the rate of physical deterioration to depreciate machines used in producing these obsolete items understates the cost of having employed the machines. There is also understatement of costs due to the obsolescence of intangible capital associated with organisational development and goodwill of buyers when changes in technologies or products undermine the profitability of established products or modes of operation.

The discussion in the second section of this chapter points out that it is possible to adjust the Sraffian reproduction cost scheme to incorporate obsolescence after the fact, once the impact of innovation on the profitability of established production processes and products is known. Guesses about future obsolescence are inherently subject to error, leading firms to various procedures for taking potential obsolescence into account when evaluating investment projects. These include evaluating projects using a payback period shorter than the project's physical life-time and adding a premium to the discount rate used in determining the expected future net revenues from the project.

For the purpose of incorporating the threat of obsolescence into determination of theoretical normal prices in Equation (7.3), a general approach is through recognising the option value of investments that embody current technologies. This option value measures the compensation required by investors to justify commitments to investment in production processes embodying the technologies, which is a reflection of the exposure to loss given the irreversible nature of the investments. Investments don't appear attractive unless the discounted value of the expected revenues from the investment exceeds the expected operating costs by an amount sufficient to cover both the amount of the investment and the option value.

When the option value is expressed on an annualised basis per unit of output, it provides a measure of the impact of obsolescence on the price required to sustain production through the replacement of worn out or obsolete production capacity. If this amount is included in the price-cost ratio, the calculated margin provides a mechanism for incorporating option values into the determination of the theoretical normal price of that product. Thus, for the ith product, $\Psi_{i,N} = 1 + \pi_{i,N}$, where the margin, $\pi_{i,N}$, is the amount of the option value on an annualised basis divided by the reproduction cost of the expected output.

While disruptive impacts of innovation might be directly felt in only a few industries during the business cycle following any particular cluster of innovations, the threat of obsolescence is likely to be more general given the uncertainty regarding which industries are to be affected by the next cluster. Also, innovations often lead to obsolescence of machines produced in the innovating industry but used elsewhere in the economy, such as has been the case with computer equipment. Thus, many diagonal elements of Ψ_N are likely to exceed the value of one due to the threat of obsolescence.

Consideration of the requirements for financing expansion of capacity provides an additional reason for expecting diagonal values of Ψ_N to exceed one. According to theories of differential firm growth, prices tend to decline towards lowest available unit cost as an innovation diffuses through the process of differential firm growth, leading to competitive elimination of marginal firms. Nonetheless, the theories suggest that in a growing industry the process stops well before profits of the innovative or progressive firms are driven to the minimum necessary for inducing replacement investment. Thus, even in the "normal" conditions of an end to the disruption caused by innovation, some heterogeneity in technology, reproduction cost and price-cost ratios remains across firms. If the highest cost firms have price-cost ratios equal to what is required to cover the ongoing threat of obsolescence, then price-cost ratios for lower cost firms exceed this level.

In reviewing the position Schumpeter takes on monopoly in his various writings, Chamberlin (1951) rejects Schumpeter's dismissal of monopoly, and especially monopolistic competition, as unimportant in determining theoretical norms. Chamberlin notes the development of Schumpeter's view of monopoly from *TED* and *BC* to *CSD* and suggests consistency with his latter view requires modifying the position that perfect competition is the theoretical norm of the economy (here referring to the economy as it is observed, which means a developing economy). Chamberlin (op. cit., p. 138) concludes,

> Nevertheless, it is clearly possible, and it is also essential, to define the static "theoretical norm" to include monopoly as well as competition, since it seems true beyond question that if the economic system were actually to "settle down," there would be nothing in the process to diminish the importance therein of either product heterogeneity or oligopoly.

While imperfect competition clearly can lead to theoretical normal prices that exceed reproduction cost, the theories of differential firm growth reviewed in the section above give differing answers as to whether price increase is more than that implied by the threat of obsolescence and the need for financing capacity expansion. Steindl's (1976 [1952]) analysis of differential firm growth has established producers holding price above unit cost after the end of the process of absolute concentration. In this stage of industry maturity, firms recognise their collective interests in limiting capacity expansion and are able to dissuade entrants through a combination of economies of scale, excess capacity and selling efforts, which implies a price-cost ratio higher than required to offset the threat of obsolescence plus finance capacity expansion sufficient to meet market growth. In contrast, Metcalfe's (1994, 1998) analysis of differential firm growth has firms continuing to invest a fixed proportion of their profits in further capacity expansion meaning the evolution of market share moves towards generating a price just equal to that required to offset the threat of obsolescence plus finance capacity expansion sufficient to meet market growth.

In classical economics free competition leads to equalisation of profit rates across industries in the long run, while in neoclassical economics free entry leads to the equivalent of all firms earning zero economic profits in the long run. There is no equivalent to the long run in the developing economy, as development is an open-ended process without any end state. As Schumpeter (1976 [1950], p. 82) puts it, 'Capitalism, then, is by nature a form or method of economic change and not only never is but never can be stationary.' The closest a developing economy gets to the equivalent of the classical or neoclassical long run is at the stage at the end of the innovation cycle when previous innovations have been widely but not fully diffused for reasons explained through this and the previous chapters. Each cycle has its own norms that correspond to this stage of economic evolution, but in each case they clearly differ from the norms of Walrasian equilibrium for the stationary economy.

Combining the various factors discussed above leads to values of $\Psi_{i,N}$ greater than one by at least enough to offset the threat of obsolescence for that industry, which is substantial in many, if not most, industries. These values may be further increased by the need to finance capacity expansion through retained profits and increased still further by mature industries maintaining prices above the level required to finance that expansion. In addition, the normal values of A_N and γ_N exceed the values associated with best-practice technology whenever the process of diffusion of innovations stops short of full adoption, which is a common outcome in models of differential firm growth. For all these reasons the theoretical normal prices for a developing economy as given by Equation (7.3) exceed those given in Equation (7.1) for a stationary economy with the same best-practice technology. Of course, as Schumpeter so persuasively argues in *CSD* the impact from innovations on the standard of living in a developing economy quickly dwarf any static advantage of lower prices enjoyed by the stationary economy.

Summary

Schumpeter's use of Walrasian equilibrium as defining theoretical normal prices for a developing economy as well as a stationary economy is fundamentally flawed, as is his use of inflection points in time-series graphs for identifying the corresponding statistical normal values. Development alters the norms applying at the transition between business cycles when one cluster of innovations has been widely diffused through the economy and another is yet to begin. The context of change in a developing economy differs from the context of continuity that is experienced in a stationary economy or a growing economy with fixed technology and preferences.

Once development is under way, decisions, especially investment decisions, are impacted by the frequency of change. If investments are reversible or easily liquidated, established businesses are able to easily adapt to changes in technology. Likewise, skilled workers are able to shift employment without loss of wages if their skills are transferrable and organisations can shift to new activities if their structures are flexible. However, the modern economy has many industries where these conditions don't hold. Instead, specific technologies are deeply embedded in the production processes, with equipment, skills and organisations all exposed to substantial loss in value when technology changes. As a result, investments in equipment, skills and organisations carry an option value representing the loss of flexibility that comes with the embodiment of specific technologies. This option value is a reflection of the threat of obsolescence and is part of the cost of operating in a developing economy.

Creative destruction involves a rise and then fall in variety in the economy as new ways of doing are introduced and eventually drive out the old. The theory of industry life cycles points to rising heterogeneity across firms during the early phase when new industries are established based on major innovations, which is followed by a shakeout eliminating large numbers of firms and concentrating the distribution of survivors around "best-practice" characteristics. Completion of the cycle involves much standardisation, so measures of firm heterogeneity stabilise at low values.

When a cluster of innovations associated with a technological breakthrough creates a range of new industries, the timing of the cycle in firm heterogeneity within the affected industries is related to the timing of Schumpeter's Kondratieff cycles. In particular, rising values of measures of heterogeneity occur in these industries during the upswing of the cycle and falling values occur in the downswing. If the number of affected industries is large, the upswing and downswing created by the cluster of innovations is reflected in rising and falling average measures of heterogeneity across all industries and low average heterogeneity occurs during the transition between cycles. Thus, measures of firm heterogeneity provide indicators of the transition between cycles as an alternative to Schumpeter's reliance on inflection points in the graphs of time-series data for economic variables.

Theories of differential firm growth provide a formal method for analysing the impact of evolutionary selection on firm performance in terms of unit cost and price. Under assumptions yielding a stationary economy as the long-run outcome, the models suggest an asymptotic approach to price equal to the lowest possible level of unit cost. This is the same outcome as with long-period equilibrium in the Walrasian model. However, when the assumptions are altered to allow for continued growth in productive capacity, economies of scale or imperfect competition, the attractor values for the long-run price and unit cost deviate from the Walrasian ideal of efficiency. Thus, the theories suggest a range of factors impact on the theoretical norm for a developing economy and cause it to deviate from Walrasian equilibrium.

Combining the influence of the threat of obsolescence and of differential firm growth with that of imperfect competition leads to the identification of norms for a developing economy that differ from those of a stationary economy. For theoretical normal prices, this means prices exceed those for a stationary economy with the same current technology. This is demonstrated through the use of Sraffa's framework for determining prices based on the production of commodities by means of commodities.

Following the approach used by Schumpeter, theoretical normal prices are interpreted as the attractors for actual prices only at the transition between the longest business cycles when the disruption from a cluster of innovation is at a minimum. Otherwise, prices move to reflect the disruptive impact of innovation and creative destruction. Analysis of this movement is the subject of the next chapter, which proposes a reconstruction of Schumpeter's price theory.

Notes

1 Wages are also likely to be affected as labour often has skills specific to the current technology of production, such as education and training in applying specific technologies in production, marketing and administration.
2 With interest payable, the depreciation charge attributable to each year rises with the age of the machine. This is because the total cost of utilising the machine, which is equal to depreciation plus interest on the remaining value of the machine, is constant over time. As the annual interest cost drops over time with the decline in the remaining value of the machine, the depreciation component of the cost of utilising the machine increases (see Sraffa, 1960, Chapter X).
3 Whenever the price of the commodity differs from its "normal", the use of old machines and their prices diverge from the normal pattern (see Kurz and Salvadori, 1995, pp. 348–51).

4 When creative destruction reduces the value of investments in embodied technology, the decline in the value of the investments may be recognised *ex post* through a revaluation of assets and associated charge against current earnings. In the extreme case, the loss of value can be so large as to lead to bankruptcy, which Schumpeter acknowledges is not an uncommon outcome of creative destruction.

5 If the changes in the relative importance of industries is part of the structural change induced by the cluster of innovations, having such changes influence the measure of firm heterogeneity is not wholly spurious.

6 Markey-Towler (2016) focuses on variation across firms in pricing strategy rather than unit cost.

7 Holm, et al. (2016) provide a general simulation approach to examining what they term confounded selection, when the selection process operates on multiple firm characteristics rather than the single characteristic assumed in simple models of replicator dynamics. They conclude, 'the simulations show quantitatively how population dynamics constrain the evolution of aggregate variables towards values that would be deemed "optimal" in an atomistic study of firm behaviour' (op. cit., p. 818).

8 For a discussion of the relationship between Steindl's treatment of dynamic competition and that of Schumpeter see Bloch (2000) and Bloch and Finch (2008).

9 Mainstream analysis of pricing is invariably cast in terms of best-practice technology without consideration of the impediments to achieving this outcome in either the short run or the long run. This promotes a misleading impression of the actual productivity of the economy and is a real impediment to the analysis of the widely observed departures from best-practice in empirical studies. Salter (1966) is a classic contribution to the study of the relationship between technical change and average productivity.

8 Reconstructing Schumpeter's price theory

Schumpeter argues the business cycle is essential to economic development under capitalism, '*The recurring periods of prosperity of the cyclical movement are the form progress takes in capitalistic society*' (Schumpeter, 1927, p. 30, italics in the original). He then starts his analysis of cyclical development from the circular flow of a stationary economy, which allows him to readily link his analysis to Walrasian equilibrium analysis of the stationary economy. However, as noted in the discussion of equilibrium versus order in Chapter 6, the equilibrium of a stationary state has no potential for change from within and is therefore not an appropriate starting point for an endogenous theory of economic development, which is what Schumpeter claims to provide.

The analysis of the previous chapter rejects perfectly competitive Walrasian equilibrium as providing an appropriate theoretical norm for a developing economy and suggests an alternative, with theoretical normal prices determined within an adapted Sraffian framework in which price exceeds reproduction cost by an amount in each industry that reflects the relevant threat of obsolescence, the requirements for the internal financing of firm growth and the degree of imperfect competition. These theoretical normal prices provide attractors for actual prices when previous innovations have largely diffused throughout the economy, leading to low heterogeneity among firms and orderly markets. Under these conditions, business conditions are "normal" and entrepreneurs can credibly calculate the expected profits from their innovations. The economy then is ripe for a new cluster of innovations as suggested by Schumpeter, but from a starting point of prices consistent with the context of a developing economy rather than starting from a stationary state that lacks evolutionary potential.

In this chapter, I propose a reconstruction of Schumpeter's price theory starting from the revised theoretical normal prices rather than from prices determined by competitive Walrasian equilibrium. I then build on Schumpeter's macro-level analysis of price movements by adopting the evolutionary "micro-meso-macro" approach to theorising proposed by Dopfer, et al. (2004) and Dopfer and Potts (2008). Post-Keynesian price theories provide the analysis of firm pricing behaviour (micro-level analysis), while both post-Keynesian and modern evolutionary theory are drawn upon for analysing innovation and creative destruction as processes driving industry and economy-wide restructuring in the price system (meso-level analysis). Finally, Schumpeter's own macro-level analysis, with amendment based on the micro and meso analysis, is applied to examine the implications of innovation and creative destruction for movements of the price level.

In the micro analysis using post-Keynesian pricing theories, firms set prices based on rules determined by administrative processes. A distinguishing feature of post-Keynesian theories is that the response to demand shocks occurs through variation in inventories, backlogs or production scheduling rather than through changing price to achieve market clearing. Radical innovation that disrupts markets poses no particular challenge in these theories. Of course, application of the pricing rules might lead to results that fail to meet firm expectations in the disrupted circumstances, but the response is a matter for firm strategic decision-making (potentially, a creative response) rather than assuming profit-maximising adaptation with full information.

Adjustment of firm pricing rules is very much the focus of the meso-level analysis of industry evolution in response to innovation and creative destruction. Post-Keynesian pricing theories have price adjustment as an emergent property, with prices or price-cost ratios stabilised until conditions change sufficiently to potentially trigger a strategic change in firm pricing rules. This contrasts with evolutionary theories with market-clearing prices, in which prices are assumed to respond quickly to changing supply or demand conditions. In either type of pricing theory, the differential impact of innovation across firms implies differential firm profitability, which in both post-Keynesian and evolutionary theories is reflected in differential expansion or contraction of the firms. Differential growth of firms together with the pattern of price adjustments are part of the process of creative destruction leading to the eventual restructuring of the industry and the economy.

In *BC* Schumpeter carries out his analysis of movements in the price level at the macro level, distinguishing this analysis from that relating to movements in the price of individual products that impact on the price system. Yet, Schumpeter relies on outcomes of the process of creative destruction to reach his conclusion there is a declining trend in the price level over the business cycle. Price adjustments at the firm and industry level flow through the economy and contribute the movements in both the price level and the price system, which is clearly demonstrated by the application of Sraffa's cost-of-production framework to integrate micro and meso analyses with Schumpeter's macro analysis.

The next section presents the micro analysis derived from post-Keynesian pricing theories, with links to both the Sraffian framework and the analysis of disruptive innovation. Following is a section devoted to meso-level analysis, examining the adjustment of prices over the course of the introduction and diffusion of innovations using both post-Keynesian and evolutionary approaches. The penultimate section integrates the micro and meso analyses with Schumpeter's macro analysis to provide a reconstructed theory of prices in motion over the course of the business cycle. A summary of the key features of the reconstructed theory concludes the chapter.

Pricing behaviour of firms (micro analysis)

As is noted in Chapter 6, Schumpeter limits his theoretical discussion of imperfect competition to equilibrium theories based on optimising behaviour by firms

operating in well understood, if not perfect, markets. The only missing information, if any, in the equilibrium theories concerns the possible reactions from rival
firms in product markets or from suppliers of inputs (especially labour). A fundamentally different type of theory starts from the premise that firms have limited
information about many aspects of their costs and the demand for their products
as well as about the reactions of rivals and suppliers. The full-cost pricing principle of Hall and Hitch (1939) is an early example of such theories, which have
collectively come to be known as post-Keynesian pricing theories.[1]

Hall and Hitch derive their full-cost pricing principle from observations formed
from surveys and follow-up interviews of managers of a sample of enterprises,
mostly manufacturing, in Britain in the 1930s. They explain the purpose of their
1939 paper as:

> to examine, in the light of the interviews, the way in which business men
> decide what price to charge for their products and what output to produce. It
> casts doubt on the general applicability of the conventional analysis of price
> and output policy in terms of marginal cost and marginal revenue, and sug-
> gests a mode of entrepreneurial behaviour which current economic doctrine
> tends to ignore. This is the basing of price upon what we shall call the 'full
> cost' principle.
>
> (Hall and Hitch, 1939, p. 12)

The procedure for determining the price that covers the full cost is then
described in the following general terms:

> prime (or 'direct') cost per unit is taken as the base, a percentage addition is
> made to cover overheads (or 'oncost', or 'indirect' cost), and a further con-
> ventional addition (frequently 10 per cent.) is made for profit. Selling costs
> commonly and interest on capital rarely are included in overheads; when not
> so included they are allowed for in the addition for profits.
>
> (op. cit., p. 19)

Prime or direct cost is the cost per unit of output for expenditure on labour, raw
materials and intermediate inputs, which is assumed to be constant over the range
of output around which the business is operating. Likewise, the percentage allowance for overheads and profit is determined based on a standard output level,
which can be the actual, estimated or full capacity output. As variations in output
within the usual operating range don't alter either unit prime cost or the percentage allowance for overhead and profit, the full-cost price remains unchanged for
output variations within this range.

Full-cost price determination shares many features with the determination of
the so-called "mark-up price". Mark-up pricing, as widely employed in modern
post-Keynesian pricing theories, is traceable back to the work of Michał Kalecki
on the impact of imperfectly competitive pricing on the distribution of income.
Kalecki (1938) argues the distribution of income in modern economies depends
on the degree of monopoly, explicitly referring to Abba Lerner's (1934) article.

Lerner measures monopoly power by the ratio of price minus marginal cost to price, which is equal to the inverse of the absolute value of the price elasticity of demand when profits are maximised. This measure of monopoly power is equal to the mark-up of price over unit prime (or direct) cost when unit prime cost equals marginal cost, a condition Kalecki argues reflects the typical condition of finished goods producers who are operating at less than full capacity.

Kalecki refines his mark-up price theory in a number of publications over several decades. Arguably, the theory loses its strong connection to profit-maximising behaviour by the individual firm and gains a justification that emphasises the sort of informational difficulties and administrative processes mentioned in Hall and Hitch (1939).[2] In one of the latest expositions of his mark-up pricing theory, Kalecki (1971, p. 44) states, 'In view of the uncertainties faced in the process of price fixing it will not be assumed that the firm attempts to maximize its profits in any precise manner.' He then goes on to compare his approach to that of full-cost price theory in the following terms:

> The degree of monopoly *may*, but need not necessarily, increase as a result of a rise in overheads in relation to prime costs. This and the emphasis on the influence of prices of other firms constitute the difference between the theory presented here and the so-called full cost theory.
>
> (op. cit., p. 51, italics in the original)

Rather than rely on an indirect connection to the price elasticity of demand, Kalecki (1971) has mark-up prices determined using a linear combination of the producer's own unit prime cost (expenditure per unit for raw materials and production labour) and the average price charged by producers of similar goods, with

$$p = mu + n\bar{p}, \ \ 0 < m, 0 < n < 1, \tag{8.1}$$

where p is the firm's price, u is unit prime cost, $\bar{p}$ is the weighted average price of all firms, m is a positive coefficient and n is positive coefficient with a value less than one (Kalecki, 1971, p. 45). The m and n coefficients capture the degree of monopoly for the firm, with an increase in either coefficient raising the firm's mark-up of price over unit prime cost as demonstrated by dividing Equation (8.1) by the firm's unit prime cost.

$$p/u = m + n(\bar{p}/u), \tag{8.2}$$

Aggregating Equation (8.1) over an industry consisting of all firms producing similar products yields

$$\bar{p} = \bar{u}(\bar{m}/(1-\bar{n})), \tag{8.3}$$

where the bar over each variable and coefficient indicates an appropriately weighted average for the industry. The average price in Equation (8.3) is equal to average unit prime cost times a mark-up factor, $(\bar{m}/(1-\bar{n}))$, which reflects the degree of monopoly for the industry determined by the pricing equations of individual firms.[3]

While full-cost pricing does not directly involve prices of other firms, a comparison of the industry average price in Equation (8.3) to a corresponding price based on full-cost price theory is still possible. A simplified version full-cost pricing equation is given by

$$p = u + qu,\tag{8.4}$$

where p is product price as before, u is variable cost per unit also as before and q is a margin to cover overheads and the conventional addition for profit. Aggregating Equation (8.4) over the firms producing similar products, yields

$$\bar{p} = \bar{u}\left(1+\bar{q}\right)\tag{8.5}$$

Solving for $\bar{p}/\bar{u}$ in Equation (8.3) and in Equation (8.5) and then equating the two solutions yields the following condition for both theories to yield the same ratio of average price to average cost:

$$\bar{p}/\bar{u} = 1+\bar{q} = \bar{m}/\left(1-\bar{n}\right)\tag{8.6}$$

Thus, for the ratio of average price to average unit cost to be the same under full-cost and mark-up pricing, one plus the average full-cost pricing margin, $\bar{q}$, must equal the ratio of the average unit cost coefficient, $\bar{m}$, to one minus the average coefficient on industry average price, $\bar{n}$.[4]

Establishing a formal correspondence between full-cost and mark-up prices provides a framework for identifying similarities and differences in the way factors impact on price determination under theories of each type. Full-cost price theories aim to closely mimic the administrative processes followed by firms in their pricing decisions, whereas Kalecki's version of the mark-up theory is a more abstract representation of the influences of a firm's own costs and the average price for related products. As noted in the quote from Kalecki above, there is more emphasis on the role of overhead costs in the full-cost theory and more emphasis on the role for prices of rivals in his own theory. Otherwise, the theories share the feature that price at the industry level is directly proportional to prime or direct cost in the short run without any immediate influence of demand on price.

Full-cost pricing theories are often expressed in terms of unit cost including overheads rather than unit direct cost and an administratively determined rate of return on capital rather than a gross profit margin. This applies particularly to theories, such as that of Lanzillotti (1958), that posit the objective of price determination as the achievement of a target rate of return. Price determination in terms of unit total cost and the administered rate of return takes the general form:

$$p = c\left(1 + kr\right),\tag{8.7}$$

where c is the unit total cost excluding a return on capital, k is the ratio of capital to total cost and r is the rate of return on capital. The correspondence between this expression and that in Equation (8.4) with the full-cost price based on unit direct cost is that the gross profit margin, q, is given by

$$q = \left[(c/u)(1+kr) \right] - 1 \tag{8.8}$$

Both of the terms in brackets on the right hand side of Equation (8.8) are greater than or equal to one, so their product is greater than or equal to one and q must be greater than or equal to zero. When there are no overhead items, $c = u$ and q equals the rate of return times the ratio of capital to total cost.

The expression in Equation (8.7) is particularly useful for linking the micro analysis based on post-Keynesian pricing theories with the expression for theoretical normal prices in Equation (7.3). Equation (8.7) relates price to the full unit cost of each commodity and the administered rate of return times the capital-to-cost ratio. In Equation (7.3), price of the ith commodity is equal to its full unit cost multiplied by $\Psi_{i,N} = 1 + \pi_{i,N}$. Thus, denoting the product of the administered rate of return and the capital-to-cost ratio for the jth firm in i^{th} industry as $k_{i,j}r_{i,j}$ and the output of the firm as $x_{i,j}$, the condition from the application of post-Keynesian pricing to yield prices at theoretical normal level for the ith industry is

$$\sum_{j=1}^{n}(x_{i,j} / \sum_{j=1}^{n}x_{i,j})r_{i,j}k_{i,j} = \pi_{i,N} \tag{8.9}$$

Wood (1975), Eichner (1976) and Harcourt and Kenyon (1976) provide post-Keynesian pricing theories in which a firm sets its administered rate of return to yield profits sufficient to allow financing of the level of capacity expansion required to achieve the firm's growth objective. If the desired rate of capacity expansion is given by g, then $g = r$ in Equation (8.7) and the higher the firm's growth objective the higher is its price for the same unit total cost and capital to cost ratio. Further, the firm's price satisfies the condition in Equation (8.9) if the planned rate of capacity expansion is equal to the normal margin for that industry divided by the firm's capital-to-cost ratio. In the meso-level analysis of the next section, Equation (8.9) is used to establish a correspondence between post-Keynesian pricing theories and the outcome of price determination in evolutionary models of differential firm growth.

Price leadership features prominently in many post-Keynesian pricing theories as a coordination mechanism for regulating the competition among firms that have heterogeneous unit costs or use differing pricing margins. Otherwise, the heterogeneity would imply different prices for similar products with price determination using Equations (8.1), (8.4) or (8.7). For example, Hall and Hitch (1939, p. 27) suggest, 'The price may be set by the strongest firm, or by a process of trial and error with all firms making some adjustments.' In this case, the price leader's unit cost and pricing margin determine the price for all firms in the industry, with the pricing margins for the followers determined by the leader's margin multiplied by the ratio of the leader's unit cost and that of the follower. The average gross profit margin for the industry, $\bar{q}$, is then equal to the leader's pricing margin, q, multiplied by the ratio of the leader's unit cost to the average unit direct cost of the followers.

Price leadership does not feature directly in Kalecki's version of mark-up pricing theory. However, Asimakopulos (1975) introduces price leadership into the theory by having a price leader with $m > 1$ and $n = 0$ in Equation (8.1), while followers have values of $m = 0$ and $n = 1$ to yield a result where there are no price differentials across firms.[5] Bloch (1990) then shows the degree of monopoly for the industry in this case is equal to the m coefficient for the leader times the ratio of the leader's unit cost to the average unit cost of the followers, which in turn equals $1 + \bar{q}$ from the full-cost approach.

The formal correspondence between post-Keynesian theories of full-cost and mark-up pricing can even be extended to include models of profit-maximising behaviour by firms. Indeed, as noted above, Kalecki starts his analysis of mark-up pricing from Lerner's (1934) analysis of profit-maximising pricing by monopolists. Cowling (1982) revives and extends the marginalist version of mark-up pricing theory from Kalecki (1938) to explicitly incorporate the modelling of oligopolistic interaction and thereby provide a theoretical framework for empirically examining long-run influences on the degree of monopoly, which can be used to consider the consequences for income distribution. Here, the price elasticity of market demand and a parameter for oligopolistic conjectures replace the firm's perceived price elasticity of demand as determinants of the size of the mark-up required to maximise profits. Whether the mark-up set by any firm is actually equal to the profit-maximising level and whether it remains so in the face of fluctuations in demand are treated as empirical, rather than theoretical, questions.

As regards full-cost price theory, Hall and Hitch (1939) suggest the standard case of an industry is an admixture of monopolistic competition and oligopoly. There is a lower limit to the price set by any firm, which is the profit-maximising price for firms acting independently, as in Chamberlin's (1933) pure model of monopolistic competition, and also a higher limit to the price, which is the joint monopoly profit-maximising price. They then state,

> The height of price (between the two limits) is determined on the "full cost" principle, conditioned by such historical accidents as (*a*) the size and efficiency of the firms in the industry at the time price stability was achieved, and (*b*) the extent of their optimism and of their fear of potential competitors as measured by the percentage addition for profits. Once this price has been fixed price competition, except in highly abnormal circumstances, ceases. Profits are reduced to normal, if at all, by an influx of firms which raises costs by reducing output per firm (increasing "excess capacity") or by competition in quality and marketing.
>
> (Hall and Hitch, 1939, p. 30)

Thus, a wide range of prices is consistent with the full-cost pricing principle, but the range is no wider than that left by profit-maximising theory prior to specifying the unobservable assumptions firms make about the reactions of rivals to changes in their own prices.

In perfectly competitive Walrasian equilibrium, competitive pressure constrains profit-maximising behaviour in the long run such that price converges on unit cost, at least in the case of industries with free entry and exit of firms. Economic profit disappears and firms earn a "normal" rate of return on their invested capital. This outcome becomes indistinguishable from that in the full-cost price theory in Equation (8.7) provided that (1) all firms are operating at the same least cost level for unit cost and the capital-cost ratio and (2) the rate of return, r, is equal to the normal rate of return. Likewise, a difference from the Kaleckian version of mark-up price theory occurs only to the extent the latter theory provides for the possibility that monopoly power may remain even in the long run and exert an upward influence on price. However, with high cost-to-capital ratios (low capital intensity) even large differences in rate of return generally translate into small differences in price, meaning that even allowing for monopoly power in any of the theories is unlikely to have large implications for the level of prices in the long run.

Correspondences across theories of the sort identified above, particularly in the overlap in forces behind the determination of prices in the long run, helps to explain much of the confused debate between proponents of the various theories. Each of the theories is able to explain a wide range of outcomes by appropriate choice of parameter values or auxiliary assumptions. When empirical outcomes lie within a range consistent with each theory, empirical evidence does not provide a basis for choosing between the theories. More generally, choosing between theories on the basis of empirical tests faces the limits pointed out by Karl Popper (1963) that such tests can at best provide refutation (usually only with a probabilistic degree of confidence) and can never prove the truth of a theory.

Schumpeter expresses great admiration for the scientific approach of the Walrasian system, which links activity throughout the economy by use of assumptions of individual optimisation and market equilibrium. He chooses to use this system as the foundation for his departure into the analysis of innovation-driven development. This leaves his analysis with the defects pointed to by Oakley (1990) (lacking a traverse from disruptive innovation to equilibrium), Metcalfe (1998) (equilibrium is incompatible with maintaining evolutionary potential as an emergent property of the economy) and Andersen (2012) (lacking a micro-evolutionary analysis consistent with his macro-evolutionary analysis). Post-Keynesian price theories provide an approach to modelling firm pricing behaviour that can avoid these defects while still incorporating Schumpeter's other insights into the impact of innovation-driven development on pricing.

Importantly, prices at the firm level are determined in both full-cost and mark-up price theory without requiring market equilibrium. Bloch and Metcalfe (2017) argue this means the theories can be applied when markets are orderly in the sense suggested by Nelson (2013) or when markets are disrupted by innovation, which provides continuity in analysing the evolutionary process of structural change following on from innovation. If each firm sets its own price using constant pricing parameters and based on normal output as in Equation (8.1) for mark-up pricing, Equation (8.4) for full-cost pricing based on unit direct cost or Equation (8.7) for full-cost pricing based on unit total cost, the average industry price changes directly only when input prices change or when there is differential growth by firms with differing pricing parameters or unit costs. Demand shifts don't directly impact on prices at the firm or industry level. Alternatively, when post-Keynesian price theories incorporate price leadership as a mechanism for coordination across heterogeneous firms, it is only changes in input prices paid by the price leader that directly affect industry price assuming no change in the price leader.

In place of determining price by the balancing of supply and demand, post-Keynesian theories rely on the application of pricing rules with constant parameters. These rules are then the subject of strategic decisions made by the firm along with decisions about other aspects of firm behaviour, such as advertising, research and development and investment in productive capacity. The firm reacts in a multi-dimensional way to its environment but without the assumptions of perfect information and foresight that characterise neoclassical analyses of firm behaviour. Creative responses to the firm's environment are possible as well as adaptive responses. Also, history can, and usually does, matter. All of this is compatible with and conducive to the analysis of innovation and creative destruction, which supports using post-Keynesian price theories for analysing firm strategy in the meso-level analysis of differential firm growth and the evolution of industry structure in the next section.

Innovation and creative destruction (meso analysis)

In the Commentary section of Chapter 4, I use Sraffa's reproduction cost framework to formalise the determination of theoretical normal prices for a stationary economy and then use this formalisation as the starting point for a critical discussion of Schumpeter's price theory. In Chapter 7, I present an alternative approach to determining theoretical normal prices for a developing economy, which leads to price determination according to Equation (7.3), repeated here as Equation (8.10).

$$\mathbf{P_N} = \Psi_N \mathbf{c_N} = ((\mathbf{I} - \Psi_N \mathbf{A_N})^{-1} \Psi_N \gamma_N) w_N, \qquad \Psi_N > \mathbf{I} \qquad (8.10)$$

In this section, I start from this equation to analyse the movement of prices and corresponding structural changes that occur with the process of innovation and creative destruction.

The introduction of innovations and their diffusion through creative destruction alter the relationships among firms within industries and the relationships between industries. Meso-level analysis of structure and structural change due to the innovation process provides the linkages between changes in microeconomic behaviour and macroeconomic performance. As Kurt Dopfer (2007, p. 75) notes, 'In the Schumpeterian programme, meso is central. Meso serves as both structural component and as process component, explaining generic structure and generic change.'

My analysis of price movements emphasises the adjustment process within an industry rather than across industries. The interaction caused by innovation and creative destruction is strongest across a group of firms selling related products or using related production processes. This analysis combines the post-Keynesian pricing rules discussed above with the industry dynamics from the section on differential firm growth in Chapter 7. Industry structure changes due to differential firm growth and this impacts on pricing rules to provide the meso trajectory of dynamic competition.

Rather than distinguish periods by a time subscript as in Chapter 4, I now distinguish in terms of phases of the cycle of innovation and creative destruction. N denotes the normal period values prevailing when innovation is at low ebb, past innovations having been largely diffused and no new innovations occurring. U denotes the period of the introduction and initial spread of the innovation through growth of the entrepreneurial firm and early imitators, while D denotes the period of domination of the innovation through further imitation and creative destruction. For innovations that occur in clusters, the subscripts correspond roughly to the normal, upswing and downswing periods in Schumpeter's two-phase business cycle.[6] The depression and recovery phases of Schumpeter's four-phase cycle don't relate directly to the process of innovation and creative destruction within industries and are left to consideration with the macro analysis in the next section.

As in the Commentary section of Chapter 4, I first use the example of a labour-saving innovation. Later, I generalise by considering other forms of innovation mentioned by Schumpeter. In the stationary state discussed in Chapter 4, all established firms use best-practice technology. However, the discussion in Chapter 7 of norms for a developing economy suggests that some residual variation in technique across firms may be consistent with a developing economy in its "normal" state.

To accommodate variation in technical coefficients across firms, the elements of $\mathbf{A}_N$ and γ_N in Equation (8.10) are expressed as weighted averages of the individual firm coefficients with weights equal to shares of industry output as follows:

$$a_{ik,N} = \sum_{j=1}^{n} a_{ik,j,N}(x_{i,j,N} / \sum_{j=1}^{n} x_{i,j,N}), \tag{8.11a}$$

$$\gamma_{i,N} = \sum_{j=1}^{n} \gamma_{i,j,N}(x_{i,j,N} / \sum_{j=1}^{n} x_{i,j,N}), \tag{8.11b}$$

There may also be variation in the price-cost ratios across firms either to offset variation in technical coefficients when there is price leadership or as residual elements representing the incomplete convergence to standard pricing practices across firms, which means diagonal elements of $\mathbf{\Psi}_N$ are also weighted averages,

$$\Psi_{i,N} = \sum_{j=1}^{n} \Psi_{i,j,N}(x_{i,j,N} / \sum_{j=1}^{n} x_{i,j,N}), \tag{8.12}$$

With this notation in place, the meso-level analysis of the impact of innovation and creative destruction proceeds by tracking the movements in values of technical coefficients, price-cost ratios and prices starting from theoretical normal values. The entrepreneurial firm, e, that introduces the labour-saving innovation into the production of commodity i has lower labour requirements per unit of output than those of any established firm, $\gamma_{i,e,NT} < \gamma_{i,j,N}$, for all j established firms. Note the labour requirement of the entrepreneurial firm is for the new technology, NT, while the established firms remain with the old technology of the "normal" starting point, N. Innovation-driven business cycles for Schumpeter are disequilibrium processes with a mix of technologies leading to competition and structural change. Analysis of these processes here simplifies by focussing on the mixing of technologies within a single industry.

In post-Keynesian price theories, cost heterogeneity generally leads to price leadership and there is also generally a pursuit of price stability, which suggests that following the innovation one or more of the established firms act as price leader. The leader sets price by applying a pricing rule that has prices rising only in response to changes in input prices, which generally have similar impact on all firms. This scenario is attractive to both the entrant and the established firms as compared to a price reduction by the price leader. The entrant is able to operate at full capacity and earn higher profits than with a price reduction, while the established firms cede sales on which they make no greater than normal profit to avoid losses they would otherwise incur from reducing price.[7]

If this price leadership scenario stays intact throughout the upswing phase, the price for all firms remains at its original theoretical normal level and the price-cost ratio for the entrepreneurial firm exceeds the average price-cost ratio of the established firms in inverse proportion to the ratio of their respective labour requirements,

$$\Psi_{i,e,U} = 1 + \pi_{i,e,U} = (\gamma_{i,N} / \gamma_{i,e,NT})(\Psi'_{i,N}) > \Psi_{i,N} = (1 + \pi_{i,N}) \tag{8.13}$$

where the U subscript is used to denote a price-cost ratio and margin specific to the circumstances of the upswing. The entrepreneurial firm's price-cost ratio in Equation (8.13) contains a margin, $\pi_{i,e,U}$, that exceeds the normal margin, $\pi_{i,N}$, thereby providing the entrepreneurial profits central to Schumpeter's theory of innovation-driven development. Still, price stability is maintained through price leadership of established firms, with the reduction in labour requirements for the entrepreneurial firm offset by a proportional increase in the firm's price-cost ratio. Markets remain orderly in Nelson's (2013) sense that most buyers and sellers are able to complete satisfactory transactions and, given the likely constraints on the expansion of the entrepreneurial firm, this order can remain for some time in spite of the heterogeneity in firm productivity and unit cost.[8]

As discussed in Chapter 7, Steindl (1976 [1952]) provides a theory of industry concentration through differential firm growth when firms have heterogeneous unit costs and corresponding profit differentials. Steindl's theory follows post-Keynesian price theory in that he emphasises price stability and price leadership, so adjustment to disruption from innovation occurs in the first instance through changes in capacity utilisation rather than price. Steindl starts with a rigid price above the unit cost of the lowest cost firms. He then works out the implications of the capacity expansion of the progressive (low-cost) firms through their internal accumulation (the investment of retained earnings while maintaining a constant debt-to-equity ratio).[9]

Steindl argues prices remain stable as long as the growth of capacity across all of the firms remains reasonably consistent with the rate of expansion of the market. There is still relative expansion of the progressive firms provided their rate of internal accumulation exceeds the rate of market expansion, which is surely the case when entrepreneurial firms have introduced major cost-reducing innovations.[10] Denoting the average labour requirement across all firms producing commodity i during this period of stable prices as $\gamma_{i,U}$, and applying Equation (8.11b) yields

$$\gamma_{i,U} = \sum_{j=1}^{n} \gamma_{i,j,N}(x_{i,j} / (\sum_{j=1}^{n} x_{i,j} + x_{i,e})) + \gamma_{i,e,NT}(x_{i,e} / (\sum_{j=1}^{n} x_{i,j} + x_{i,e})), \tag{8.14}$$

Where $x_{i,j}$ is the output of an established firm and $x_{i,e}$ is the output of the entrepreneurial firm.

The corresponding average price-cost ratio is

$$\Psi_{i,U} = \sum_{j=1}^{n} \Psi_{i,j,N}(x_{i,j} / (\sum_{j=1}^{n} x_{i,j} + x_{i,e})) + \Psi_{i,e,U}(x_{i,e} / (\sum_{j=1}^{n} x_{i,j} + x_{i,e})), \tag{8.15}$$

With the relative expansion of the entrepreneurial firm, the last term in parentheses in Equations (8.14) and (8.15), which represents the market share of the entrepreneurial firm, is growing. The expanding market share of the entrepreneurial firm lowers the average labour requirements below the prior normal level, $\gamma_{i,N}$, for the industry and correspondingly raises the average price-cost margin above $\Psi_{i,N}$. Yet, for the economy as a whole there is no change in the price level or the price system, with

$$P_N = P_U = \Psi_U c_U = (I - \Psi_U A_N)^{-1} \Psi_U \gamma_U) w_N,$$
$$\gamma_U < \gamma_N, \Psi_U > \Psi_N > I \tag{8.16}$$

If many industries are experiencing innovations simultaneously as in Schumpeter's clustering of innovations, there may be implications for the prices of the means of production (in this case the wage rate for the single homogenous primary input of labour) but these are considered in the next section on macro analysis.

With the average price-cost ratio in the ith industry exceeding the normal level in Equation (8.16), the average margin added to unit cost, $\pi_{i,U}$, exceeds the normal price-cost margin, $\pi_{i,N}$, and is more than sufficient to finance capacity expansion in line with market growth. Growth by the entrepreneurial firm is a cumulative process, as the higher the share of the entrepreneurial firm the higher is the industry average price-cost ratio and the greater is the rate of capacity expansion for the industry as a whole. Eventually excess capacity emerges in the industry, which may be aggravated by the entry of imitators and the conversion of established firms to the new technology. While initially the established firms accept the burden of excess capacity to maintain price stability and market order, the situation is dynamically unstable.

Steindl argues accumulation of unutilised capacity beyond desired levels eventually leads to aggressive price or selling competition. This may be initiated by high-cost firms with excess capacity and falling market shares or by low-cost firms pursuing sales growth in line with their relatively fast capacity expansion. In any event, a drop in the average rate of return on capital across the industry is necessary to reduce the rate of expansion of capacity and bring it in line with the exogenously determined rate of expansion of the market.[11]

In terms of the adapted Sraffian framework, aggressive competition reduces the average margin of price over cost from the level associated with price stability in the upswing of the cycle, $\pi_{i,U}$, to a new lower level, $\pi_{i,D}$. Downward pressure on the margin continues until the margin is in line with the requirements for financing capacity growth equal to the growth of the market. This may still involve price leadership with the margins of the entrepreneurial firm and the established firms falling proportionally or it may involve a greater decline for the entrepreneurial firm (and its imitators) as they move to attract customers from the established firms. In terms of the revised Sraffian framework, the reduction in industry average price-cost margin means that the reduction in average labour requirements is no longer fully offset by higher price-cost margins, so that prices in the ith industry decline as does the price vector for the full economy, with

$$\mathbf{P_U} > \mathbf{P_D} = \psi_D \mathbf{c}_D = ((\mathbf{I} - \psi_D \mathbf{A_N})^{-1} \psi_D \gamma_D) w_N, \quad \gamma_D < \gamma_U, \psi_D \leq \psi_U \qquad (8.17)$$

In addition to being linked to the downswing phase of Schumpeter's business cycle, the subscript D on the price-cost margin also stands for disorder. Once price stability is abandoned, there is no clear focal point for prices in the market. The heterogeneity of unit cost, profits and growth rates across firms combined with a likely unevenness in the distribution of excess capacity undermines the common interests of sellers. Price leaders may emerge to provide some degree of coordination, but any leadership position is susceptible to challenge from firms whose administered processes lead to a lower preferred price. Instability in prices with a downward bias is likely for a substantial period and overreaction means the original normal price-cost margin for the industry, $\pi_{i,N}$, may not provide a lower bound. The market is disorderly in the sense that many sellers are in the position of having levels of unutilised capacity well above desired levels, while buyers are faced with unstable prices.

Susceptibility to outbursts of aggressive competition continues as long as $\pi_{i,D}$ remains above the level required to finance capacity expansion equal to the growth of market demand, which may continue for some time. As $\pi_{i,D}$ falls, the price obtainable by the non-reforming established firms falls below their normal unit cost, at which point they are unable to finance replacement investment or repay debt. Further declines in $\pi_{i,D}$ then bring the obtainable price below their

shutdown level of operating unit cost. The absolute decline and eventual elimination of these non-reforming established firms increases the level of $\pi_{i,D}$ as the
weights of high-cost firms are declining, thereby prolonging the period over
which $\pi_{i,D}$ remains above $\pi_{i,N}$. This struggle for growth by the entrepreneurial
firm and imitators alongside the struggle for survival by the established firms is
the phase of diffusion of the innovation that Schumpeter captures so aptly in the
phrase, creative destruction.[12]

In Steindl's analysis, the reduction in output from the highest cost producers
followed by their elimination implies absolute concentration of the industry. As
the industry concentrates and the share of high-cost firms shrinks, surviving firms
recognise their common interests and desist from further expanding capacity
beyond what is required to maintain their desired capacity utilisation ratio. This
condition, which Steindl refers to as industry maturity, allows a restoration of
price stability under the leadership of the low-cost firms.

Steindl suggests the process of absolute concentration stops before all firms
with higher costs are driven from the market, at which point the average labour
requirement for the industry remains above the best-practice level.[13] Correspondingly, the level at which price is stabilised remains above the lowest obtainable
unit cost. There remains an element of profit due to imperfect competition, but
the profit is not sufficient to attract entry or induce any of the surviving firms to
aggressively compete and thereby upset the price stability.[14]

The average price-cost margin prevailing during the phase of industry maturity
represents a new normal for the industry and is denoted as $\pi_{i,NN}$, with the extra N
here indicating that it is a new normal. The new normal margin may be higher,
lower or equal to the old normal level, $\pi_{i,N}$, depending on the evolution of the
threat of obsolescence, financing needs and imperfection of competition. However, the margin is low enough that the resulting price-cost ratio, $\Psi_{i,NN}$, rises by a
smaller proportion than the reduction in unit cost from the original innovation, so

$$\mathbf{P_N} > \mathbf{P_{NN}} = \Psi_{NN}\mathbf{c_{NN}} = ((\mathbf{I} - \Psi_{NN}\mathbf{A_N})^{-1}\Psi_{NN}\gamma_{NN})\mathbf{w_N},$$
$$\gamma_{NN} < \gamma_N, \Psi_{NN} < \Psi_N(\gamma_N / \gamma_{NN}) \tag{8.18}$$

Otherwise, the unstable circumstances of the aggressive competition of the downswing continue. Schumpeter's conclusion that the process of innovation and
creative destruction imparts a downward bias to prices over the course of the
business cycle remains safe, at least for the case of labour-saving process innovation in a single industry.

An alternative to assuming the pattern of pricing behaviour in Steindl's analysis
is to assume firms continually set prices low enough to fully utilise their productive capacity. As discussed in Chapter 7, this is the scenario analysed in the theory
of industry evolution as a replicator process with differential firm growth. Firms
grow or decline in proportion to their current profits or losses, much as in Steindl's
theory. Also as in Steindl, when innovation leads to cost differences across firms,

low-cost entrepreneurial firms expand relative to the high-cost established firms based on their higher profit rates and greater ability to finance expansion of production capacity, which implies a growing share of low-cost firms and a rising rate of growth of industry capacity that eventually exceeds the rate of growth of the market.

Setting price to maintain the balance between sales and productive capacity for each firm yields a different price movement over time from Steindl's theory and this has implications for industry profitability and growth as well as for excess capacity. Rather than prices remaining stable with price leadership as in Steindl's theory, average price decreases as soon as the growth of industry capacity equals the growth of the market. Competitive pressure is continuous rather than being at least temporarily suppressed through the build-up of excess capacity. Accordingly, the industry average price-cost margin is lower than in Steindl's analysis, which leads to slower growth of industry productive capacity. Indeed, the average price-cost margin rises above the normal level, $\pi_{i,N}$, only to the extent that falling prices or increasing selling effort increases the rate of growth of industry sales. The combination of a slower growth of productive capacity and a faster growth of sales ensures that the utilisation of productive capacity remains at the desired level.

Metcalfe (1998) shows that, without increased selling effort and other complicating factors, the rate of price decrease for balancing industry sales growth with industry capacity expansion follows Fisher's Principle and is proportional to the variance in unit cost across firms. In the example of the introduction of a labour-saving innovation by a single entrepreneurial firm, the variance of unit cost across firms initially is low because the entrepreneurial firm share is low, so following Fisher's Principle, there is initially a low rate of decrease in average industry price. The rate of price decline rises as the entrepreneurial firm's market share rises, which implies the rate of industry average price decrease is accelerating. However, as the entrepreneurial firm and imitators move towards a dominant market share with the decline and eventual elimination of high-cost firms, the variance of unit cost reaches a maximum and then continually declines, which implies a deceleration in the rate of average price decrease for the industry.

There are up, down and stabilising phases in the industry average price-cost margin in Metcalfe's analysis, which can be separated using $\pi_{i,U}$, $\pi_{i,D}$ and $\pi_{i,NN}$ following the approach applied to Steindl's analysis. However, the industry average price-cost margin is lower in each phase than in Steindl's theory. Price stability in Steindl's theory as compared to price decreases in Metcalfe's theory implies that $\pi_{i,U}$ is higher and rises faster with Steindl, both because price is higher for all firms and because the expansion of capacity by low-cost firms is greater. This also implies that $\pi_{i,D}$ starts higher but is prone to sharp declines relative to the steadily falling value in Metcalfe's theory. Finally, $\pi_{i,NN}$ is higher in Steindl's theory given the element of imperfect competition when the industry reaches maturity and firms behave cooperatively maintaining excess capacity, which compares to the assumptions of continued reinvestment of profits in expanding capacity and the balanced growth of productive capacity and demand in Metcalfe's theory.

The timing of the transition between the phases of rising, falling and stabilising price-cost margins also differs between the theories. In Steindl's theory the upswing ends when rising excess capacity or other factors trigger a breakdown in cooperative pricing behaviour, leading to a phase of erratically declining price-cost margin after which the price-cost margin stabilises at a new normal level when cooperation returns. In Metcalfe's theory the upswing ends when the variance of unit cost is at a maximum, while the price-cost margin stabilises when the variance of unit cost is at low ebb. Transitions in Metcalfe's theory are determined solely by the differential growth of firms with heterogeneous levels of unit cost, whereas Steindl requires a change in pricing strategy by leading firms. The link between the two theories is through the process of differential firm growth based on internal accumulation, which means in both theories low-cost firms are the leading firms and their pricing is impacted by the growth of their productive capacity relative to the market.[15]

The theories of Steindl and Metcalfe apply more broadly to the meso analysis of the impact of innovation than just to the example of a labour-saving process innovation. In addition to saving labour, innovations may save on intermediate inputs (including capital equipment). Suppose an innovation reduces intermediate inputs used in the production process of the ith commodity, so that $a_{ik,e,NT} < a_{ik,j,N}$. The analysis of the impact on unit cost, price-cost margins and prices in the industry using the input proceeds much the same as with the example of a labour-saving innovation, except that a variant of Equation (8.11a) is used in working out the impact of differential firm growth on industry average intermediate input requirements in place of the variant of Equation (8.11b) given in Equation (8.14) for working out the impact on industry average labour requirements. The impact on industry average price-cost margins then follows in parallel to the analysis using Equation (8.15) for working out the impact of a labour-saving innovation.

One important difference between an innovation-saving intermediate input and one saving labour is that a reduction in use of intermediate input necessarily involves more than a single industry. The industry that produces the input faces changed demand conditions, with the impact negative or positive depending on how much the output of the using industry expands. As variations in industry demand have no direct impact on prices in post-Keynesian pricing theories, there is no basis in these theories for expecting immediate price changes in the industry producing the intermediate input. However, to the extent that direct costs of production fall in the using industry, an immediate fall in the price of those products is expected unless there is price rigidity at the original "normal" price.

Innovations affecting the productivity of an intermediate input can have quite broad impact in the economy, as in the example of computers. Indeed, historians and long-wave theorists have pointed to examples of innovations in intermediate inputs, such as steel and steam engines as well as computers, as representing new general purpose technologies (see, for example, Lipsey, et al., 2005). Introduction of such technologies provides a technological explanation for the appearance of the clusters of innovations that Schumpeter associates with waves of entrepreneurial activity. Of course, the timing of the introduction and spread of a general purpose technology may still depend on the restoration of normal business conditions at the end of the Kondratieff business cycle.

Process innovations that save on labour or intermediate input are examples of the case of new methods of production included by Schumpeter (1961 [1934], p. 66) in the list of five cases of innovations covered by his concept of economic development. Another case in this list is the development of new sources of supply of raw materials. In terms of the Sraffian framework, raw materials are themselves produced means of production. Each raw material has its price included as an element of the price vector, $\mathbf{p}$, its technical requirements for other commodities as inputs included as a row in the matrix, $\mathbf{A}$, its labour requirements as an element in the vector, γ, and its price-cost ratio as a diagonal element of Ψ. If a new source of supply represents a reduction in the labour or technical coefficients in the production structure, then its impact on price-cost ratios and prices can be analysed as above.

Another aspect of opening up of new sources of supply of raw materials is greater availability of primary inputs used in the production of the raw materials. Prominent in the historical examples of new sources of supply of raw materials Schumpeter refers to in *BC* are the opening up of new lands, such as the American west or Argentina as sources of supply of agricultural products to the rest of the world (Schumpeter, 1939, pp. 319–20). Also mentioned are discoveries of new mineral deposits, such as copper deposits in Arizona and Montana (Schumpeter, 1939, p. 423).

Including innovations that affect the availability of primary inputs in the meso analysis is best handled through modification of the Sraffian framework to include multiple primary inputs. Extension of the Sraffian framework to include land or natural resource deposits used as primary inputs in the production of raw materials or to include multiple types of labour (for example, agricultural versus industrial) is straightforward. In place of the single vector, γ, of primary input, there is a matrix, Γ, with each column of the matrix representing a different primary input and corresponding to the single input price there is a vector of input prices, $\mathbf{w}$, with an element for each column of the Γ matrix. The matrix of input-output coefficients, $\mathbf{A}$, and the matrix of price-cost ratios, Ψ, aren't directly affected.

When the new source of supply of a raw material leads to lower prices for the primary inputs used in production of that raw material, the price of the raw material falls as do other commodity prices to the extent that the raw material is used in their own production process or in the processes used to produce any of their intermediate inputs. The impact of this type of innovation in terms of the Sraffian framework involves an eventual move to a new normal in which technical relationships and price-cost ratios remain unchanged and commodity prices are reduced in relation to their direct and indirect use of the primary input, with

$$\mathbf{P_N} > \mathbf{P_{NN}} = \psi_{NN}\mathbf{c_{NN}} = ((\mathbf{I} - \psi_N\mathbf{A_N})^{-1}\psi_N\Gamma_N)\mathbf{w_{NN}}, \quad \mathbf{w_{NN}} < \mathbf{w_N} \qquad (8.19)$$

Where $\mathbf{w_{NN}}$ is the vector of prices of primary inputs after the introduction of a new source of supply for the kth input reduces its price so that $w_{k,NN} < w_{k,N}$. The adjustment of the input price occurs over a period of time related to the need for investment in production capacity, transport and distribution systems, but the adjustment process in primary production need not follow the same cyclical process as for industrial production. The timing and path of the price adjustments is not further considered here.[16]

At the head of Schumpeter's list of cases of innovation in *TED* is the introduction of new products. Incorporating new products into the Sraffian framework involves extending the dimensions of the input-output matrix, $\mathbf{A}$.[17] An extra row for each new product gives its requirements for intermediate inputs and an extra column gives the amount of the new product used in other products (all equal zero if the new product is solely a consumer good). There is also an extra element in the vector of labour requirements, γ, which gives the labour requirement per unit of output for the new product, an extra diagonal element in the matrix, $\mathbf{\Psi}$, which gives the price-cost ratio for the new product, and an extra element in the price vector, $\mathbf{p}$, for the price of the new product.

As production of the new product constitutes a new industry, meso-level analysis based on theories of differential growth of firms within an industry, such as those of Steindl and Metcalfe, doesn't apply. Rather, the meso-level analysis proceeds in terms of the evolution of the structure of the economy rather than the structure of the industry. Differential firm growth still is at the heart of the analysis, but it is growth of the innovating firm and its imitators relative to the rest of the economy that is of interest.

If the new product yields entrepreneurial profit in Schumpeter's sense of a super-normal return, its price exceeds its reproduction cost by more than in comparable industries. To keep the analysis straightforward, assume that in the upswing of the new industry the price-cost ratio for the new product, z, exceeds that of all other products being sold at their theoretical normal prices, $\Psi_{Z,U} > \Psi_{j,N}$ for all $j \neq z$. The higher price-cost ratio in the z industry provides for faster growth of production capacity than for non-innovating industries. As a result, the average price-cost ratio in the economy grows much as the price-cost ratio for an industry experiencing innovation in production technology grows with the rising output share of the innovating firm. However, there is no direct comparison of price vectors $\mathbf{p}_N$ and $\mathbf{p}_U$, as occurs in Equation (8.16), for the introduction of the new product $\mathbf{p}_U$ contains an extra element, the price of z, that is not present in $\mathbf{p}_N$.

In place of theories of differential firm growth within an industry, theories of industry life cycle provide guidance as to the pattern of diffusion of the new product through creative destruction. As noted in the section 'Firm Heterogeneity, Industry Maturity and the Business Cycle', in Chapter 7, the first stage of the industry life cycle according to Klepper (1997) is characterised by an initially low volume of output, high rates of entry of new firms and challenges to product design. This initial stage includes the upswing phase for the price-cost ratio of the industry with the high value of $\Psi_{Z,U}$, yielding the profit that attracts entry and finances a high rate of expansion for firms with desirable product designs.

In the second stage of the industry life cycle, output growth is high, product design stabilises and a shakeout of firms occurs. This is a characterisation of aggressive competition and suggests a fall in the price-cost ratio of the leading firms, which encourages high growth in their sales to meet the rapid expansion of their productive capacity and also leads to the elimination of marginal firms. As with the analysis of differential firm growth within an industry, the falling price-cost ratio for leading firms eventually lowers the average price-cost ratio for the industry in spite of the offsetting impact of the elimination of marginal, presumably low price-cost ratio, firms. The decline in the average price-cost ratio for the new product z, that is $\Psi_{Z,D} < \Psi_{Z,U}$, implies a decline in the overall price vector, $\mathbf{p}_D < \mathbf{p}_U$, given that technology, input prices and price-cost ratios for other products remain constant.[18]

The third and final stage of the industry life cycle is characterised by slowing output growth, reduced entry and stabilising market shares. The price-cost ratio for this new normal, $\Psi_{Z,NN}$, can be higher, lower or equal to $\Psi_{Z,D}$. If, as in Metcalfe's analysis, the reduction in growth means a lower financing requirement for expanding productive capacity, the price-cost ratio may be below that occurring during the downswing stage. However, if firms refrain from expanding production capacity beyond the growth of the market as in Steindl's analysis, the price-cost ratio may stabilise at a level above that occurring in the downswing. In either case, this stage of industry maturity has reduced heterogeneity among firms and less pressure for further creative destruction, so it can be considered to represent a new theoretical normal for the industry.

Ambiguity regarding the comparison of the new normal price-cost ratio to its downswing value means there is no clear implication for new product industries contributing to a further decline in prices beyond that achieved in passing from the upswing phase to the downswing phase. It is also not possible to make any general inference about the contribution of the new product to the result trend in price movements over the full cycle, as the new product only comes into existence and impacts on aggregate prices during the cycle. Nonetheless, new products are often essential elements in the transformation of technologies that have massive impact on costs across the whole economy, as with the examples of steel, electric motors and computers.[19] Inability to generalise at the theoretical level clearly doesn't imply insignificance at the practical level. Rather, the impact of new products on the price level is necessarily an object for historical study.

The final item in Schumpeter's list of cases of innovation in *TED* is carrying out a new organisation of an industry, with the example given of creating or destroying a monopoly position. In *BC*, the related case of setting up new business organisations is added, with department stores as an example. If the new modes of organisation involve the introduction of new products, production methods or sources of supply, this aspect of their impact can be analysed in the same way as is done above for these cases separately.

To the extent that innovations in mode of organisation affect product market relationships, rather than products, technical conditions of production or input prices, their impact in terms of the Sraffian framework is limited to changes in the price-cost ratio. For the innovation to be attractive to the entrepreneurial firm, the firm's price-cost ratio exceeds the normal level, $\Psi_{i,e,U} > \Psi_{i,N}$. A similar condition applies to another of Schumpeter's cases of innovation, that of entering a new market, where the entry is attractive to the entrepreneurial firm if $\Psi_{i,e,U} > \Psi_{j,N}$, for all $j \neq i$. Both cases parallel the relationship in Equation (8.13) for the case of a labour-saving technical change, except there is no offsetting change in labour requirements and, accordingly, $p_U > p_N$ rather than $p_U = p_N$.

Beyond the initial period of the introduction of a new mode of business organisation, the impact of such innovations is not subject to analysis in a way comparable to process or product innovations. Changes in market relationships don't easily fit into the analysis of price determination with differential firm growth applied to those categories of innovations. They may instead lead directly to a new normal for the industry, much as in the case of new sources of supply leading to lower prices for primary inputs. However, rather than pushing product prices down as occurs with $w_{k,NN} < w_{k,N}$, a one-off rise in the price-cost ratio with $\Psi_{i,NN} = \Psi_{i,e,U} > \Psi_{i,N}$ implies a positive impact on the new normal price vector compared to the original. Alternatively, a process of creative destruction may occur driving down the price-cost ratio back toward the original normal level, so $\Psi_{i,NN} \leq \Psi_{i,D} < \Psi_{i,e,U} > \Psi_{i,N}$, which implies an ambiguous impact on prices in the new normal versus the original normal.

Schumpeter is clearly aware that achieving entrepreneurial profit from innovations in business organisation depends on creating a wedge between price and cost. Yet, he carefully avoids acknowledging that price might rise without any change in unit cost. In *TED* when discussing of 'the introduction of large-scale manufacturing businesses into an economic system in which they were previously unknown' (Schumpeter, 1961 (1934), p. 133), he considers as an innovation 'the aim of which is to produce a unit of product with less expense and thus create a discrepancy between their existing price and their new costs' (ibid.). No consideration is given to the possibility that price might rise without any change in cost.

Developments in business organisation feature prominently in Schumpeter's discussion of monopolistic practices in *CSD*. Here, Schumpeter acknowledges price is above unit cost without insisting the gap is due to a reduction in cost. However, he still argues,

> There cannot be any reasonable doubt that under the conditions of our epoch such superiority is as a matter of fact the outstanding feature of the typical large-scale unit of control, though mere size is neither necessary nor sufficient for it. These units not only arise in the process of creative destruction and function in a way entirely different from the static schema, but in many cases of decisive importance they provide the necessary form for the achievement. They largely create what they exploit.
>
> (Schumpeter, 1976 [1950], p. 101)

As noted in Chapter 6, Schumpeter goes on to reach the conclusion that in the context of the modern epoch, 'perfect competition is not only impossible but inferior' (op. cit., p. 106).

Schumpeter's view is clearly that innovations in the mode of organisation of business have been beneficial, whether or not they lead to reduced product prices over the course of the introduction and diffusion of the innovation. Others have not seen these innovations as so benign. For example, in discussing the role of the modern large-scale corporation, Baran and Sweezy (1966, p. 82) suggest that, 'Schumpeter's perennial gale of creative destruction has subsided into an occasional mild breeze.' Their view is that profit margins have a secular tendency to rise due to the domination of economic activity by a few large corporations, which contributes to an upward secular trend for prices set by these firms.

In his speculation about the future of capitalism in *CSD*, Schumpeter accepts the force of entrepreneurship and creative destruction is undermined by the modern large-scale enterprise.

> Since capitalist enterprise, by its very achievements, tends to automatize progress, we conclude that it tends to make itself superfluous – to break to pieces under the pressure of its own success. The perfectly bureaucratized giant industrial unit not only ousts the small or medium sized firm and "expropriates" its owners, but in the end it also ousts the entrepreneur
>
> (Schumpeter, 1976 [1950], p. 134)

While entrepreneurs and creative destruction seemed to have survived so far, there has also been a rising share of industrial output contributed by large corporations, now mostly multinational in focus. The effect is a tendency to increase the average price-cost ratio over the world economy to the extent that these large industrial corporations depend on higher than average price-cost ratios to fund their research and development laboratories, marketing and advertising expenditures and centralised administration. Whether there is an offsetting trend in production cost is a question for historical examination.

Overall, the meso analysis of the various cases of innovation suggests that during the upswing phase following the introduction of innovations the impact on price determination in directly affected industries is small and the direction ambiguous. In the case of process innovations, the application of post-Keynesian price theory suggests price leadership keeps prices stable, while with market-clearing prices there is downward movement in prices from the start but the initial rate of decline is low. No direct comparison of prices before and after innovation is possible in the case of new products, as the new product doesn't enter into the original price vector. New sources of supply of primary inputs may lead to lower product prices, especially if the new sources are generally available to producers rather than only a single producer, but the full impact requires investments in production capacity, transport and distribution systems that take time. On the other hand, innovations in business organisation might, at least initially, lead to increased prices. Thus, stable, falling or rising prices within an industry during the upswing phase are possible and the impact of a cluster of innovations on the price vector for the whole economy depends very much on the mix of innovations.

Substantial downward pressure on prices in directly affected industries occurs for most cases of innovations discussed above as the diffusion process gathers pace in the downswing phase. This is clearly the case for process innovations in the post-Keynesian analysis of Steindl (1976 [1952]), with aggressive price competition ensuing only after the accumulation of substantial unutilised capacity in the industry. In Metcalfe's analysis of differential firm growth applied to cost heterogeneity resulting from process innovations, the rate of price decrease reaches a maximum when the low-cost entrepreneurial firm and its imitators have grown substantially, such that the variance of firm size is at a maximum. In the case of new product innovations, price declines also occur only after a period of price stability and can accelerate substantially if the production process for the new product requires less input as the design characteristics stabilise and there is learning by doing or supplemental process innovations. The cases of new sources of inputs and innovations in business organisation are less clear, but the decline in input prices from a new source can extend substantially beyond the initial period and there are certainly examples of substantial price reductions with the diffusion of innovations in business organisation, such as with department stores and supermarkets.

Comparing the prices in the original theoretical norm to those in the new norm at the end of the diffusion process, all the cases of innovation examined above suggest a reduction in price in the directly affected industries aside from, possibly, the case of innovation in business organisation. Thus, the meso-level analysis of innovations generally supports Schumpeter's argument that innovations contribute to a downward trend in prices over the full length of Kondratieff cycles. However, Schumpeter's analysis of the downward trend is s properly considered as part of the macro analysis for the reconstructed price theory, which is presented in the section below.

Price-level cycles and trends (macro analysis)

As noted in Chapter 4 and further discussed in Chapter 5, Schumpeter has a credit theory of inflation and deflation in the price level. The rise in the price level in the upswing of the business cycle results from the expansion of bank credit and the autodeflation of the downswing primarily results from the subsequent withdrawal of this extra credit. This credit expansion and contraction is an endogenous response to the financing needs of entrepreneurial ventures, with the repayment of the credit plus interest out of entrepreneurial profits.

Importantly, for Schumpeter money is not simply a veil over the production process of the economy. The expansion of credit is a necessary accompaniment to the introduction of innovations. Entrepreneurial firms use newly created credit to purchase means of production as a precursor to implementing their innovations in the form of new production processes, new products or new ways of connecting markets or otherwise organising business. Net revenues from the improved processes, products and organisations make the process sustainable and entrepreneurs in aggregate are more than able to repay with interest the credit advanced from banks. The inflation associated with the introduction of innovations is temporary and no Ponzi schemes or asset bubbles are involved in Schumpeter's cyclical behaviour of prices.

As in the Commentary of Chapter 4 and in Schumpeter's analysis, prices of primary inputs (the means of production) are the main actor in generating the cyclical upswing of the price level in the reconstruction of Schumpeter's price theory. Starting from the theoretical normal prices for a developing economy, as expressed in Equation (8.10), a rise in the wage rate from w_N to w_U with price-cost ratios constant results in a proportional rise in the price of all produced commodities, $p_U > p_N$. This satisfies Schumpeter's concept of a rise in the price level in the sense of a decline in the purchasing power of money, no matter which prices are used to determine the value of money.[20]

By providing a clear link from input prices to product prices, post-Keynesian price theories provide a micro analysis supporting Schumpeter's macro reasoning regarding price movements in the business cycle upswing. In the post-Keynesian theories, average industry price generally moves proportionally with unit cost at normal output. Technology and price-cost ratios are assumed constant in the short run, which implies the only source of short-run variation in product price is variation in the prices of labour and raw materials.

The meso analysis of the section above further shows price leadership delays the downward impact on prices from improvements in production technology in the form of reduced labour requirements or lower technical coefficients for intermediate inputs. The decline in labour requirements for the entrepreneurial firm is offset by an increase in the firm's price-cost ratio in Equation (8.16), preventing the growing output of the entrepreneurial firm from having a deflationary impact on prices. A parallel result is found for the case where an innovation lowers technical coefficients.

Replacing the assumption of price stability under a price leader with an assumption that prices are adjusted to maintain balance between the growth of productive capacity and the growth of market demand, as in Metcalfe's (1998) evolutionary theory, leads to the price of the entrepreneur's product declining as soon as production with the labour-saving innovation starts at the entrepreneurial firm. However, when the entrepreneurial firm is small, its output has very little impact on industry average price regardless of whether products are homogenous or differentiated. Only as the market share attributable to the new low-cost production method rises with the higher than average growth of the entrepreneurial firm, and with imitation, does the decline in the price of the industry's output become substantial and begin to noticeably affect prices in industries using this product as an input.

A rising price level in the cyclical upswing and a falling price level in the downswing are the outcomes of the application of the micro and meso post-Keynesian theories as with the two-phase cycle of Schumpeter's pure model of the business cycle. The force of innovation operates to give the business cycle a shape in which the beginning and end of the cycle occur at the boundary of the smoothed times-series graph of the price level, which implies the transition between cycles occurs at the lower boundary where the price level is growing at a rate equal to the result trend inflation rate for the full cycle.

Schumpeter's second approximation to the business cycle in Chapter IV of *BC* has four phases, with depression and recovery added to the initial prosperity and recession. Depression is attributed to 'The cyclical clusters of errors, excesses of optimism and pessimism and the like' (Schumpeter, 1939, p. 146). Businesses expand in prosperity on the expectation the rise in demand from the introduction of the cluster of innovation will continue indefinitely. When prices fall in the downswing, businesses that have borrowed for expansion and speculators who have borrowed based on asset inflation are subject to liquidation, thereby providing the impulse to overshooting that constitutes the depression phase of Schumpeter's cycle. Panic and crisis may, but need not, ensue. Schumpeter expects the depression phase to run its course, which allows the system to enter the recovery or revival phase.

The secondary phenomena of the four-phase business cycle complicate Schumpeter's pure model, but Schumpeter abdicates responsibility for explaining these phenomena, suggesting 'Our analysis adds nothing to this well-known piece of mechanism except the ignition of it and the means of distinguishing it from the more fundamental process which sets it in motion' (Schumpeter, 1939, p. 145). Post-Keynesian price theories have been developed precisely to deal with the determination of prices under conditions in which supply and demand do not balance, so they are particularly useful for extending Schumpeterian price theory to the depression and revival phases of the business cycle.

As an example, post-Keynesian theories linking pricing to investment behaviour readily generate the pattern of depression and recovery described by Schumpeter. For example, sharp and erratic declines in price feature in the downswing of industry price cycles in Steindl's (1976 [1952]) analysis. When prices drop sharply, so do profits and investment while marginal firms are eliminated through bankruptcy. When many industries are affected together by a cluster of innovations, an economy-wide wave of liquidations is possible if not probable. Depression ensues possibly accompanied by panic and crisis. Once prices are stabilised in industry maturity, the force for further liquidations is removed and normality returns, albeit with increased industry concentration and price-cost ratios.[21]

Post-Keynesian pricing theories also provide an explanation for the behaviour of money and real wage rates during the downswing of the business cycle. Money wages are determined at the industry level in bargaining between a small group of firms and their counterpart labour unions (see, for example, Sarantis, 1991). Price leadership with a fixed price-cost margin means an industry-wide increase in wage rates is readily reflected in increased prices to cover the increased costs, diminishing the incentive for firms to resist wage increases and explaining the tendency of wage rates to stay up in recession and depression. However, with the diffusion of innovations average industry price-cost ratios fall during the downswing phase of the cycle in almost all cases of innovations analysed in the meso analysis of the previous section. Falling price-cost ratios imply increased purchasing power for a given money wage rate, so the real wage increases in the downswing in the business cycle whether money wage rates rise or decline.[22]

Schumpeter's model of the business cycle is based on observations about the credit arrangements, firm pricing behaviour and government regulation of prices characterising the nineteenth and early part of the twentieth century, but he recognises the evolutionary process alters social, cultural and political behaviours as well as institutional arrangements. As is discussed in Chapter 5, he acknowledges the emergence of persistent inflationary pressure after the Second World War in 'March into Socialism' (Schumpeter, 1950). In the event, no downward trends in aggregate price indexes for major industrial countries are detectable over any substantial number of years over the second half of the twentieth century and so far into the twenty-first century, with the notable exception of Japan. There have been rises and falls in the rate of inflation, which may very well correspond to appropriately dated Kondratieff cycles, but no choice of beginning and end dates yields a downward result trend for the price level over a full cycle.

In view of the experience of continual inflation in the twentieth century, Schumpeter's argument that there is a downward result trend for the price level over the course of a Kondratieff cycle requires revision. The meso analysis of the last section, which abstracts from changes in primary input prices due to the influence of money or credit, leads to the result that $p_N > p_{NN}$ for all cases of innovation with two exceptions. Exceptions are for the case of new product innovation (for which no comparison is possible as the new product is not part of the original normal price vector) and for the case of innovations in business organisation (for which any relationship is recognised as possible when comparing the vector of prices for the original theoretical norm at the beginning of the cycle to the corresponding vector for the new theoretical norm at the end of the cycle). The meso analysis thus broadly supports Schumpeter's argument regarding the downward result trend in the price level over the course of business cycles, as long as the argument is interpreted as conditional on unchanged prices of primary inputs and on having industry price cycles highly correlated to yield a corresponding cycle for the full economy.

As an alternative to stating the downward result trend for the price level is conditional on unchanged primary input prices, the result can be stated in terms of relative prices or, more precisely, in terms of the purchasing power of incomes. Using the result for the case of a labour-saving innovation from Equation (8.18) to solve for p_{NN}/w_{NN} and then combining with the solution for p_N/w_N from Equation (8.10), yields

$$\frac{p_N}{w_N} = \left(I - \Psi_N A_N\right)^{-1} \Psi_N \gamma_N > \frac{p_{NN}}{w_{NN}} = \left(I - \Psi_{NN} A_N\right)^{-1} \Psi_{NN} \gamma_{NN},$$

$$\gamma_{NN} < \gamma_N, \Psi_{NN} < \Psi_N \left(\gamma_N / \gamma_{NN}\right) \tag{8.20}$$

Equation (8.20) implies each product price in the new theoretical norm when divided by the wage rate is no higher than in the original theoretical norm and at least one such price is lower in the new norm. Thus, the meso-analysis supports the conclusion that the purchasing power of the wage rate rises over the full course of an industry price cycle, at least for the case of labour-saving innovations. A similar argument can be made for the case of innovations that reduce requirements for intermediate inputs with $A_{NN} < A_N$.

Unfortunately, extending the result for a single input as given in Equation (8.20) to the case of multiple inputs encounters difficulties. The vector of the requirements for the single labour input and wage rate in Equation (8.20) can be replaced by a matrix of input requirements and a vector of input prices as is utilised in Equation (8.19). However, the ratio of two vectors, the product price vector and the input price vector, has no unambiguous meaning in terms of purchasing power.

A ratio of index numbers can be used in place of the price-vector ratio, but this encounters the cautions invoked by Schumpeter in Chapter VIII of *BC*. In particular, prices of different primary inputs evolve quite differently over time. For example, the wage rates of low-skilled workers have fallen substantially relative to those of at least some high-skilled workers in recent decades.[23] Thus, the precise meaning of a rise in the purchasing power of the wage rate demonstrated in Equation (8.20) doesn't easily extend to the analysis with multiple primary inputs.

One complication affecting differential movement in prices of primary inputs is a dichotomy in price determination for raw materials and finished manufacturing goods as in Kalecki's (1971) pricing theory. Prices of manufactures are determined by applying a fixed price-cost margin to unit cost as in other post-Keynesian pricing theories, but prices of raw materials from agriculture, forestry, fishing, mining and fossil fuels are determined competitively by the forces of supply and demand. Fluctuations in aggregate demand have no direct impact on the prices of manufactures in the framework of Equation (8.20), but have a pro-cyclical impact on the prices of raw materials.[24] Implicitly, the price-cost ratios and/or the returns to suppliers of primary inputs (landowners, resource deposit owners and workers) to the raw material sector are also pro-cyclical.

Overall, applying the reconstruction of Schumpeter's price theory yields many features of his business cycle in prices, but without implying a downward result trend in the price level. There is an upswing phase in which the prices of all products rise with competition for the means of production followed by a downswing phase in which a decline in price-cost ratios accompanies the process of creative destruction. The downward result trend for the price level is reinterpreted as implying an upward result trend for the purchasing power of money wage rates, which means the result doesn't depend on the institutional arrangements of banking, credit and money remaining as in Schumpeter's time.

Adding post-Keynesian micro and meso analysis to Schumpeter's macro reasoning helps explain the otherwise anomalous behaviour of real wage rates Schumpeter observes for industrial countries in the prosperity phase of Kondratieff cycles. The strong link from wage rates to manufactured goods prices combined with the delayed downward influence of improved production technology on prices of manufactures using that technology is conducive to wage-price spirals. Money wage rates increase with the increased competition for means of production followed by proportional manufacturing price increases and yet more competition for labour, promoting another round of wage increases. Also having an upward influence on unit cost and prices of manufactures is the pro-cyclical movement in raw material prices. If the spiral continues through the upswing of the Kondratieff cycle, a corresponding period of slow growth in real wage rates occurs of the sort observed in Schumpeter's data on wage rates and price levels in *BC* (see the discussion in the 'Commentary on Money and the Price Level' in Chapter 5).

The vector of theoretical normal prices in the adapted Sraffian framework of Equation (8.10) is determined by particular values of technical coefficients, price-cost ratios and the wage rate. In practice these values are historically determined unlike the corresponding values in a perfectly competitive Walrasian general equilibrium, which are uniquely determined by given preferences, technology and factor endowments.[25] Historical study of each industry is needed to determine the values corresponding to normal conditions and this can only be done at the conclusion of a cycle as the normal values change between cycles.

The end of the business cycle occurs in Schumpeter's theory when the economy approaches the neighbourhood of equilibrium, which is revealed by historical analysis and the use of Frisch's method of locating inflection points in the smoothed time-series graphs for aggregate economic variables. The alternative suggested by the meso analysis of the previous section is associating the end of the cycle with widespread industry maturity. In a mature industry, price-cost ratios and technical coefficients are stabilised by reduced firm heterogeneity after innovations have diffused through the economy and creative destruction has removed marginal firms.

In Steindl's analysis of industry concentration, the pricing rule stabilises when an industry reaches maturity after the elimination of high-cost producers, leaving a relatively homogenous group of firms that have achieved close to the lowest costs across the group. There is also a tendency towards stability in price-cost ratios as well as low variance in unit cost across firms at the end of the diffusion process in Metcalfe's (1998) analysis of differential firm growth as high-cost firms shrink or are eliminated by the faster growth of their low-cost competitors. Thus, the relatively full diffusion of innovations as measured by a low level of firm heterogeneity within industries is the observable condition indicating achievement of statistical normal values of the technical coefficients and price-cost ratios. As minimal variance remains in technical coefficients, unit cost or price-cost ratio across surviving firms, choosing between the values for the best-performing firm, the average firm or any arbitrary firm makes less difference than at other points of the cycle. This means the normal values of these variables are less susceptible to mismeasurement, even when there is no theoretical basis for choice among alternative measures or when the theoretically preferred measure is not available.

There are practical difficulties with determining what level of firm heterogeneity constitutes normality, particularly in view of the various dimensions in which heterogeneity can be measured, such as cost, product quality and provision of ancillary services. There is also the problem of defining the scope of the industry and making adjustments for niche markets. Using time-series data helps, but then there is the problem of distinguishing between local and global minima or maxima.

Adoption of post-Keynesian pricing rules widely through the economy contributes to the stability of the price system even with changing input prices as long as the movements in prices of different inputs don't diverge too greatly. If there is endemic inflation as experienced through most of the twentieth century, application of post-Keynesian pricing rules lead to individual product prices increasing more or less in tandem with the general rate of increase of input prices without much impact on relative prices. Arguably, this type of stability in the price system makes calculation of profits from innovations reasonably reliable and is conducive to an upsurge in innovative activity. However, stability of pricing rules occurs only with industry maturity and for some period into the upswing of a cluster of innovations. Stability of pricing rules is least likely in the downswing phase and in any following periods of depression.

Steindl argues that once prices are stabilised in maturity, the economy is prone to stagnation as established firms refrain from rapidly expanding productive capacity. In contrast, Schumpeter argues that the restoration of normality allows entrepreneurs to reliably calculate profits from their innovations and convince bankers to finance their enterprises.[26] Schumpeter's argument can be applied in a modern setting by changing the party to be convinced, which is more likely to be a venture capitalist or a corporate investment committee than a bank. Regardless of who needs convincing, Schumpeter's argument implies the endogenous business cycle starts anew with first few and then many entrepreneurs, both inside and outside established firms, introducing innovations.

Summary

The reconstruction of Schumpeter's price theory presented in this chapter is a theory of prices in motion. The business cycle, which is the form growth takes under capitalism according to Schumpeter, begins with an upsurge in entrepreneurial activity made possible when current prices approach their normal values. Innovations lead to upward pressure on prices of means of production and to increased price-cost ratios for entrepreneurial firms. Aggressive competition in the process of creative destruction then pushes price-cost ratios down towards new normal levels and leads to prices that reflect structural adaptation to diffusion of the innovations. The price level for the new normal may be higher or lower than the original, but the purchasing power of the wage rate is higher.

Schumpeter argues theoretical normal prices are determined by perfectly competitive Walrasian equilibrium, with the price of each product equal to its reproduction costs. This may be appropriate for starting from a stationary economy but is not appropriate for starting from an economy that has already experienced development. To reflect the circumstances of a developing economy, the reconstructed price theory starts with theoretical normal prices exceeding reproduction costs by amounts that reflect the option value associated with the threat of obsolescence, the financing requirements for growth of entrepreneurial firms, and the existence of imperfect competition.

The reconstructed price theory then follows the micro-meso-macro approach of evolutionary theorising. In the micro analysis, firms set prices using administered pricing rules of the type specified in post-Keynesian price theories. As a result, rather than have prices adjust to clear the market in the short run, adjustments are made to production levels, inventories or backlogs. The essential characteristics of the pricing rules are (1) prices are cost determined in the sense that they vary proportionally with average direct cost in the short run, (2) demand exerts no direct influence on price and short-run fluctuations in output have no immediate influence on price and (3) price leadership determines industry price, especially when products are homogenous and there is cost heterogeneity across firms in the industry.

The administrative processes of firms incorporate strategies for dealing with any excess supply or demand that appears when the pricing rule doesn't balance demand for the firm's product with its desired capacity utilisation. Firms that distribute their output through downstream merchandisers hold inventories or excess production capacity to enable them to respond to fluctuating demand without altering price, while firms engaged in producing to order generally maintain order books for similar purposes. These mechanisms as well as longer term adjustments in production capacity, supply chain, distribution channels, marketing strategies and product development provide alternatives to price adjustment when markets are disrupted by innovation and creative destruction.

At the meso level, Steindl's (1976 [1952]) theory of industry concentration is used in applying post-Keynesian pricing theory to the analysis of structural change following the introduction of input-saving innovation. Cost heterogeneity leads to differential rates of growth across firms within an industry and to three phases of pricing behaviour; price rigidity in the phase of relative concentration, aggressive price competition in the phase of absolute concentration and price rigidity once the industry matures and sellers recognise their common interests. Price decreases are an emergent property of the process of industry concentration in this analysis. Price decreases also occur in Metcalfe's (1998) analysis of differential firm growth, but the assumption that prices are set to balance the rate of growth of capacity with the exogenously determined rate of growth of market demand means the price decreases are continual and the rate of price change is determined according to Fisher's Principle.

Extension of the meso analysis to other cases of innovation considered by Schumpeter generates diverse results. Innovations in opening up new sources of supply of primary inputs tends to reduce product prices, but there is no clear parallel to the input-saving case in terms of a cyclical pattern to the decline. New product prices have a downward trajectory from some point after introduction, but the prices at the end of the cycle can't be compared to those at the start when the product didn't exist. Finally, innovations in business organisation can lead to decreases or increases in product prices, without necessarily having a cyclical pattern or a determinant result trend.

For at least input-saving innovations, combining the micro and meso analyses of the reconstructed price theory with elements of Schumpeter's macro analysis generates price cycles that have at least some of the characteristics Schumpeter attributes to the movement of prices over the business cycle. If primary input prices rise in the upswing of the business cycle under the pressure of competition for the means of production, then application of post-Keynesian pricing rules with fixed margins and unit costs calculated for standardised output results in product prices generally rising in proportion to the input prices. Declines in price-cost margins during the process of creative destruction contribute to a decline in product prices in the downswing of the business cycle, which can lead to forced liquidations and depression, if not panic and crisis. Finally, a downward result trend is expected over the full course of the cycle, at least when product prices are measured relative to the wage rate.

Importantly, the reconstruction of Schumpeter's price theory incorporates many features of the modern economy that Schumpeter acknowledges, especially in *CSD* and other of his later writings. These include imperfect competition and associated pricing practices, such as price stabilisation and price leadership, which are standard features in the post-Keynesian price theories. Also, in the reconstructed theory changes in pricing rules are an emergent property, which provides scope for history to matter in the meso analysis of structural change, a feature essential to any evolutionary analysis. Further, the reconstructed theory provides a reinterpretation of Schumpeter's downward result trend for the price level in terms of rising purchasing power of the wage rate, which applies even with changes in the institutional arrangements determining monetary policy and fits with observations Schumpeter makes about persistent inflationary pressure in *CSD* and 'March into Socialism' (Schumpeter, 1950).

Notes

1 The main categories of post-Keynesian theories are administered pricing, full-cost or normal cost pricing, target rate-of-return pricing and mark-up pricing. For a discussion of the various theories and the relationships among them see Lee (1998).
2 This is the position taken by Peter Kriesler (1987) against an argument in Basile and Salvadori (1984–85) favouring continuity in the justifications Kalecki uses in the various presentations of his pricing theory.
3 Kalecki (1971, p. 46–47) uses the expression in Equation (8.3) to show the magnitude of the ratio of price to unit direct cost for an individual firm depends on the ratio of the industry average price to the firm's unit direct cost as well as on the firm's m and n coefficients. This introduces an influence from prices of other firms directly into determination of each firm's mark-up factor, which is absent from other post-Keynesian pricing theories. There has been considerable discussion of the relation of Kalecki's pricing equation to the other post-Keynesian pricing theories as well as its relation to marginalist pricing (see, for example, Kriesler, 1987, Lee, 1998).
4 The weighting factors used to determine average values differ across coefficients. For the m and q coefficients the weighting factor is the share of the firm in the total costs of the group of firms, while for the n coefficient the weighting factor is the firm's share in group revenue. The cost and revenue shares are equal only if price-cost ratios are the same for all firms.
5 Kalecki restricts the value of the m and n coefficients for firms in Equation (8.1) to lie between zero and one in order to ensure the degree of monopoly for the industry

in Equation (8.3) is a positive number greater than one, but Basile and Salvadori (1984–85) show Kalecki's analysis can be generalised to include boundary values of $m = n = 0$ and $n = 1$.

6 Schumpeter recognises that innovation and creative destruction occur over time, but the length of the intervals is ill-defined, especially when he adopts the approach of overlapping cycles of differing duration in Chapter V of *BC*. The important analytical distinction in terms of denoting changing values of the parameters of the price system is between phases of the cycle, not any particular calendar period.

7 Here, I implicitly assume constant returns to scale in the sense that unit labour require-ments or technical coefficients in the input-output matrix are unaffected by the change in scale of operation by the established firms. A separate issue is whether the firm is committed to paying for inputs whether used or not, such as with labour contracts or equipment leasing. To the extent that established firms are disadvantaged by reducing output their willingness to cede sales is undermined and the phase of aggressive com-petition discussed below may be brought forward in time.

8 In post-Keynesian theory firms operate with bounded rationality, imperfect information and limited access to capital, which mean they rely, at least in part, on retained profits to provide internal finance of capacity expansion. Stability and order can prevail without necessarily satisfying the conditions for either short-run or long-run equilibrium of a model with optimisation based on perfect foresight and perfect capital markets.

9 David Levine (2005) points to the potential for using Steindl's analysis of capitalist dynamics to enrich the classical theory of price determination based on the require-ments of reproduction. Instead of simple or extended reproduction, prices are deter-mined in Steindl's analysis as an element of structural transformation. The implications of Steindl's analysis for price determination within Sraffa's framework of classical reproduction prices are formalised in the following paragraphs.

10 Steindl suggests that relative expansion requires some special selling effort on the part of the progressive firms, but this is neglected here to simplify the analysis.

11 A similar result linking profit rates to growth of the market at the firm level is obtained in post-Keynesian price theories that have price determined by the internal financing required to achieve the firm's growth objectives, such as the theories of Wood (1975), Eichner (1976) and Harcourt and Kenyon (1976) discussed in the previous section.

12 Downie (1958) provides an interesting analysis of the differential firm growth induced by innovation and extends Steindl's analysis to consider how the pressure on estab-lished firms encourages their efforts to introduce further innovations, which introduces the possibility of delay, perhaps even indefinite delay, in the elimination of marginal firms.

13 The best-practice technology at this point may have improved substantially beyond the level at the time of introduction of the labour-saving innovation due to learning by doing, economies of scale and supplemental innovations. These complications are ignored in the analysis above in order to simplify the exposition, but may serve in prac-tice to substantially extend the process of diffusion of the innovation and increase the magnitude of its impact on price. The best-practice firm at the end of the process may not even be the original innovator.

14 Sylos-Labini (1962) provides a similar characterisation of a stable pricing outcome for an industry with cost heterogeneity due to technological differences across firms. However, Sylos-Labini's theory focuses more on entry conditions for the industry and less on the dynamic process associated with the elimination of high-cost firms. See Bloch (2016a) for a detailed discussion of the similarities and differences between Sylos-Labini and Steindl related to the analysis of innovation and creative destruction.

15 There is also a relationship to post-Keynesian theories of pricing of Wood (1975) and others discussed above that determine prices to meet requirements for financing the desired growth of the firm. Metcalfe (1998, pp. 56–57) explicitly notes the relationship between his price theory and that of Wood.

16 This treatment implicitly assumes a uniform price for each primary input, whereas variation in price is common. Where prices vary, especially across countries, there may also be variation in the price-cost ratios or prices of raw materials and also the finished products directly or indirectly using these raw materials. Schumpeter (1939, pp. 266–70, pp. 319–25) discusses the impact of the opening up of new lands as leading to agrarian depressions through depressed prices for agricultural outputs without focussing attention on the implications for the prices of products using these outputs as raw materials.

17 If the new product has uses closely related to those of an existing product, a less radical approach is to include the new product as a variety of the existing product. To be able to earn a super-normal profit, the new product variety presumably is more useful to buyers than the old, which is formalised as less input per unit of output and the analysis of impact on prices proceeds as above for a reduction in intermediate input required for producing an established product.

18 There may also be substantial reductions in production cost in the shakeout phase of the life cycle for new product industries. The stabilisation of product design allows the achievement of economies of scale within the individual firm and external economies for all firms in the industry. Some of these gains are reflected in lower direct labour requirements, while other gains occur through reductions in technical coefficients for producing the new product or through reductions in either labour requirements or technical coefficients for intermediate inputs. Such changes may induce further reductions in the overall price vector along the lines of the price reductions occurring in Equation (8.17).

19 Sraffa (1960, p. 8) distinguishes between basic and non-basic commodities, with basic commodities being direct or indirect inputs into all other commodities. A change in the production conditions for a basic commodity affects all prices in the economy, whereas a change in production conditions for a non-basic commodity affects only the price of that commodity and those dependent on the non-basic in their production. Steel, electric motors and computers are examples of commodities that are basic (or nearly basic) commodities in a modern economy, which means their introduction alters the price structure of the economy in a generic way that the introduction of pure consumption goods, say movies or computer games, does not.

20 If allowance is made for a variety of primary inputs as in Equation (8.19) with the matrix of primary input requirements, Γ, and vector of input prices, $\mathbf{w}$, then prices of various commodities rise more or less than average depending on the size of the price increase of the primary inputs they use most heavily both directly and indirectly. However, all commodity prices rise or at least stay constant as long as there are no primary inputs with declining prices, which means the changes in the price system can still be considered to satisfy Schumpeter's concept of a declining value of money.

21 See Courvisanos (1996, 2012) for an extended discussion of investment behaviour in Steindl's analysis and how it links with Schumpeter's theory of innovation-driven growth and the business cycle.

22 In *BC* Schumpeter attributes the tendency of real wages to rise in cyclical downswings primarily to falling prices, noting when money wages don't rise in recession, 'The fruits of innovation and induced developments would entirely be harvested in the form of increased "purchasing power" of the unit of income' (Schumpeter, 1939, p. 573, quotation marks in the original). Schumpeter points in particular to the chart of English real wage rates allowing for unemployment (Chart XXXI, op. cit., p. 571), which shows an increase of about 25 percent in real wages during the depression phase of the second Kondratieff.

23 For a discussion of inequality in the movement of wage rates for various types of labour across a range of countries and a discussion of the influence of technology and institutions, including minimum wage laws, as drivers of relative wage rates see Piketty (2014, Chapter 9).

24 Bloch and Sapsford (2000) apply Kalecki's theory to explaining differential movements in the price of raw materials and manufactured goods over the second half of the twentieth century, while Bloch and Sapsford (2013) apply Kalecki's theory together with Schumpeter's business cycle theory to explaining cycles in the price of raw material relative to manufactures over the three-and-a-half centuries from 1650.

25 All firms operate with best-practice technology in Walrasian equilibrium, but in a developing economy best-practice may not be the attractor value towards which firms are converging according to the theory of industry dynamics and, even if best-practice is the attractor value, the convergence process can stop well short of this outcome.

26 In the Introduction to the 1976 edition, Steindl acknowledges that he was wrong to deny the stimulation given to investment by innovations (Steindl, 1976 [1950], p. xii). However, he doesn't follow Schumpeter in associating the introduction of innovations to there being normal business conditions.

9 Summing up

Theory of prices in motion

Schumpeter's approach to price theory diverges from both classical and neoclassical theory, which address price determination in terms of long-run tendencies and market equilibrium, respectively. Instead, Schumpeter treats prices as determined by the process of development of the economy, which is a process of transformation occurring over historical time. What Schumpeter provides is a theory of prices in motion.

Long-run or "natural" prices in classical economics are determined by the difficulty of production, in particular by the amount of labour time expended in the production of each commodity and this reflects the fixed endowments of nature and the state of technology. Neoclassical economics has market equilibrium prices determined by fixed consumer preferences as well as factor endowments and technology. Schumpeter's great insight is that capitalism is a self-transforming system in which endowments, preferences and, especially, technology are all malleable through the innovations introduced by entrepreneurs. Schumpeter's price theory is focussed on explaining the movements in prices that are essential to the introduction and diffusion of innovations in a process occurring in historical time and following recurrent, although not necessarily regular, patterns.

In summarising the content of the earlier chapters, I first recap the main points from Schumpeter's price theory before reviewing the strengths and weaknesses of the theory. I then review how my proposed reconstruction presented in Chapter 8 addresses weaknesses while maintaining key elements of Schumpeter's vision. I close the chapter with a few reflections on Schumpeter's contributions.

Key points of Schumpeter's price theory

Schumpeter's price theory, the direct subject of Chapter 4, is part of his holistic theory of capitalist development incorporating his theory of innovation-driven growth as discussed in Chapter 2, his theory of the business cycle as discussed in Chapter 3 and his theory of money, banking and credit as discussed in Chapter 5. Innovations financed by bank credit impact both on the money supply and on the production process, which leads to cyclical behaviour of the price level and structural change in the price system. The combination of monetary and real phenomena distinguishes Schumpeter's theory from purely monetary theories of the price level and from neoclassical theories of relative prices based on assumptions regarding fixed endowments, technology and preferences.

Schumpeter starts the economy in a stationary state with prices determined by perfectly competitive long-run general equilibrium. There is a clearly understood and accepted value of money (the inverse of the price level) and an equilibrium set of relative prices (the price system), which are taken as the normal values for the economy. Schumpeter then notes a capitalist economy in equilibrium provides fertile ground for the introduction of innovations as entrepreneurs are readily able to calculate the potential profits from their innovations and these calculations provide a credible basis to secure financing from banks. Thus, equilibrium, or even being in the neighbourhood of equilibrium, stimulates innovation.

Extra purchasing power created through using bank credit to finance innovations puts upward pressure on the prices of means of production, which are assumed to be otherwise fully employed. The extra purchasing power then flows through to support increased prices of consumer goods to match the higher cost of means of production, which implies a reduced value of money (a higher price level). There is also a change in the mix of output, with lower output from those established firms who have lost access to means of production and, eventually, higher output from innovators. Price changes in affected markets are diverse, so the price system is disrupted.

Innovations tend to be cumulative. Entrepreneurs initially face stiff resistance to change in the status quo, but success of a few encourages the efforts of others. In addition, rising prices and incomes stimulate secondary expansions and also encourage speculation on asset prices. These secondary phenomena add to the boom conditions of the prosperity phase of the business cycle, putting additional upward pressure on the price level and further disrupting the price system. Innovations and their diffusion destroy equilibrium, at least the type of long-period equilibrium that determines theoretical normal prices in Schumpeter's theory.

Movements in the price system and price level away from equilibrium values reduce the flow of innovations by making the profitability of innovations more difficult to assess for both entrepreneurs and bankers. Extension of credit to additional entrepreneurs is restricted, although credit for established businesses and speculators may continue to expand. Then, as successful entrepreneurs start repaying their outstanding loans, there is downward pressure on the total amount of credit outstanding.

Declines in credit outstanding and money in circulation lead to the recession phase of the business cycle with autodeflation in the price level. There is also an output expansion from innovators, which is greater than the decline in output of established firms. With the removal of extra credit and money, the extra output means a lower price level is required for equilibrium according to the quantity equation. Thus, Schumpeter concludes that the price level has a downward result trend over the full course of the Kondratieff cycle.[1]

Creative destruction also occurs in recession, with competition between the products of innovators and established firms displacing their competition for means of product. Competition among producers and products is disruptive of the price system. Relative prices are in flux throughout the cycle and only approach their normal values when the economy is in the neighbourhood of equilibrium at the end of the cycle.

The dialectical relationship between innovation and equilibrium in Schumpeter's theory provides the endogenous mechanism responsible for the business cycle being the form taken by growth and development under capitalism. Importantly, this is an out-of-equilibrium process in which both prosperity and recession are essential elements. The cumulative nature of innovations pushes the economy towards unsustainable acceleration in prosperity, while the resulting disruption of equilibrium ensures an eventual decline in innovative activity leading to recession and, possibly, depression.

In his pure model of the two-phase business cycle, Schumpeter has price and quantity movements interacting within the monetary tie of the quantity equation. In the prosperity phase of the cycle, the price level rises with the expansion of credit and money while there is no clear change in aggregate output (innovative industries expanding and at least some established industries contracting). In recession, the price level falls along with the contraction of credit and money, while output expansion from innovative industries exceeds the output decline in established industries (this displacement is the form progress takes according to Schumpeter). Any inflationary tendency from the expansion of credit is temporary, while the change in composition and magnitude of aggregate output is permanent.

Schumpeter's extended model of the business cycle (the second approximation) includes phenomena usually following on from, but not necessary to, the process of innovation-driven growth. These secondary phenomena include expansion of non-innovating industries in response to prosperity as well as speculative activity induced by the expectation the upsurge will continue indefinitely. They tend to exacerbate price increases in the upswing of the cycle and may generate some extra employment and output, especially if the upswing starts with less than full employment. The main impact of the secondary phenomena is that they set the conditions for the depression and revival phases of the cycle. In the depression phase, the liquidation of the unwarranted and speculative investments pushes both price and output down in tandem, especially in a crisis or panic, while the revival phase is cast as an across-the-board return towards equilibrium conditions with both prices and output rising.

Schumpeter argues classical statistical analysis of time-series data is inappropriate as the theoretical norms of variables are changing over the course of the business cycle, so the assumption of stochastic variation around a fixed mean is invalid. Instead, Schumpeter uses the historical analysis in *BC* to demonstrate the working of his theory for the cycles experienced up to the 1930s. In this analysis, cyclical movement in the price level is related to movements in credit and money, while changes in relative prices (the price system) reflect restructuring of the economy with the changes in production processes, products and organisation of markets introduced by the particular innovations characterising each Kondratieff cycle.

Strengths

Above all else, Schumpeter's vision is what distinguishes him from his contemporaries. Where others see still photographs Schumpeter sees moving pictures. From his earliest writings through his posthumously published *HEA* Schumpeter shows a clear understanding and appreciation of the virtues of the Walrasian system of competitive general equilibrium, with supply and demand finely balanced for each commodity and primary input. However, he quickly realises the limits of this static picture and begins working on a theory of capitalist motion, which continues to occupy him throughout his life.

Schumpeter sees profit-seeking behaviour extending beyond the limited horizon of maximisation of gains subject to constraints of technology, resource endowments and consumer preferences. There are also gains, sometimes very large gains, to be had from breaking these constraints through innovations in production processes, products, sources of supply and forms of organising businesses and markets. However, there are psychological, social and economic resistances to change, so the process of introducing innovations is neither easy nor smooth. Also, entrepreneurs who bring innovations to life are predominantly outsiders, who need to convince bankers to finance the acquisition of means of production through the extension of credit.[2]

Once introduced, innovations secure their place in the economic system through creative destruction of established ways of doing things. The business cycle is an inevitable consequence of this evolutionary process, as innovations force their way into the economy through credit expansion creating boom conditions and recession is required to liquidate superseded products and producers. Excesses of reckless lending and speculation followed by crises and panics are not a necessary part of the process, but are likely given the institutional structure of capitalist banking. Economic change is neither smooth nor without negative impacts, so Schumpeter suggests the process should be characterised as economic evolution rather than economic progress.

The scope of Schumpeter's vision of evolutionary change is broad, extending beyond the confines of the economy to culture, politics and institutions. Particularly important for price theory is his analysis of the institution of money, which is most extensively detailed in *TM*. Schumpeter explains the autonomy of money as reflecting its determination by social practice (as in the rise of metallic money) or by a social entity (such as a central bank). Yet, the role of banks as deposit takers and credit providers opens the way to an additional function as financiers of entrepreneurs, which is crucial to the disruption of the circular flow and the continuation of economic evolution.

Application of Schumpeter's theory provides a much richer explanation of the quantitative expansion of the world economy than Solow's (1957) simple growth accounting framework for neoclassical growth theory. Moreover, his theory extends to structural changes in what is produced, how it is produced and where it is produced, changes that have transformed agrarian rural societies to industrialised urban societies and seen the rise and fall of leading economies. Through the breadth of his vision of social transformation, Schumpeter takes economic analysis beyond the narrow confines of present circumstances (or expanded reproduction based on capital accumulation) to consider the transformative forces creating those circumstances and shaping future circumstances.

Weaknesses

Given the breadth of Schumpeter's vision of capitalist development it is not surprising his theory of this process has weak points. In his effort to extend the scope of economic theorising Schumpeter understandably draws on elements of theories designed to deal with narrower conceptions of the economic problem, particularly the Walrasian theory of perfectly competitive general equilibrium. Also, in spite of his efforts in *BC* to flesh out the skeleton of the theory presented in *TED*, there are inevitable gaps in Schumpeter's analysis. Finally, while Schumpeter never repudiated or acknowledged the need for major revision of the theory he puts forth in *TED* and *BC*, some points he makes in later publications do not fit easily with his earlier assumptions about competition and the monetary mechanism.

Walrasian equilibrium provides a theoretical norm for prices in Schumpeter's theory. This is problematic as has been noted in many commentaries on Schumpeter's work and in the discussion in Chapter 6. From an evolutionary perspective, a major difficulty is equilibrium is inconsistent with endogenous change because, as Schumpeter notes in *HEA*, an equilibrium position has no tendency to change from within.

Schumpeter attempts to finesse the theoretical and practical problems associated with achieving equilibrium through employing the concept of the neighbourhood of equilibrium. Aside from the obvious obfuscation, Schumpeter ignores the possibility that norms for a developing economy differ systematically from those for a stationary economy. Development brings with it an ongoing threat of obsolescence through creative destruction and irreducible imperfections in competition, both of which impact on the normal values of price-cost margins.

The primary focus of Schumpeter's analysis is explaining movements in macroeconomic magnitudes, such as the price level, aggregate output, employment and amount of money in circulation. There is some discussion of the behaviour of firms, especially entrepreneurial firms and banks, and of competitive dynamics, especially the process of creative destruction, but no systematic theory covering the micro and meso aspects of economic development. His theory is left without adequate depth to examine whether various components of the theory are internally consistent. As an example, the micro and meso analyses within the theory are inadequate to provide Schumpeter with the foundation for determining whether a developing economy has the same or different theoretical norms as a stationary economy.

Schumpeter emphasises the difference between invention and innovation and places the explanation for innovation clearly within the scope of his theory. However, he says little about the drivers of invention, particularly the generation and diffusion of knowledge. With the shift from the individual entrepreneur to the industrial research laboratory, invention and innovation are increasingly integrated into a single process. Also, Schumpeter glosses over whether technological breakthroughs are inherently cumulative, which for long-wave theorists generally provides an explanation of the clustering of innovations without recourse to psychological or sociological explanation of the cumulative nature of entrepreneurial activity.

Secondary phenomena dominate in the depression and revival phases of Schumpeter's business cycle, but he notes with regard to secondary phenomena, 'Our analysis adds nothing to this well-known piece of mechanism except the ignition of it and the means of distinguishing it from the more fundamental process which sets it in motion' (Schumpeter, 1939, p. 145). As in the case of taking the theoretical norm for a developing economy to be the same as for a stationary economy, Schumpeter is assuming too much by taking the well-known piece of mechanism to be unaffected by altering the process that puts it in motion.[3] Minsky argues forcefully in favour of combining Schumpeter's emphasis on innovation with Keynes' emphasis on disjuncture between asset prices and product prices, particularly paying attention to innovations in financial instruments and institutions.

In *BC* Schumpeter notes his theory of economic development poses difficulties for interpreting time-series data. Yet, he insists the result trend for any economic variable drawn through points of equilibrium (or intervals corresponding to neighbourhoods of equilibrium) has economic significance and suggests that these points can be discerned from the application of Frisch's method of normal points (indicated by inflection points on smoothed graphs of time-series data) or by historical analysis. Schumpeter admits Frisch's method is highly susceptible to error and, as pointed out by critics, his historical analysis lacks objective criteria for dating business cycles.

Application of Schumpeter's theory to the interpretation of time-series graphs is further complicated because his analysis suggests key economic magnitudes have different timing, amplitude, shape and result trend for their time-series graphs. In particular, movements in the price level and aggregate output are non-synchronous in his analysis of the pure model of the two-phase business cycle. Also, confounding are Schumpeter's cautions against the use of aggregate series, which he terms synthetic and claims can provide spurious results. He glosses over most of these difficulties in *BC* with his historical analysis and in interpreting the time series for economic magnitudes in Chapters VIII through XIII, no doubt contributing to the poor reception afforded the book.

Reconstruction

My discussion of the reconstruction of Schumpeter's price theory starts with rejecting the proposition of identical norms for developing and stationary economies. Instead of Schumpeter's theoretical norm for a developing economy being given by perfectly competitive general equilibrium, I suggest a norm based on the concept of industry maturity. Instead of a statistical norm given by points of inflection in time-series graphs of the price level, my suggested norm is a mature economy with stable industry structure for the economy and low variation in characteristics such as size, productivity and profitability across firms within each industry. Finally, the common-sense or businessman's norm of "normal" profits is not zero economic profit as asserted by Schumpeter, but rather includes premia associated with the threat of obsolescence, an irreducible level of imperfect competition and, in growing markets, a contribution towards financing continued expansion of production capacity.

Order, rather than equilibrium, is what characterises the theoretical norm for the reconstruction of Schumpeter's theory. Equilibrium is a condition without any tendency to change from within and, as such, is inconsistent with evolutionary theorising. Order, in the sense of a rough matching of the quantities of goods sought by buyers and the planned output by sellers at prices and other conditions acceptable to both, is a condition consistent with dynamic forces that would, without external shocks, continue to alter quantities and prices over time.

Markets are usually orderly aside from when they are experiencing the disruptive impact of innovation or general economic crisis. A cluster of innovations initially disrupts only a small part of economic activity, but the effects spread with the process of the diffusion of the innovation and the ensuing transformation of economic structure. Theories of industrial dynamics characterise the end state of the process of diffusion within an industry as industry maturity, with characteristics including standardisation of products and processes, small numbers of surviving firms (aside from situations in which there are many niche markets) and incremental (rather than radical) innovations.

My suggested reconstruction of Schumpeter's price theory builds on the Sraffian framework of reproduction prices. Within this framework Schumpeter's theoretical normal prices for a stationary economy are set by equating price to reproduction cost for each commodity without any profits. The reconstruction, in contrast, has theoretical normal prices for a developing economy exceeding reproduction costs by amounts reflecting the threat of obsolescence, the internal financing of capacity expansion to meet market growth and irreducible elements of imperfect competition. Such theoretical normal prices are the values approached when the process of creative destruction has completed its work and the industrial structure of the economy has matured.

I organise the discussion of a reconstructed price theory using the micro-meso-macro approach of modern evolutionary theorising. In the micro analysis prices are set using fixed mark-ups on unit operating costs as in post-Keynesian pricing theories. The meso analysis examines the industrial dynamics resulting from responses to excess supply or demand conditions that emerge from the introduction and diffusion of innovations. Combining changes in firm pricing rules from the meso analysis with Schumpeter's banking, credit and monetary theory provides a macro analysis in which there is cyclical movement in the price level and disruption in the price system.

The output price dynamics generated from the reconstruction of Schumpeter's price theory mimic those he derives for the price level and the price system in *BC*.

However, his conclusion regarding a downward result trend for the price level over each Kondratieff cycle is qualified to recognise the impact of shifting social, cultural and political conditions as well as changes in institutional arrangements affecting wage setting, price determination and the role of banks and financial markets. The micro and meso analyses of the reconstructed theory additionally provide a clearer basis for analysing the movement of real wage rates over the course of the Kondratieff cycle.

My discussion of reconstructing Schumpeter's price theory covers only a limited number of theories of firm pricing behaviour and industrial dynamics. There is also only a limited treatment of the role of demand, or of technological trajectories, or of knowledge generation and transmission, all topics that have been or are becoming increasingly important to evolutionary economists. Furthermore, I focus on product markets, largely neglecting input and asset markets. There is clearly much potential for further development within the micro-meso-macro approach or with alternative approaches, such as agent-based modelling or stock-flow consistent modelling. What I hope to have demonstrated are the possibilities for addressing weaknesses in Schumpeter's price theory without losing his vision of capitalist development driven by innovation.

Final reflections

At the most basic level Schumpeter's essential contribution to price theory is his emphasis on the instability of capitalism, which is reflected in both the price level and the price system. Historical evidence certainly supports the proposition that the price level and the price system are unstable. Schumpeter addresses the challenge to understand the forces driving this motion.

Schumpeter continues a tradition of price theories incorporating price dynamics, including Smith's analysis of market versus natural prices and Marshall's analysis of the movement between short-period and long-period equilibrium prices. Schumpeter's theory is best understood in terms of an open evolutionary process rather than in terms of movements away from and back to an unchanging equilibrium. This process impacts on both the "norms" underpinning the process and on the pattern of movement towards these norms.

Schumpeter erred in relying on perfectly competitive long-run general equilibrium for determining theoretical normal prices, but not in emphasising the unevenness over both time and industry in the adjustment of prices towards normal values. He provided important hints for the micro and meso analysis of the process of adjustment, but also left large gaps. Identifying appropriate norms for a developing economy and filling the gaps in micro and meso analysis are important and interrelated tasks in the further development the theory of prices in motion that he gave us. My discussion of reconstructing his theory provides examples of how these tasks may be addressed, but only scratches at the surface of the possibilities.

Schumpeter certainly was correct in his insight that prices only occasionally approach their theoretical normal values. Transformation of the economy with the disruptive introduction and diffusion of innovations drives prices away from theoretical normal values and also changes the values approached at the end of the process. Importantly, the theoretical normal prices in Schumpeter's theory are attractor values that are usually approached from a single direction (for example, costs and prices approach their normal values from above) rather than being centres of gravity with fluctuations evenly distributed above and below the normal value.

Poor understanding of the process generating observed prices leads to errors in the interpretation and statistical analysis of price dynamics, which affects decision-making, especially regarding investment and public policy decisions that use current and past price information to project into the future. Schumpeter provides a start to developing a proper understanding of this process through his theory of prices in motion. Much remains to be done.

Notes

1 As discussed in Chapter 5, Schumpeter is hardly a monetarist, but he does view the efficiency of payments in the economy as determining the income velocity of circulation of money when the economy is in equilibrium. He further assumes money in circulation returns to its starting level at the end of the cycle when innovative activity and credit to entrepreneurs are at cyclical lows. A higher output (income) then implies a lower price level to satisfy the money tie between purchasing power and nominal income.
2 As Heinz Kurz (2012, p. 892) puts it, 'Schumpeter deserves credit for having intuitively seen that the complexity of the economic world allows for phenomena that are not covered by the conventional marginalist doctrine.'
3 Here, Schumpeter is relying on the mechanics of conventional theories, in spite of distinguishing his theory from monetarist and Keynesian theories of the business cycle that cast the business cycle as a response to exogenous shocks in the balance between money supply and demand or in aggregate demand, respectively. Schumpeter's theory is also different from modern real business cycle theory, which casts the business cycle as a response to exogenous shocks in productivity (aggregate supply).

References

Acs, Zoltan J. and Audretsch, David B. (1988a), 'Testing the Schumpeterian Hypothesis', *Eastern Economic Journal*, 14(2): 129–40.

Acs, Zoltan J. and Audretsch, David B. (1988b), 'Innovation in Large and Small Firms: An Empirical Analysis', *American Economic Review*, 78(4): 678–90.

Aghion, Philippe and Howitt, Peter (1992), 'A Model of Growth through Creative Destruction', *Econometrica*, 60(2): 323–51.

Aghion, Philippe and Howitt, Peter (1998), *Endogenous Growth Theory*, Cambridge, MA, MIT Press.

Andersen, Esben Sloth (2004), 'Knowledges, Specialization and Economic Evolution: Modelling the Evolving Division of Human Time', in J. Stanley Metcalfe and John Foster, editors, *Evolution and Economic Complexity*, Cheltenham, UK, Edward Elgar: 108–47.

Andersen, Esben Sloth (2012), 'Schumpeter's Core Works Revisited – Resolved Problems and Remaining Challenges', *Journal of Evolutionary Economics*, 22(4): 627–48.

Andrews, David (2015), 'Natural Price and the Long Run: Alfred Marshall's Misreading of Adam Smith', *Cambridge Journal of Economics*, 39(1): 265–79.

Asimakopulos, Anthony (1975), 'A Kaleckian Theory of Income Distribution', *Canadian Journal of Economics*, 8(3): 313–33.

Baran, Paul A. and Sweezy, Paul M. (1966), *Monopoly Capital*, New York, Monthly Review Press.

Barney, Jay (1991), 'Firm Resources and Sustained Competitive Advantage', *Journal of Management*, 17(1): 99–120.

Basile, Liliana and Salvadori, Neri (1984–85), 'Kalecki's Pricing Theory', *Journal of Post Keynesian Economics*, 7(2): 249–62.

Baumol, William J. (2002), *The Free Market Innovation Machine*, Princeton, Princeton University Press.

Binswanger, Mathias (1996), 'Money Creation, Profits and Growth: Monetary Aspects of Economic Evolution', in Ernst Helmstädter and Mark Perlman, editors, *Behavioral Norms, Technical Progress, and Economic Dynamics*, Ann Arbor, University of Michigan Press: 413–37.

Bloch, Harry (1990), 'Price Leadership and the Degree of Monopoly', *Journal of Post Keynesian Economics*, 12(3): 439–51.

Bloch, Harry (2000), 'Schumpeter and Steindl on the Dynamics of Competition', *Journal of Evolutionary Economics*, 10(2): 311–28.

Bloch, Harry (2016a), 'Post-Keynesian Pricing with a Schumpeterian Twist', in Jerry Courvisanos, James Doughney and Alex Millmow, editors, *Reclaiming Pluralism for Economics*, London, Routledge: 203–20.

Bloch, Harry (2016b), 'Prices in Motion: Schumpeter's Contribution to Price Theory', *Metroeconomica*, 67(4): 742–67.

Bloch, Harry and Finch, John (2008), 'Schumpeter and Steindl on Growth and the Transformation to Maturity in Capitalism', *History of Economics Review*, 47(Winter): 1–19.

Bloch, Harry and Metcalfe, Stan (2011), 'Complexity in the Theory of the Developing Firm', in Cristiano Antonelli, editor, *Handbook on the Economic Complexity of Technological Change*, Cheltenham, UK, Edward Elgar: 81–104.

Bloch, Harry and Metcalfe, Stan (2015), 'Restless Knowledge, Capabilities and the Nature of the Mega-Firm', in Andreas Pyka and John Foster, editors, *The Evolution of Economic and Innovation Systems*, Heidelberg, Springer: 431–53.

Bloch, Harry and Metcalfe, Stan (2017), 'Innovation, Creative Destruction and Price Theory', *Industrial and Corporate Change*, forthcoming.

Bloch, Harry and Sapsford, David (2000), 'Whither the Terms of Trade? An Elaboration of the Prebisch-Singer Hypothesis', *Cambridge Journal of Economics*, 24(4): 503–17.

Bloch, Harry and Sapsford, David (2011), 'Terms of Trade Movements and the Global Economic Crisis', *International Review of Applied Economics*, 25(5): 461–81.

Bloch, Harry and Sapsford, David (2013), 'Innovation, Real Primary Commodity Prices and Business Cycles', in Esben Andersen and Andreas Pyka, editors, *Long Term Economic Development*, Berlin, Springer: 175–89.

Chamberlin, Edward H. (1933), *The Theory of Monopolistic Competition*, Cambridge, MA, Harvard University Press.

Chamberlin, Edward H. (1951), 'The Impact of Recent Monopoly Theory on the Schumpeterian System', *Review of Economics and Statistics*, 33(2): 133–38.

Courvisanos, Jerry (1996), *Investment Cycles in Capitalist Economies*, Cheltenham, UK, Edward Elgar Publishing.

Courvisanos, Jerry (2012), *Cycles, Crises and Innovation*, Cheltenham, UK, Edward Elgar Publishing.

Cowling, Keith (1982), *Monopoly Capitalism*, London, Macmillan Press.

Dangel-Hagnauer, Cécile (2013), 'Schumpeter's Institution of Money: Slipping off the Border of Economic Theory and Landing in Economic Sociology', *European Journal of the History of Economic Thought*, 20(6): 1000–31.

De Vecchi, Nicoló (1995), *Entrepreneurs, Institutions and Economic Change: The Economic Thought of J.A. Schumpeter (1905–1925)*, Cheltenham, UK, Edward Elgar Publishing.

Dopfer, Kurt (2007), 'The Pillars of Schumpeterian Economics: Micro, Meso, Macro', in Horst Hanusch and Andreas Pyka, editors, *Elgar Companion to Neo-Schumpeterian Economics*, Cheltenham, UK, Edward Elgar Publishing: 65–77.

Dopfer, Kurt (2012), 'The Origins of Meso Economics: Schumpeter's Legacy and Beyond', *Journal of Evolutionary Economics*, 22(1): 133–60.

Dopfer, Kurt, Foster, John and Potts, Jason (2004), 'Micro-Meso-Macro', *Journal of Evolutionary Economics*, 14(3): 263–80.

Dopfer, Kurt and Potts, Jason (2008), *The General Theory of Economic Evolution*, London, Routledge.

Dosi, Giovanni, Nelson, Richard R. and Winter, Sidney G. (2002), *The Nature and Dynamics of Organizational Capabilities*, Oxford, Oxford University Press.

Downie, Jack (1958), *The Competitive Process*, London, Duckworth.

Eichner, Alfred S. (1976), *The Megacorp and Oligopoly*, Armonk, NY, USA, M.E. Sharpe.

Festré, Agnès and Nasica, Eric (2009), 'Schumpeter on Money, Banking and Finance: An Institutionalist Perspective', *European Journal of the History of Economic Thought*, 16(2): 325–56.

Fischer, David Hackett (1996), *The Great Wave: Price Revolutions and the Rhythm of History*, Oxford, Oxford University Press.

Foster, John (2015), 'Joseph Schumpeter and Simon Kuznets: Comparing Their Evolutionary Economic Approaches to Business Cycles and Economic Growth', *Journal of Evolutionary Economics*, 25(1): 163–72.

Freeman, Christopher (1990), 'Schumpeter's *Business Cycles* Revisited', in Arnold Heertje and Mark Perlman, editors, *Evolving Technology and Market Structure*, Ann Arbor, University of Michigan Press: 17–38.

Freeman, Christopher (2007), 'A Schumpeterian Renaissance?' in Horst Hanusch and Andreas Pyka, editors, *Elgar Companion to Neo-Schumpeterian Economics*, Cheltenham, UK, Edward Elgar Publishing: 130–41.

Freeman, Christopher, Clark, John and Soete, Luc (1982), *Unemployment and Technological Innovation*, London, Frances Pinter.

Freeman, Christopher and Louçã, Francisco (2001), *As Time Goes By*, Oxford, Oxford University Press.

Frisch, Ragnar (1931), 'A Method of Decomposing an Empirical Series into Its Cyclical and Progressive Components', *Journal of the American Statistical Association*, 26(173, supplement): 73–78.

Gatti, Domenico Delli, Gallegati, Mauro and Minsky, Hyman (1996), 'Financial Institutions, Economic Policy, and the Economic Behavior of the Economy', in Ernst Helmstädter and Mark Perlman, editors, *Behavioral Norms, Technical Progress, and Economic Dynamics*, Ann Arbor, University of Michigan Press: 393–411.

Graham, Frank D., Daughtery, Carroll R., Sweezy, Paul M. and Tarshis, Laurie (1938), 'Wage Policies', *American Economic Review*, 28(1, supplement): 155–58.

Haas, David (2015), 'Diffusion Dynamics and Creative Destruction in a Simple Classical Model', *Metroeconomica*, 66(4): 638–60.

Hall, Robert L. and Hitch, Charles J. (1939), 'Price Theory and Business Behaviour', *Oxford Economic Papers*, 2: 12–45.

Harcourt, Geoffrey C. and Kenyon, Peter (1976), 'Pricing and the Investment Decision', *Kyklos*, 29(3): 449–77.

Harrod, Roy F. (1939), 'Price and Cost in Entrepreneur's Policy', *Oxford Economic Papers*, 2: 1–11.

Hart, Neil (2013), *Alfred Marshall and Modern Economics: Equilibrium Theory and Evolutionary Economics*, Basingstoke, Palgrave Macmillan.

Heertje, Arnold (1981), *Schumpeter's Vision: Capitalism, Socialism and Democracy after Forty Years*, East Sussex, UK, Praeger Publishers.

Holm, Jacob R., Andersen, Esben S. and Metcalfe, J. Stanley (2016), 'Confounded, Augmented and Constrained Replicator Dynamics, *Journal of Evolutionary Economics*, 26(4): 803–22.

Innis, Harold A. (1940), 'Review of *Business Cycles: A Theoretical, Historical and Statistical Analysis of Capitalist Process* by Joseph A. Schumpeter', *Canadian Journal of Economics and Political Science*, 6(1): 90–96.

Kalecki, Michał (1938), 'The Determinants of the Distribution of National Income', *Econometrica*, 6(2): 97–112.

Kalecki, Michał (1971), *Selected Essays on the Dynamics of the Capitalist Economy 1933–1970*, Cambridge, Cambridge University Press.

Keynes, John M. (1936), *The General Theory of Employment, Interest and Money*, London, Macmillan Press.

Kleinknecht, Alfred (1987), *Innovation Patterns in Crisis and Prosperity*, London, Macmillan Press.

Klepper, Steven (1997), 'Industry Life Cycles', *Industrial and Corporate Change*, 6(1): 145–81.

Knell, Mark (2015), 'Schumpeter, Keynes and the Financial Instability Hypothesis', *Journal of Evolutionary Economics*, 25(1): 293–310.

Knight, Frank H. (1971 [1921]), *Risk, Uncertainty and Profit*, Chicago, University of Chicago Press.

Kondratieff, Nikolai D. (1935), 'The Long Waves of Economic Life', *Review of Economics and Statistics*, 17(6): 105–15.

Kriesler, Peter (1987), *Kalecki's Microanalysis*, Cambridge, Cambridge University Press.

Kurz, Heinz D. (2008), 'Innovations and Profits: Schumpeter and the Classical Heritage', *Journal of Economic and Behavioral Organization*, 67(1): 263–78.

Kurz, Heinz D. (2012), 'Schumpeter's New Combinations: Revisiting His *Theorie der wirtschaftlichen Entwicklung* on the Occasion of Its Centenary', *Journal of Evolutionary Economics*, 22(5): 871–916.

Kurz, Heinz D. (2013), ' "New Combinations" in the Economy and in Economics: A Tribute to Stanley Metcalfe', *Economics of Innovation and New Technology*, 22(7): 653–65.

Kurz, Heinz D. and Salvadori, Neri (1995), *Theory of Production*, Cambridge, Cambridge University Press.

Kuznets, Simon (1940), 'Schumpeter's *Business Cycles*', *American Economic Review*, 30(2): 257–71.

Lakomski-Laguerre, Odile (2016), 'Joseph Schumpeter's Credit View of Money: A Contribution to a "Monetary Analysis" of Capitalism', *History of Political Economy*, 48(3): 489–514.

Lange, Oscar (1941), 'Review of *Business Cycles: A Theoretical, Historical and Statistical Analysis of Capitalist Process* by Joseph A. Schumpeter', *Review of Economics and Statistics*, 23(4): 190–93.

Lanzillotti, Robert F. (1958), 'Pricing Objectives in Large Corporations', *American Economic Review*, 48(5): 921–40.

Leathers, Charles G. and Raines, J. Patrick (2004), 'The Schumpeterian Role of Financial Innovations in the New Economy's Business Cycle', *Cambridge Journal of Economics*, 28(5): 667–81.

Lee, Frederic S. (1998), *Post Keynesian Pricing Theory*, Cambridge, Cambridge University Press.

Lerner, Abba P. (1934), 'The Concept of Monopoly and the Measurement of Monopoly Power', *Review of Economic Studies*, 1(3): 157–75.

Levine, David P. (2005), 'Reproduction and Transformation in the Theory of the Market: Observations on Josef Steindl's Theory of Capitalist Dynamics', in Tracy Mott and Nina Shapiro, editors, *Rethinking Capitalist Development*, London, Routledge: 11–22.

Lipsey, Richard G., Carlaw, Kenneth I. and Bekar, Clifford T. (2005), *Economic Transformations*, Oxford, Oxford University Press.

Loasby, Brian J. (1996), 'The Imagined, Deemed Possible', in Ernst Helmstädter and Mark Perlman, editors, *Behavioral Norms, Technical Progress, and Economic Dynamics*, Ann Arbor, University of Michigan Press: 17–21.

Marget, Arthur W. (1951), 'The Monetary Aspects of the Schumpeterian System', *Review of Economics and Statistics*, 33(2): 112–21.

Markey-Towler, Brendan (2016), 'The Law of the Jungle: Firm Survival and Price Dynamics in Evolutionary Markets', *Journal of Evolutionary Economics*, 26(3): 655–96.

Marshall, Alfred (1920), *Principles of Economics*, eighth edition, London, Macmillan Press.

Mayhew, Anne (1980), 'Schumpeterian Capitalism versus the "Schumpeterian Thesis"', *Journal of Economic Issues*, 14(2): 583–92.

McGraw, Thomas K. (2007), *The Prophet of Innovation: Joseph Schumpeter and Creative Destruction*, Cambridge, MA, Harvard University Press.

Mensch, Gerhard (1979), *Stalemate in Technology*, English translation of Das Technologische Patt, Frankfurt, Umschau Verlag, 1975, Cambridge, MA, Ballinger.

Messori, Marcello (1997), 'The Trials and Misadventures of Schumpeter's Treatise on Money', *History of Political Economy*, 29(4): 639–73.

Metcalfe, J. Stanley (1994), 'Competition, Fisher's Principle and Increasing Returns in the Selection Process', *Journal of Evolutionary Economics*, 4(4): 327–46.

Metcalfe, J. Stanley (1998), *Evolutionary Economics and Creative Destruction*, London, Routledge.

Metcalfe, J. Stanley (2007), 'Alfred Marshall's Mecca: Reconciling the Theories of Value and Development', *Economic Record*, 83(supplement): S1–S22.

Metcalfe, J. Stanley (2008), 'The Broken Thread: Marshall, Schumpeter and Hayek on the Evolution of Capitalism', in Yuichi Shinoya and Tomatsu Nishizawa, editors, *Marshall and Schumpeter on Evolution*, Cheltenham, UK, Edward Elgar Publishing: 116–44.

Metcalfe, J. Stanley (2012), 'J. A. Schumpeter and the Theory of Economic Evolution: One Hundred Years beyond the *Theory of Economic Development*', Papers on Economics and Evolution, #1213, Max Planck Institute of Economics, Jena, Germany.

Metcalfe, J. Stanley (2014), 'Capitalism and Evolution', *Journal of Evolutionary Economics*, 24(1): 11–34.

Metcalfe, J. Stanley and Steedman, Ian (2013), 'Exploring Schumpeterian Dynamics: Innovation, Adaptation and Growth', *Evolutionary and Institutional Economics Review*, 10(2): 149–78.

Minsky, Hyman P. (1986), 'Money and Crisis in Schumpeter and Keynes', in Hans-Jürgen Wagener and Jan W. Drukker, editors, *The Economic Law of Motion of Modern Society*, Cambridge, Cambridge University Press: 112–22.

Minsky, Hyman P. (1990), 'Schumpeter: Finance and Evolution', in Arnold Heertje and Mark Perlman, editors, *Evolving Technology and Market Structure*, Ann Arbor, University of Michigan Press: 51–74.

Nelson, Richard R. (2012), 'Why Schumpeter Has Had so Little Influence on Today's Main Line Economics, and Why this May be Changing', *Journal of Evolutionary Economics*, 22(5): 901–16.

Nelson, Richard R. (2013), 'Demand, Supply, and Their Interaction on Markets, as Seen from the Perspective of Evolutionary Economic Theory', *Journal of Evolutionary Economics*, 23(1): 17–38.

Nelson, Richard R. and Consoli, David (2010), 'An Evolutionary Theory of Household Consumption Behavior', *Journal of Evolutionary Economics*, 20(5): 665–87.

Nelson, Richard R. and Winter, Sidney G. (1982), *An Evolutionary Theory of Economic Change*, Cambridge, MA, Harvard University Press.

Oakley, Allen (1990), *Schumpeter's Theory of Capitalist Motion: A Critical Exposition and Reassessment*, Aldershot, Hants, Edward Elgar Publishing.

Pasinetti, Luigi L. (1977), *Lectures on the Theory of Production*, New York, Columbia University Press.

Patinkin, Don (1965 [1956]), *Money, Interest and Prices*, New York, Harper and Row.

Perez, Carlota (1983), 'Structural Change and the Assimilation of New Technologies in the Economic and Social System', *Futures*, 15(4): 357–75.

Perez, Carlota (2002), *Technological Revolutions and Financial Capital*, Cheltenham, UK, Edward Elgar Publishing.

Pigou, Alfred C. (1928), 'An Analysis of Supply', *Economic Journal*, 38(150): 238–57.

Piketty, Thomas (2014), *Capital in the Twenty-First Century*, Cambridge, MA, Belknap Press of Harvard University Press.

Popper, Karl R. (1963), *Conjectures and Refutations*, London, Routledge and Kegan Paul.

Price, George R. (1972), 'Fisher's "Fundamental Theorem" Made Clear', *Annals of Human Genetics*, 36(2): 129–40.

Raffaelli, Tiziano (2003), *Marshall's Evolutionary Economics*, Abingdon, UK, Routledge.

Ramazzotti, Paolo (2004), 'What Do Firms Learn? Capabilities, Distribution and the Division of Labor', in J. Stanley Metcalfe and John Foster, editors, *Evolution and Economic Complexity*, Cheltenham, UK, Edward Elgar Publishing: 38–61.

Rosenberg, Hans (1940), 'Review of *Business Cycles: A Theoretical, Historical and Statistical Analysis of the Capitalist Process* by Joseph A. Schumpeter', *American Historical Review*, 46(1): 96–99.

Rothbarth, Erwin (1942), 'Review of *Business Cycles: A Theoretical, Historical and Statistical Analysis of the Capitalist Process* by Joseph A. Schumpeter', *Economic Journal*, 52(206–07): 223–29.

Salter, Wilfred E.G. (1966), *Productivity and Technical Change*, Cambridge, Cambridge University Press.

Samuelson, Paul A. (2015), 'The Harvard-Circle', *Journal of Evolutionary Economics*, 25(1): 31–36.

Sarantis, Nicholas (1991), 'Conflict and Inflation in Industrial Countries', *International Review of Applied Economics*, 5(2): 155–69.

Schumpeter, Joseph A. (1926 [1912]), *Theorie der wirtschaftlichen Entwicklung*, Leipzig, Duncker and Humboldt.

Schumpeter, Joseph A. (1917–18), 'Das Sozialprodukt und die Rechenpfennige: Glossen und Beiträge zur Geldtheorie von heute', *Archiv für Sozialwissenschaft und Sozialpolitik*, 44: 627–715.

Schumpeter, Joseph A. (1927), 'The Explanation of the Business Cycle', *Economica*, 21: 286–311.

Schumpeter, Joseph A. (1928), 'The Instability of Capitalism', *Economic Journal*, 38(151): 361–86.

Schumpeter, Joseph A. (1930), 'Mitchell's Business Cycles', *Quarterly Journal of Economics*, 45(1): 150–72.

Schumpeter, Joseph A. (1961 [1934]), *The Theory of Economic Development: An Inquiry into Profits, Credit, Interest, and the Business Cycle*, translation of second German edition of Schumpeter, (1926 [1912]) by Redvers Opie, London, Oxford University Press.

Schumpeter, Joseph A. (1935), 'The Analysis of Economic Change', *Review of Economics and Statistics*, 17(4): 2–10.

Schumpeter, Joseph A. (1939), *Business Cycles: A Theoretical, Historical and Statistical Analysis of the Capitalist Process*, volumes 1 and 2, New York, McGraw-Hill.

Schumpeter, Joseph A. (1941), 'Alfred Marshall's *Principles*: A Semi-Centennial Appraisal', *American Economic Review*, 31(2): 236–48.

Schumpeter, Joseph A. (1947), 'The Creative Response in Economic History', *Journal of Economic History*, 7(2): 149–59.

Schumpeter, Joseph A. (1949), 'The Historical Approach to the Analysis of Business Cycles', *Universities-National Bureau Conference on Business Cycle Research*, November 25–27, Reprinted in Clemence (1951): 308–15.

Schumpeter, Joseph A. (1950), 'March into Socialism', *American Economic Review*, 40(2): 446–56.

Schumpeter, Joseph A. (1976 [1950]), *Capitalism, Socialism and Democracy*, third edition, New York, Harper and Row.

Schumpeter, Joseph A. (1951), 'Preface to Japanese Edition of *Theorie der wirtschaftlichen Entwicklung*', in Richard V. Clemence, editor, *Essays of J.A. Schumpeter*, Cambridge, MA, Addison-Wesley Press: 158–63.

Schumpeter, Joseph A. (1954), *History of Economic Analysis*, Oxford, Oxford University Press.

Schumpeter, Joseph A. (1956), 'Money and the Social Product', *International Economic Papers*, 6: 148–211 (translation of Schumpeter (1917–1918) by Arthur Magret).

Schumpeter, Joseph A. (1970), *Das Wesen des Geldes*, edited from a 1930 manuscript by Fritz Karl Mann, Gottingen, Vandenhoeck and Ruprecht.

Schumpeter, Joseph A. (1990), *L'Essenza della Moneta*, Italian translation of Schumpeter (1970) by E. Dal Bosco, Turin, Cassa di Risparmio di Torino.

Schumpeter, Joseph A. (1991), 'Money and Currency', *Social Research*, 58(3): 499–543.

Schumpeter, Joseph A. (1996), *Trattato Della Moneta: Capitoli Inediti*, Italian translation of additional material for Schumpeter (1970), by L. Berti and M. Messori, Naples, Edizioni Scientifiche Italiane.

Schumpeter, Joseph A. (2005a), 'Development', *Journal of Economic Literature*, 43(1): 108–120.

Schumpeter, Joseph A. (2005b), *Théorie de la Monnaie et de la Banque*, 2 volumes, French translation of Schumpeter (1970) and Schumpeter (1996) by Claude Jaeger and Odile Lakomski-Laguerre, Paris, France, Cahiers d'Economie Politique-L'Harmattan.

Schumpeter, Joseph A. (2014), *Treatise on Money*, English translation of Schumpeter (1970) by Ruben Alvarado, Aalten, the Netherlands, Wordbridge Publishing.

Shackle, George L. S. (1965), *A Scheme of Economic Theory*, Cambridge, Cambridge University Press.

Shah, Parth J. and Yeager, Leland B. (1994), 'Schumpeter on Monetary Determinacy', *History of Political Economy*, 26(3): 443–64.

Solow, Robert M. (1957), 'Technical Change and the Aggregate Production Function', *Review of Economics and Statistics*, 39(3): 312–20.

Sraffa, Piero (1960), *Production of Commodities by Means of Commodities*, Cambridge, Cambridge University Press.

Steindl, Josef (1976 [1952]), *Maturity and Stagnation in American Capitalism*, New York, Monthly Review Press.

Swedberg, Richard (1991), *Schumpeter: A Biography*, Princeton, NJ, Princeton University Press.

Sweezy, Paul M. (1939), 'Demand Under Conditions of Oligopoly', *Journal of Political Economy*, 47(4): 568–73.

Sylos-Labini, Paolo (1962), *Oligopoly and Technical Progress*, Cambridge, MA, Harvard University Press.

Tichy, Gunther (1984), 'Schumpeter's Monetary Theory – An Unjustly Neglected Part of His Work', in Christian Seidl, editor, *Lectures on Schumpeterian Economics*, Berlin, Springer-Verlag: 125–138.

Tylecote, Andrew (1992), *The Long Wave in the World Economy*, London, Routledge.

Ülgen, Frank (2014), 'Schumpeterian Economic Development and Financial Institutions: A Conflicting Evolution', *Journal of Institutional Economics*, 10(2): 257–71.

Warburton, Clark (1953), 'Money and Business Fluctuations in the Schumpeterian System', *Journal of Political Economy*, 61(6): 509–22.

Wood, Adrian (1975), *A Theory of Profits*, Cambridge, Cambridge University Press.

Index

For Product Safety Concerns and Information please contact our EU
representative GPSR@taylorandfrancis.com
Taylor & Francis Verlag GmbH, Kaufingerstraße 24, 80331 München, Germany

www.ingramcontent.com/pod-product-compliance
Ingram Content Group UK Ltd.
Pitfield, Milton Keynes, MK11 3LW, UK
UKHW020951180425
457613UK00019B/618